"Not knowing just how he could best be launched on his tales, I feigned a matter of business; told him of my surveying, and asked vague questions about the district."

— H.P. Lovecraft, "The Colour Out of Space"

TOUR DE LOVECRAFT

- THE DESTINATIONS -

BY KENNETH HITE

FOR PRESTON —
ENJOY THE RIDE!! ..

ATOMIC
OVERMIND
PRESS

Tour de Lovecraft: The Destinations
is published by Atomic Overmind Press

Book Layout and Design by Hal Mangold
Cover by Ivan Dixon
Interior illustrations by Domenico Nezitti and Toren Atkinson
Cartography by Mark Richardson and Kenneth Hite

Earlier versions of the essays "Antarctica," "Antiquity," "Arabia," "Arkham," "Boston," "Dreamland," "Dunwich," "Hyperspace," "Kingsport," "New York City," "The Pacific Ocean," "Pnakotus," "Vermont," and "The Woods" appeared in *Weird Tales* magazine between 2007 and 2012 as the "Lost in Lovecraft" column.

Atomic Overmind Press
143 Wesmond Dr.
Alexandria, VA 22305

Visit us online at **www.atomicovermind.com**.

10 9 8 7 6 5 4 3 2 1

Stock number AOP1009, April 2021.

ISBN: 978-0-9896155-5-6

Printed in Lithuania.

H. P. Lovecraft

ALSO BY KENNETH HITE

Books and Games from Atomic Overmind Press

Tour de Lovecraft: The Tales
Cthulhu 101
Dubious Shards
The Tarot of Cthulhu

Adventures Into Darkness
(for *HERO System*, *Mutants & Masterminds*, and *Truth & Justice*)

The Day After Ragnarok
(for *Savage Worlds*, *Fate*, and *HERO System*)

Lovecraftian Children's Books from Atlas Games

Where the Deep Ones Are
The Antarctic Express
Cliffourd the Big Red God
Goodnight Azathoth

From Osprey Publishing

The Nazi Occult
The Cthulhu Wars: The United States' Battles Against the Mythos
[with Kennon Bauman]

From Arc Dream Publishing

The King in Yellow: Annotated Edition, by Robert W. Chambers

FOR DONOVAN LOUCKS,
TOUR GUIDE EXTRAORDINAIRE

CONTENTS

FOREWORD

By Nick Mamatas

How does one introduce a book such as this? "Ken Hite sure read a lot of Lovecraft! And now, the scenery!" Thank you, that'll be one hundred dollars, please.

Does Hite know his Lovecraft, and his geography? Of course he does. But the question this introduction must answer is "So what?"

H. P. Lovecraft, who died obscure and who is now breathtakingly famous, has been overstudied even as he remains underrated. Where academe ignored him, fan-scholarship blossomed. Now a few scholarly presses are sufficiently interested to publish collections of critical material, or Lovecraft's correspondence with figures local to this or that university, but most Lovecraft scholarship is written outside of the requirements of academic research. As such, there are qualitative differences between what one might find in a peer-reviewed journal, and critical material along the lines of this book as well as the bookshelves of stuff by S. T. Joshi et al. Popular criticism of Lovecraft is less interested in what we used to call "theory" and more in the cataloging and evaluation of works, in biocriticism, and in—horrors!—evaluation of story values, writing ability, and the like.

Lovecraft himself was a famous amateur. His interests in science, architecture, history, politics, and amateur publishing all inform both his creative work and the sad shape of his career. It was also amateur activity from his friends and correspondents that saved his career and built for him a posthumous reputation. But you know all this. You don't end up with this particular title in your hands without already having spent a decade or more steeped like a teabag in the black waters of the Dreamlands.

What will you get out of Ken Hite's close examination of place in Lovecraft's work, of his chart about the moon and what words Lovecraft uses to describe it, or the chart about deep time? A lot.

As the real-estate hucksters say right before you click "Skip Ads" on YouTube: "Let me explain."

Lovecraft has become an intriguing figure for the philosophical movement called Speculative Realism. Of course, as the movement contains more than one philosopher, there are of course different schools of thought within the movement, but the basic idea is that people cannot know very much, if anything, about the material universe. There are certain correlations between our sensory experiences and cognitive interpretations and what is out there, but only correlations. The extent to which the correlations are valid, and if they exist in any real way themselves is one of the major debates within Speculative Realism. Of course, the idea of an unknowable universe comes from Kant; the new breed of speculative realists just point to him and say that he shut down the philosophical project entirely…then they point to themselves and say "Hmm, so what are we doing then?"

What they're doing is considering what is left. Is the issue really the mind and its inability to apprehend objects…or is it that the mind itself is just another object, albeit a squishy one we ride around inside of? Can science really tell us how the object interfaces with the mind? Don't be so fast to say, "Of course!" nerd. Consider one of Lovecraft's favorite things: ice cream. There is a raft of associations with ice cream—the endless flavors and variants (gelato, ice milk, superpremium with the high buttermilk fat content), the ice cream bars shaped like Spider-Man's head, ice cream sold out of trucks that perhaps play "The Entertainer" or "Turkey in the Straw", those nice white "ice-cream suits" bankers wear in the Cayman Islands, etc.

And to know about ice cream you'd thus also need to know about buttermilk, chocolate, Ben and Jerry and who they are and thus perhaps what the Grateful Dead was and what it's like in Vermont, and also who Spider-Man is and perhaps Ray Bradbury as Stuart Gordon made a film of his short story about a white suit and thus also what children are and who adults are and how they're both allowed to enjoy ice cream just as Lovecraft did but too much enthusiasm for ice cream as an adult suggests a certain childishness—Lovecraft was a teetotaler and not much for sex, just like a child himself—and the weather in the Cayman Islands (and why there are so many banks there, which brings up the questions of taxes, capital, government...) which is rather the opposite of New England which is where they eat the most ice cream not despite the fact that it is cold but because of it and then we're back to buttermilk fat content and how burning fat helps keep a body warm, and hey who was from New England again, ah yes one Howard Phillips Lovecraft....

Philosophy has, in the past and even today, decided to deal with this problem by shaking a fist at that old devil language. We're all familiar with this as Lovecraftians—all the worst Lovecraftian fictions make the mistake of opening up the *Necronomicon* or some other cursed manuscript and showing us readers a few lines from the text. It's always so disappointing, because language has some pretty severe limits. It is better not to know, as Lovecraft teaches us.

And yet, Lovecraft in his own fiction deals with the issues of incomprehensibility of the universe and the inadequacy of language by turning up the volume, the treble, the bass. Everything's up to eleven. This is why minor thinkers and the semiliterate dismiss him as a bad writer, when in truth he is a "difficult writer" along the lines of the modernist avant-garde. He's not a kid playing with a thesaurus, it's all purposeful.

And the same with Kenneth Hite and this book. While academic criticism of Lovecraft amounts to a reason to perform a cosmic shrug for tenure, enthusiast criticism knows that it is in a war against the infinite universe. The web of associations that is supposed to make knowledge ever contingent and always tentative is inverted and commandeered—Hite uses the quantum computer of his mind to create a traveling salesman program to explore the entire Lovecraftian universe, and thus the entire universe through the lens of Lovecraft. You know the stories, but you don't know the world outside, and this book will give you a little glimpse of the universe in which your wet little brain is still somehow trapped despite the cosmos being infinite.

TOUR DE LOVECRAFT
- THE DESTINATIONS -

INTRODUCTION

"One thing that influences [my style] is my extreme & lifelong geographic sensitiveness. I have never been tremendously interested in people, but I have a veritably feline interest in & devotion to places. The greater number of my dreams & visions are fantastic syntheses, etherealisations, & rearrangments of the landscape & architectural impressions which impinge on me during waking hours; & during those waking hours there is no pleasure which can compare with the experience of seeing strange old towns & houses & scenic vistas. These things are, & always have been, the most potent stimuli my imagination can possibly encounter; hence they usually form the points of departure for my excursions into the outside cosmic gulfs."

— H.P. Lovecraft, letter to Clark Ashton Smith (January 17, 1930)

Howard Phillips Lovecraft (1890-1937) is justly hailed as the progenitor of, to use Fritz Leiber's phrase, a "Copernican Revolution" in horror. Over the course of a few dozen tales, he shifted the focus of fear from the supernatural and the Earthly to the alien and the cosmic. Recognizing that mere ghosts and vampires were increasingly passé, he forced a "demythologization" of horror into the realm of the scientific that spawned not only his "Lovecraft Mythos" eidolons, but the Freudian horrors of Robert Bloch and Thomas Harris, the sheerly existential and Heisenbergian terrors of Thomas Ligotti, and perhaps even the "non-fictional" paranoia of Whitley Strieber and John Keel.

But almost as important, and almost certainly more influential, Lovecraft also brought horror fiction down to Earth, to precisely pinpointed street hill-tops and street corners, or at least to places that should be on the map, if you looked hard enough. Not for him the storm-soaked Gothic wilds of Italy or Germany, or the nebulous no-places of Poe. (Poe, after all, boasted: "Horror is not of Germany, but of the soul.") Only seldom do his horrors haunt "strange far places" such as Geneva or Transylvania—or Antarctica. And even when they do, they do so through the eyes of stolid New England Yankees, connected by tenure or blood to Providence or Arkham. And having seen the horrors, they, like Lovecraft, bring them home. To his home, specifically, to "the familiar Old Providence" and its New England hinterlands.

True, Machen had the same instinct on occasion, and Stoker was clever enough to briefly bring a foreign vampire into the beating heart of Victorian London, but Lovecraft went local more intensely, more often, and more powerfully than either. Only M.R. James, that poet of the ghostly landscape, can be considered his peer in joining the physical essence of a specific location with the supernatural effect of it—and James' stories, unlike Lovecraft's, never moved beyond the chapel into the cosmic. Also, M.R. James' fictitious locations—Burnstow and the rest—only lightly wash their originals with horror. Lovecraft sinks the fictitious foundations of his own Arkham country deep into history and geography. The railway-obsessed and urgently domestic Victorians originated this "fictional-factual" setting method: Elizabeth Gaskell's Cranford (1851), Charles Dickens' Coketown (1853), and Anthony Trollope's Barchester (1855). Lovecraft, for all his expressed contempt for Victorian values, recognized a good trick for achieving simultaneous verisimilitude and phantasy when he saw it.

Lovecraft believed that the qualities of a place—real or fictitious—depended on their interrelationships: the "settled adjustment" of the population, the natural landscape, and the architecture mediating between them. He built his terrors from the terroir, so to speak, of the setting, linking his most enormous themes to its smallest details: gambrel roofs and the sounds of birdsong. Hence, this unsung "Second Copernican Revolution" of weird fiction was no less influential for all the occasional Aristarchuses and Nicolases of Cusa before it. Without Lovecraft's Providence, there would be no Ramsey Campbell Midlands, no Poppy Z. Brite New Orleans ... no Stephen King Maine.

"With me, the very quality of being cosmically sensitive breeds an exaggerated attachment to the familiar and immediate—Old Providence, the woods and hils, the ancient ways and thoughts of New England."

— H.P. Lovecraft, letter to August Derleth (November 21, 1930)

The only equal of Lovecraft as a New England horrorist is Nathaniel Hawthorne, and not all of Hawthorne by far. However, a few masterpieces such as *The House of the Seven Gables,* which Lovecraft read as part of a complete study of Hawthorne in 1920, were enough to eventually divert Lovecraft's course from the dreamlands of Dunsany and the purple tarns of Poe into the Miskatonic Valley. If regional fiction had survived its critical high water mark in the 1930s and 1940s, Lovecraft might receive as much praise for blending horror with the regional as he does now for blending the supernatural with science fiction. But the prestige of regional fiction receded with the rise of mass culture and mass media, leaving horror alone on its former turf. Novels are about people, now, and usually people alienated from their surroundings at that.

Thus literary discussion of Lovecraft too often neglects the physical environment, the specific settings of his stories. Critics tend to leave the street grid of Innsmouth and the borders of Leng to obsessive nerds like me, and concentrate on Lovecraft as psychological or cosmic horrorist. This is not a universal truth, of course: Peter Cannon, Robert Waugh, and even S.T. Joshi once in a blue moon examine the ground under our fictive feet before haring off in search of green meadows of the mind. Steven Mariconda, for example, reminds us of the importance of "background" to Lovecraft, the complete effect of ancestry, geography, folkways, and architecture not just on his personality but on his fiction. Throughout this Tour, I try to call attention to the signs erected in the landscape before I got there.

"My New England is a dream New England—the familiar scene with certain lights and shadows heightened (or meant to be heightened) just enough to merge it with things beyond the world."

— H.P. Lovecraft, letter to Bernard Austin Dwyer (June 1927)

In her unjustifiably neglected essay "Lovecraft and Landscape," Angela Carter writes that, "Since Lovecraft's geography is that of dream, it has the uncanny precision of dream." Precision means something, it literally conveys meaning, in dreams and in literature. My aim is to map Lovecraft's geography, to provide a topographic chart of his creations and thus perhaps survey his works from a new angle. The word "topography" comes from the Greek *topos* ("place") + *graphein* ("writing"), and "writing about place" is the core of this Tour.

Following the German literary historian Ernst Robert Curtius, critics sometimes refer to literary topoi, the plural of topos.[1] This usage comes from classical rhetoric, in which certain arguments or images recurred so often they were called *koinoi topoi*, "common places." Curtius noted that hundreds of images, motifs, and phrases recurred throughout Western literature, becoming commonplace topoi worthy of study outside their specific usage in a given work. On the vastly smaller scale of one author's corpus, that's what this Tour does: study common places, the topoi that recur in Lovecaft in story after story.

Rather than hunt down every use of "eldritch" or even every mention of Cthulhu, I'm restricting myself to the question of those literally common places in Lovecraft. How do they change? How do they stay the same? What might they mean or indicate? I don't know if we'll find any answers, or if our grubby samples and faded photographs will satisfy the armchair psychiatrists and parlor philosophers who never want to go outside or walk down the street at night. But unlike travellers in Dunwich, we won't be afraid to ask directions. And like Randolph Carter, we may just yet find Lovecraft's sunset city. We just need to wake up and look around us.

---

1. The literary topos closely resembles the postmodern concept of the trope. The word trope comes from the Greek *tropos*, meaning "turning, direction, path," which is nicely geographical as well. From Shakespeare's time until about 1975, "trope" in literary terms simply meant "metaphor" or "figure of speech," referring either to the tendency of speech to turn down a familiar path, or to the turning of words to point at meaning. Now it seems to refer to the same tendency, except about story fragments, what folklorists call motifs. Feel free to grump that people who say "trope" really mean "motif" or "topos" if you want to with my blessing, but this is not the Sentinel Hill I want to die on.

THE WOODS

"But the true epicure in the terrible, to whom a new thrill of unutterable ghastliness is the chief end and justification of existence, esteems most of all the ancient, lonely farmhouses of backwoods New England; for there the dark elements of strength, solitude, grotesqueness and ignorance combine to form the perfection of the hideous."

— H.P. LOVECRAFT, "THE PICTURE IN THE HOUSE"

The very first time Lovecraft puts us down in the Miskatonic Valley, we go astray trying to take "the shortest cut to Arkham." We're lost in the woods, looking at "The Picture in the House," the 1920 story that serves as well as anywhere to begin our second Tour de Lovecraft. It begins with one of the great opening lines in an oeuvre not shy of them: "Seekers after horror haunt strange far places." The trouble is that in the delight of the phrase, readers can miss the paragraph's (and the author's) further point—that your own backyard is scarier still, if you stop to look.

And our unnamed narrator does stop to look, and he sees a picture, Plate XII in the *Regnum Congo*, depicting a cannibal butcher shop of the Anziques … in a clearing in a forest. Which is to say, right where we are now, albeit eight levels from us. We read about the picture, as written by Lovecraft, as relayed by the narrator, as described by the old cannibal, as illustrated by "the brothers De Bry," from text printed in a Latin edition, of a book originally written in Italian, by an author (Filippo Pigafetta) telling another traveler's (Duarte Lopez') story.[2]

The secret of immortality, the black horror at the heart of life itself, thus

---

2. And since Lovecraft never actually saw a copy of *Regnum Congo*, but depended on descriptions and some reproductions in book by Thomas Huxley, that's either one or two more levels in there somewhere.

lies at the center of an intertextual labyrinth—and in the center of "lawless luxuriances of green" along a "remote, devious, and problematical course" through a forested maze. Even this early in his career, Lovecraft interplays his geographies and his narratives, composing a fugue of unreality and hideous hints. This interleaved, almost archaeological, narrative joins us— also guilty onlookers at a potential cannibal butchery—the narrator, and the Anziques … in the woods.

> *"They stood quite still and looked at the forest,*
> *Saw how high were the great cedars,*
> *And gazed upon the entrance to the forest.*
> *There, where Humbaba was wont to tread,*
> *Was a fine path; straight it was and easy to travel.*
> *They saw also the Cedar Mountain, where lived the gods…"*

> — EPIC OF GILGAMESH (ROBERT TEMPLE, TRANS.)

Lovecraft is hardly alone at setting such things in the woods, or even starting them there. The most famous wrong turning in the woods, of course, is Dante's, who finds himself "in a dark wood, as the straight way was lost." The result is a vision of Hell, much like that of our Arkham-bound narrator. The midnight forest, the labyrinthine elder ruin, the dark tangle of Arkham streets: Angela Carter reminds us they all lead into the same maze for Lovecraft, the maze where you can lose your self and find a monstrous secret at the center. The wood holds dark sorcery—the Druid woods of Lucan's *Pharsalia* (65 A.D.) conceal, Dunwich-style, "altars horrible / On massive stones upreared / sacred with blood of men." The forest contains, even nurtures a doom. It may be as deserved as Dante's Hell, as Tacitus' Germani who wait to punish decadent Rome, as Birnam Wood ready to flow down upon the guest-slaying Macbeth.

The woods are also the home of a strange figure, the Wodewose, or Wild Man of the Woods. He can be a man-eating ogre like the old man in "Picture" or the witch in Grimm's fairy tales. He might be a wild, prophetic figure like the Welsh Myrddin or Chretien's Yvain. He might partake of both, like Pan or the Green Knight. Enkidu begins as an ogre, and becomes a hero; reflecting that path, the Wild Man of the Woods becomes the Noble Savage. Enkidu becomes Natty Bumppo. Sometimes, as with Lord Greystoke, the Noble Savage is actually a Savage Noble: Robin Hood, or Duke Senior in the Forest of Arden from *As You Like It*. In all these cases, the Man in the Woods is outside time, unbounded by law, in a constant state of Misrule—just as Lovecraft's old man is immortal, white-bearded but lively … and a cannibal.

"Branching away now and then were narrow, half-concealed roads that bored their way through solid, luxuriant masses of forest among whose primal trees whole armies of elemental spirits might well lurk."

— H.P. LOVECRAFT, "THE WHISPERER IN DARKNESS"

Dante's—and Lovecraft's—wood also holds demons and devils, beginning with Humbaba, who haunts the Cedar Forest and makes even great Gilgamesh nervous at the "fine path" leading ever deeper inward. Hawthorne's "Young Goodman Brown" (1835) meets the Devil in the woods, Cooper's Hawkeye duels with his own nemesis Magua in the forest, and the family in Flannery O'Connor's "A Good Man is Hard to Find" (1953) meets their death there. American authors like Hawthorne, Cooper, O'Connor, and Lovecraft especially felt the pull of what, in *Supernatural Horror in Literature,* Lovecraft called "the vast and gloomy virgin forests in whose perpetual twilight all terrors might well lurk."

He goes on to note that American forests came pre-stocked with "hordes of coppery Indians whose strange, saturnine visages and violent customs hinted strongly at traces of infernal origin…" Robert E. Howard's subtly ambivalent "Beyond the Black River" (1935) transposes the Indians to the white-skinned (but "dark") Picts, and the American forest to primeval Hyboria. This quintessentially colonialist transference echoes Conrad's *Heart of Darkness* (1902) and its racial Misrule echoes Lovecraft's description of Plate XII, in which the Anziques are depicted "with white skins and Caucasian features" although the old man believes they are "kinder like Injuns ... even ef they be in Afriky." Again, the forests of the Congo and the Miskatonic valleys become the same.

> *"In the tunnels of that twisted wood, whose low prodigious oaks twine groping boughs and shine dim with the phosphorescence of strange fungi, dwell the furtive and secretive Zoogs; who know many obscure secrets of the dream world and a few of the waking world, since the wood at two places touches the lands of men, though it would be disastrous to say where."*

> — H.P. LOVECRAFT, *THE DREAM-QUEST OF UNKNOWN KADATH*

The forests in Lovecraft—and woods or forests appear in over a third of his tales—serve similar functions. To Lovecraft, as to Mircea Eliade, "the forest is a symbol which contains death." In "The Thing on the Doorstep," Ephraim Waite's cult center lies "in the heart of the Maine woods," and we've already noted the parallels between Lucan's grove and the "forested sides" of the hills in "The Dunwich Horror." In "The Tomb," the "hideous soul of the forest" calls Jervas Dudley to self-discovery and undeath. Those "mazes of the wooded hollow," like the Arkham woods in "Picture," and the "wild maze of hills" around the uncanny "Tree on the Hill," hold minotaurine hybrid realities. In "The Call of Cthulhu," the forest shelters the altar and alien idol of Cthulhu; Legrasse pursues the cult "through the terrible cypress woods where day never came."

This reveals Old Castro, the mad priest of Cthulhu, as a Wild Man of the Woods, and true to form he provides an oracle of mankind's doom and Cthulhu's rising. If Old Castro is Enkidu, then Shub-Niggurath, "the Black Goat of the Woods" is Humbaba. Other Lovecraftian Wodewoses are more ambivalent—the tower of "The Outsider" lies among "terrible trees"—or even positive—in "The Silver Key" the woods surround Randolph Carter's Arkham house, and Carter himself at times. But mostly the Lovecraftish woods hold ogres like our cannibal, or hordes of "strange, saturnine" beings such as the degenerate Martenses of "The Lurking Fear," in which tale Lovecraft tells us that Tempest Mountain lies amid "miles of primeval forest" and that the Martense mansion itself is "forest-swathed."

Although Lovecraft doesn't make the vegetation level explicitly clear, Harley Warren meets his death in the "Big Cypress Swamp," which implies trees and big ones to boot. Lovecraft's woods bloat: the trees in Dunwich "seem too large," and the trunks around the blasted heath grow "too big for any healthy New England wood." Even in the urban jungle of Boston's North End, Richard Upton Pickman paints "deep woods" into the background of his ghoul portraits. In *Charles Dexter Ward*, we learn (delightfully enough, from Judge *Hathorne*) that "fortie Witches and the Blacke Man were wont to meete in the Woodes behind Mr. Hutchinson's house." Again, in "The Whisperer in the Darkness," like Hawthorne's Devil, the Mi-Go make "surprising offers to lone travelers on roads and cart-paths in the deep woods."

> *"Then I saw that dark westward tangle of glens and slopes for myself, and ceased to wonder at anything beside its own elder mystery. It was morning when I saw it, but shadow lurked always there. The trees grew too thickly, and their trunks were too big for any healthy New England wood. There was too much silence in the dim alleys between them, and the floor was too soft with the dank moss and mattings of infinite years of decay."*
>
> — H.P. LOVECRAFT, "THE COLOUR OUT OF SPACE"

But perhaps the most famous, and in a way the most perplexing, Lovecraftian forest is the one that begins "The Colour Out of Space." You know the one, the forest "west of Arkham," where "the hills rise wild, and there are valleys with deep woods that no axe has ever cut." (This is more than a little reminiscent of Lucan's Druid "grove / Which from the earliest time no hand of man / Had dared to violate." But we stray, again, from our path.) What, you may ask, is this earthy, Earthly forest doing here, in the quintessential alien, cosmic tale of extraterrestrial terror? It's not even a permanently evil forest. Lovecraft assures us that "these were not haunted woods, and their fantastic dusk was never terrible till the strange days." And besides, they're all going underwater: "miles of old wood … to be blotted out" by the new reservoir.

The woods in this vale, in this tale, are twofold. First, it happens here, because like the not-quite shortcut to Arkham in our earlier tale, the woods in "Colour" are a liminal zone, a borderland between rule and Mis-rule. (In what may be an arch reference to that earlier story, Lovecraft describes the countryside as "too much like some forbidden woodcut in a tale of terror.") This is true of forests all across the tales. Lovecraft puts an Enchanted Wood on the boundary of Dreamland; he puts "The Tomb" (leading between death and life, between dream and reality, between past and present) in "the darkest of the hillside thickets." His Mi-Go haunt woods "above the limits of normal hill-climbing," along two edges at once. Forests run along the wall of sleep: like the Colour, Joe Slater is found in the woods, "unconscious in the hollow of a tree." The resurrected Joseph Curwen lives on Lockwood Street. (What do you lock? A door.) In 1692, his partner Hutchinson lived on the *edge* of "the Woodes."

And second, the Forest is symbolically the reversal—the *blasphemous* reversal, as the atheist Lovecraft would so often, and so oddly, put it—of the Garden. The trees grow "too thickly," after all. The Colour falls to earth on a farm in the woods belonging to—the Gardner (Gardener) family. It is the *fiat lux*, the "let there be light" (but what light) of a new Creation, a re-replacement of the firmament with the Chaos that once "moved upon the face of the deep." (And at the end, the deep will move over its face, in yet another reversal.) The entire Bible is recreated here in the "blasted heath" (a reversal of a reversal—a place where nothing grows, in the midst of forest that should be Gardened) as the Colour's exodus from space is marked by a "pillar of smoke" like the Godhead above the fleeing Hebrews.

Three "wise men" from Arkham attend the Colour's birth, which occurs in June, on the opposite side of the calendar from Christmas. It poisons the well of life. Unlike the old man in "Picture in the House," the Colour does not even offer a blasphemous sacrament of immortality, but changes flesh and blood to inert matter in a lengthy first and last supper. It does not die on the Tree but lives on in the trees, the "fat oaks that shine and move as they ought not to do at night." There are twelve witnesses (seven live and five dead) to the Colour's Ascension, which happens in November, six months away from May. At the end, there shall be no Revelation, but instead a great covering up. The Garden is sealed by fire; the Forest is concealed by water, a mirror to the alien sky.

Arkham

"Now I found myself upon an apparently abandoned road which I had chosen as the shortest cut to Arkham ..."

— H.P. Lovecraft, "The Picture in the House"

With those words, Lovecraft introduces his signature setting to the rest of the world. Five of Lovecraft's tales are set primarily in Arkham— "The Unnamable," "Herbert West—Reanimator," "The Silver Key," "The Dreams in the Witch House," and "The Thing on the Doorstep"—more than Boston, or New York, or even Providence. Arkham also serves as a major counterpoint to the primary setting in "The Dunwich Horror" and "The Colour Out of Space," and takes a turn as the backdrop in "The Shadow Out of Time." It has become a permanent part of the atlas of the imagination, alongside Hobbiton and Atlantis and Trantor.

"[My] mental picture of Arkham is of a town something like Salem in atmosphere [and] style of houses, but more hilly [and] with a college ... I place the town [and] the imaginary Miskatonic ... somewhere north of Salem—perhaps near Manchester..."

— H.P. Lovecraft, letter to F. Lee Baldwin (April 29, 1934)

His acolytes, not content with climbing Federal Hill or exploring Red Hook, have tried to pin Arkham to their own maps as well. Will Murray presented an ingenious argument that Lovecraft initially sited Arkham in central Massachusetts, specifically where the similar-sounding town of Oakham sits ten miles east of the Quabbin Reservoir. And indeed, any ordinary reading of "The Colour Out of Space" (speaking of reservoirs) implies an Arkham amid the wild hills far from the sea. But against that, we have numerous descriptions of Arkham as a river port hard by coastal Kingsport and Innsmouth, and Lovecraft's own description in letters (to Donald Wandrei in 1927 and August Derleth in 1931, among others) of seaboard Salem as "my Arkham." Salem certainly has its own Witch House, and (according to an HPL letter of 1927) a tree-split grave slab in Salem's Charter Street Burying Ground served as the model for the one in "The Unnamable." Perhaps it's not entirely the narrator's fault, in "The Picture in the House," that he gets lost looking for Arkham.

> *"What lay behind our joint love of shadows and marvels was, no doubt, the ancient, mouldering, and subtly fearsome town in which we live— witch-cursed, legend-haunted Arkham, whose huddled, sagging gambrel roofs and crumbling Georgian balustrades brood out the centuries beside the darkly muttering Miskatonic."*
>
> — H.P. LOVECRAFT, "THE THING ON THE DOORSTEP"

Though it's not quite clear why one might be in a hurry to get to Arkham at all, given its unpleasant associations with "traditions of horror, madness, and witchcraft," in Nathaniel Peaslee's words. Even its creator seems repulsed by the town: Lovecraft calls it "terrible," "haunted," and "crumbling," a "black city" with a "brooding, festering horror" to it. In "The Dreams in the Witch House," Walter Gilman encounters "an ancient crone" in the "dark tangle of lanes near the abandoned wharves." He had sought geometry and history, communing with the ancient soul of Arkham in "shadowy tangles of unpaved musty-smelling lanes." Arkham is a maze, a labyrinth, the man-made image of the hideous woods, and like them holds a dark secret at its heart.

Arkham's "centuried gambrel roofs," those "huddled, sagging," "tottering," "hoary," "moss-grown," and "clustering" constructions, signify the horror in tale after tale. They, and Arkham, are crouched and old in the way of the Old Ones and the cannibal in the woods, a baleful "hoary" age. In "The Dreams in the Witch House," "changeless" Arkham's gam-brel roofs are explicitly linked with Arkham's other great evil, witches: they "sway and sag over attics where witches hid from the King's men in the dark, olden days of the Province." Arkham, where children disap-pear every May Eve, is "witch-cursed" or "witch-accursed" or "witch-haunted" (twice in "The Silver Key") or "whisper-haunted," or "legend-haunted." This connection, by the way, points to the special horror of the gambrel roof; it is a relic of the "ghastly, festering" Puritan seventeenth century, not the glorious Augustan eighteenth, where Lovecraft fancied himself at home.

> *"[T]he pastures slope up to the ridge above the Miskatonic and give a lovely vista of Arkham's white Georgian steeples across leagues of river and meadow. Here he found a shady road to Arkham, but no trail at all in the seaward direction he wished."*
>
> — H.P. LOVECRAFT, "THE STRANGE HIGH HOUSE IN THE MIST"

That century, however, Arkham also represents, significantly in its "white Georgian steeples," and even the "crumbling Georgian balustrades" in "The Thing on the Doorstep." Arkham is part of the "breathlessly lovely panorama" in "The Silver Key," and part of the sunset city likewise seen by Randolph Carter in *The Dream-Quest of Unknown Kadath*. But it is not merely lovely in the dream or Dunsanian tales, it is representative of order and sanity in the later Miskatonic stories. Even its "labyrinthine water-front alleys" shelter Gilman from Keziah's gaze, human architecture and urbanity briefly hiding its residents from the Outside.

In "The Shadow Over Innsmouth," Arkham is the bright mirror held up to Innsmouth's even more shadowy and decrepit nature. The Arkham-born grocery clerk shows "brightness and affability" and at-tends a decent church (Asbury Methodist Episcopal) in Arkham rather than the debased cults of Innsmouth. Even in a "dark Arkham" tale like "The Thing on the Doorstep," Innsmouth is still worse; as Upton reminds us, "Arkham folk avoid going to Innsmouth whenever they can." In "The Dunwich Horror," Arkham is not merely the "good twin" to decadent Dunwich, but its antidote: Arkham kills both sons of Yog-Sothoth, and "the Arkham men" are embodiments of order and reason. Meanwhile, "The Festival" tells us that compared to Kingsport, Arkham is "broad-minded," with better hospitals.

Not only is Arkham wise and caring, but it is conventional and even bland, cynically laughing at meteor stories and uncomprehending of Kingsport's temporal drifts. "They must have lied when they said the trolleys ran to this place," muses the narrator, prefiguring the contrast in "The Whisperer in Darkness" between remote Vermont and Wilmarth's native Arkham, part of the "mechanised, urbanised" region of New England. By this 1930 tale, even the trains run to Arkham; there's a stodgy, respectable commuter train into Boston (the 8:07).[3] "Changeless" "hoary" Arkham has become one of "the sections which modernity has touched," no doubt featuring "foreigners and factory-smoke, bill-boards and concrete roads."[4] A year later, in "Dreams in the Witch House" we return to "eldritch brown houses of unknown age [that] leaned and tottered and leered mockingly through narrow, small-paned windows." There Walter Gilman studies hyper-modern mathematics and medieval metaphysics alike.

"About 'Arkham' and 'Kingsport'—bless my soul! but I thought I'd told you all about them years ago! They are typical but imaginary places—like the river 'Miskatonic,' whose name is simply a jumble of Algonquin roots."

— H.P. LOVECRAFT, LETTER TO AUGUST DERLETH (NOVEMBER 6, 1931)

Perhaps we can resolve this duality dilemma not by locating Arkham the place, but by reading Arkham the sign. Robert Marten believes that "Arkham" comes not from the location "Oakham" but from the name of

---

3. By 1933 and "The Thing on the Doorstep," there's also an 8:20 p.m. night train to Boston, with continuing service to New York City.

4. On the evidence of "Dreams in the Witch House," Arkham has a substantial Polish community by 1930.

the Rhode Island township of "Arkwright," in metropolitan Providence, named for the proto-industrialist Richard Arkwright. Lovecraft may or may not have taken his fiction's name from Arkwright, but unlike Dunwich (a real town in Suffolk), he could not have taken it from England, either. (The closest homonym is the tiny living of Arkholme in Lancashire.) It's perhaps more likely, and certainly more interesting, that Lovecraft built the name deliberately.

Let's start with the easy half, -ham. It has two possible Anglo-Saxon derivations: from *hám*, or "home," as in Nottingham; or from *hamm*, or "enclosure" (cognate with "hemmed in"), as in Oakham. (As the Massachusetts-Bay Puritans came mostly from East Anglia, we can omit the derivation from the Norse *holm*, or "island," most common in the North, as in Durham.) And then there's the Ark. Here, also, we have two options: the Ark of the Covenant, preserving Law and Order against the wilderness; and the Ark of Noah, carrying bestial survivals away from righteous wrath and disaster. Is Arkham the enclosure of the Ark, the shelter for ancient lore safe from mundane gaze? Or are its "ancient, cryptically brooding hills" the resting place of those who fled the Flood, the home of primordial evils and ancient witchcraft?

> *"It was always a very bad time in Arkham, even though the fine folks up in Miskatonic Avenue and High and Saltonstall Streets pretended to know nothing about it."*
>
> — H.P. LOVECRAFT, "THE DREAMS IN THE WITCH HOUSE"

Arkham is "crumbling" and "changeless," rational and mad. Its "labyrinthine alleys" conceal and reveal the horror. It is what Robert H. Waugh has called the "double city," both ideal and shadow, both personal and fancied. (Prefiguring Waugh, Barton Levi St. Armand also identifies the horror-attraction of opposites—Jung's *mysterium coniunctionis*—as a key to Lovecraft's creations.) In "The Dreams in the Witch House," Arkham stretches back into "the monstrous past," and perhaps those "centuries of dark brooding had given [Arkham] a peculiar vulnerability" to Yithian influence, as Peaslee suggests. Consider Arkham as a magnet, or vortex, or weak spot in space-time, drawing alien shadows and heroic Armitages alike.

In *At the Mountains of Madness,* the brig that transmits Dyer's (the one who dies?) messages from the camp at Kadath to academic civilization, the intermediary between Hell and the waking world, is named the *Arkham.* The eponymous city likewise speaks to two realms, even as its name carries two burdens. Its police raid Walpurgis Night revelers on Meadow Hill but "never believed such things." Perhaps, much as Arkham switches from rustic backwater to bustling coastal railhead, and from witch-haunted blight to Georgian bulwark, it is both home and enclosure to both Arks.

Lovecraft begins by littering the hinterland of Arkham with unnatural survivals—the immortal cannibal, Herbert West's zombies, the Unnamable in the burying ground—like jetsam on the slopes of Ararat. (The *Arabian Nights*-obsessed HPL would perhaps have known of the Arabic legend that some monsters survived the Flood by clinging to the Ark in the darkness.) But soon enough, Arkham becomes a shelter, an enclosure, first against the chaotic floodwaters underlying Kingsport and later, literally—like the Biblical Ark of the Covenant—against the hosts of Dagon. The sign changes, or is lettered on both sides, but the name remains the same.

DREAMLAND

"Why the beings and the sculptures lingered so late in the world, even until the coming of men, none can tell; unless it was because the land of Mnar is very still, and remote from most other lands, both of waking and of dream."

— H.P. LOVECRAFT, "THE DOOM THAT CAME TO SARNATH"

Finding the "first appearance" of Lovecraft's Dreamlands involves a perhaps appropriately murky exploration. For instance, his first three mature tales—"The Tomb," "Dagon," and "Polaris"—all involve dream visions that may or may not also be travel narratives. The first explicit mention of "lands of dream" (a notion Lovecraft took from Dunsany, or perhaps from Winsor McKay?) in Lovecraft's fiction is in "The Doom that Came to Sarnath," but the only tale explicitly set in the Dreamlands is *The Dream-Quest of Unknown Kadath*. On the other hand, out of Lovecraft's fifty-one solo stories,[5] forty feature or mention dreams, and five more mention nightmares. Of the six remaining, two—"The Cats of Ulthar" and "The Other Gods"—are conventionally considered "Dreamland" stories, though that convention, like the "pink marble city of the clouds" Serranian, dissolves if you examine it too closely.

---

5. This number includes the 49 standard solo tales in, e.g., the Penguin Classics Lovecraft, plus his early, disavowed weird tale "The Transition of Juan Romero" and his long and flavor-filled dream transcript "The Very Old Folk." It doesn't include his pre-1917 juvenilia, fragments ("Azathoth," "The Book," "The Descendant," "The Evil Clergyman," "The Thing in the Moonlight"), sonnet cycle (*The Fungi From Yuggoth*) or other poetry, lesser prose poems ("Ex Oblivione," "Memory," "What the Moon Brings"), comic pieces ("Old Bugs," "Sweet Ermengarde"), racist satire ("The Street"), or proto-Borgesian 'non'-fictions ("A Reminiscence of Samuel Johnson," "History of the *Necronomicon*," "Ibid.").

Lovecraft explicitly locates Leng, Kadath, Sarnath, and Lomar in both his "real world" and in the Dreamlands. Even Randolph Carter, the soul-symbol of the Dream Cycle, spends at least half his time in waking world adventures. Further, Lovecraft drew elements of many of his stories, including "The Statement of Randolph Carter," "Nyarlathotep," and "The Call of Cthulhu," from his own dreams. In that last story, the sculptor Wilcox recounts his (and Lovecraft's) dream, which was "sent by" Cthulhu in some occult fashion. In a sense, Lovecraft's entire cosmos, from "changeless, legend-haunted" Arkham to the vaults of Zin, is a Dreamland.

The boundary between "Dreamland" stories and "Mythos" stories is so thin as to be risible. As thin, indeed, as one suspects Lovecraft considers the boundaries between the mundane world and any of his higher dimensions: the ultra-violet, hyperspace, the Dreamlands, the past of "He," or the chaos outside Erich Zann's window. Or, to be sure, the boundaries between life and death in "Cool Air" or madness and reality in "Hypnos" or tale and truth in "Quest of Iranon" or man and monster in "Shadow Over Innsmouth" or science and blasphemy in "The Dunwich Horror." Thin-ness of boundaries, the lack of walls—of sleep or otherwise—seems to be a huge meta-concern spanning all of Lovecraft's work.

> *"They reminded him, too, that not only had no man ever been to Kadath, but no man had ever suspected in what part of space it may lie; whether it be in the dreamlands around our own world, or in those surrounding some unguessed companion of Fomalhaut or Aldebaran. If in our dreamland, it might conceivably be reached…"*

> — H.P. LOVECRAFT, *THE DREAM-QUEST OF UNKNOWN KADATH*

Dreamland, meanwhile, is somewhere else. It is on the other side of the Gates of Deeper Slumber, and through a ghoul-burrow, and just that side of the Tanarian Hills, and through the Enchanted Wood. And that's just in one novel, the *Dream-Quest*. In "The White Ship" Basil Elton takes a White Ship across the Southern Sea to what might be Dreamland. King

Kuranes of "Celephaïs" merely nods off and "journeys" there, although the specific "there" seems to vary with his age. The Dreamland is both the "inner world" and "around our world," and there are other "regions of dream" that aren't it at all. Dreamland has its own Moon and Saturn, at least, and there are other dreamlands entirely "surrounding some unguessed companion of Fomalhaut or Aldebaran."

Parts of it resemble Earth—such as the patch of Cornwall dreamed into existence by Kuranes—and parts of it might even be on Earth, such as Randolph Carter's Novanglian "sunset city," which he reaches not by falling asleep but by waking up. Jason Eckhardt points out that Dreamland resembles an "exploded" or "expanded" New England, despite its Symbolist coloration. Ulthar, for example, has not just cats and notaries but "old peaked roofs and overhanging upper stories." Inganok, the northernmost human city in the Dreamlands, has a central Temple (church) square complete with bell tower, and the taciturn residents keep to themselves in "pride and secrecy," and keep the old rhythms of life. In the Dreamlands, the gods look like New Englanders, with narrow eyes, pointed chins, thin noses, and long ears.

> *"It was very strange, but as the riders went on they seemed to gallop back through Time…"*

> — H.P. LOVECRAFT, "CELEPHAÏS"

Perhaps more of Dreamland than we, or Randolph Carter, suspect lies on the Earth. Ulthar, for example, receives a visit from a young cat-fancier named Menes who (we are led to infer) will grow up to be that Menes who became the first Pharaoh of Egypt, dating the events of "The Cats of Ulthar" to approximately 3100 B.C. Sarnath and Ib are explicitly dated to "ten thousand years ago," and in *At the Mountains of Madness*, Ib joins such faultlessly terrestrial locations as Atlantis, R'lyeh, Lomar, and Arabia's Nameless City. *At the Mountains of Madness* also incidentally further confounds the locations of Kadath and Leng, both occasional features of the Dreamlands, by identifying them with the Old Ones' Antarctic conurbation.

"The Other Gods" situates Kadath among such Dreamland environs as Hatheg-Kla, Ulthar, and so forth, but then sets them all "in the youth of the world." Dreamland, in other words, is an ancestral memory-plane, or even the ancient world itself—note that Lomar, visited in dreams by the narrator of "Polaris," turns out to be an ancient (fl. 24,000 B.C.) country. In this context, it is perhaps significant that Lovecraft's Commonplace Book story-seed for "Celephaïs" reads: "Man journeys into the past— or imaginative realm—leaving bodily shell behind." And indeed, when Kuranes makes his final trip to Celephaïs, the riders escorting him seem "to gallop back through Time" past "houses and villagers such as Chaucer or men before him might have seen."

> "Then he saw a sort of grey phosphorescence about, and guessed they were coming even to that inner world of subterrene horror of which dim legends tell, and which is litten only by the pale death-fire wherewith reeks the ghoulish air and the primal mists of the pits at earth's core."
>
> — H.P. LOVECRAFT, *THE DREAM-QUEST OF UNKNOWN KADATH*

But is Kuranes really traveling to the distant past on his final ride? It is, after all, his final ride because his hashish-stupefied "bodily shell" has fallen over an English cliffside somewhere. In short, Kuranes dies and goes to the Dreamlands. Something similar happens to Richard Upton Pickman, who is dragged into a tunnel in his Boston cellar only to emerge as a ghoul in the Dreamlands, a tough enough trick to manage even without adding time-travel to the mix. Barzai the Wise falls "into the sky" above Kadath, into a "damnable pit." George Wetzel's bravura essay "The Cthulhu Mythos" identifies the Dreamland directly with Hell, or rather with Elysium and Tartarus intermixed.

The ghouls, and their vast piles of bones in the Vale of Pnath, usher in this hellish atmosphere. Moreover, the Dreamlands of the *Dream-Quest* are full of "daemon" entities, "gargoyles," and other infernal signifiers, lurking in omnipresent pits, abysses, and gulfs. Like Dante's inferno, the way to the Dreamland lies both in the middle of a wood and in the "inner world." (Better yet, Mt. Ngranek lies within "the primal mists of the earth's core.") Like Avernus, one descends (770 steps) into Dreamland, although contra Virgil, the descent is not as easy as all that.

"A blessed haze lies upon all this region, wherein is held a little more of the sunlight than other places hold, and a little more of the summer's humming music of birds and bees; so that men walk through it as through a faery place, and feel greater joy and wonder than they ever afterward remember."

— H.P. LOVECRAFT, *THE DREAM-QUEST OF UNKNOWN KADATH*

Can these three Dreamlands be reconciled? Can the Dreamland be an amorphous parallel dimension, and the ancient past, and the pit of Tartarus all at once? What else might come from dreams and fancies, or the past, or Hell? A sampling of answers: According to the Edwardian anthropologist W.Y. Evans-Wentz, changelings are made while children are asleep. On the Isle of Skye, falling asleep on a fairy mound results in being taken to Fairyland. As the Irish author 'A.E.' put it: "Many go to the Tir-na-nog in sleep, and some are said to have remained there." Shakespeare's fairy encounters occur in an Enchanted Wood (zoog-free) during a midsummer night's dream.

So much for dreams. What of the past? The Irish *Book of Conquests* tells of the primordial Tuatha de Danaan, who retreated inside the hills to become the Daoine Sidh, or fairies, keeping their ancient world alive there. Lovecraft and Arthur Machen, among others, took this to mean that the "little people" were ancient survivals of a "Mongolian" race of pre-Britons. And Hell? Again, Evans-Wentz reports beliefs across the Celtic world identifying the fairies with the spirits of the dead. The sluagh of the Highlands are the evil dead; Finvarra's troops in Ireland are likewise sinister sorts. Lady Wilde even reports an Irish legend that the fairies are fallen angels. And of course Hell, Faërie, and Lovecraft's Dreamland are all underground realms.

Like Lovecraft's ghouls, fairies snatch trespassers and feed them a transforming food that keeps them in Fairyland forever. The merchants of Dylath-Leen, and the slavers from the Moon, and the night-gaunts, all likewise kidnap passersby in fine fairy style. The fate of Iranon in his eponymous quest resembles that of King Herla, who aged to dust upon return from Faërie. Like "Tir-na-nog," the fairies' Land of Youth, Ooth-Nargai holds "only perpetual youth." Sona-Nyl, where "there is neither time nor space," sounds like the eternal twilight realm of infinite meadows and forests tucked inside a fairy mound.

The peculiar behavior of time and space in the Dreamland likewise tracks the tales of a night's dancing that lasts seven years, or of fairy rides across all England in a night. Dreamland and Fairyland overlap thoroughly, albeit mysteriously. Lovecraft read Machen and A.E., and the Anglo-Irish Lord Dunsany was of course familiar with the renaissance in Irish fairy lore that was occurring all around him. Exactly how the sidhe became the ghouls, or the redcaps the gugs, we may never know. But it seems as clear as the River Skai that whether by design, inspiration, or Dunsany, Lovecraft had discovered Fairyland, and dreamed himself its creator.

THE MOON

"I hate the moon—I am afraid of it—for when it shines on certain scenes familiar and loved it sometimes makes them unfamiliar and hideous."

— H.P. LOVECRAFT, "WHAT THE MOON BRINGS"

The moon shifts under (or over) our analysis: as one of the oldest, most powerful symbols in all of human culture, it's hard to pin Lovecraft down when he uses it. Furthermore, it's an entirely natural descriptive feature of stories—like most horror stories—happening at night. We should keep in mind the wise caveat of T.R. Livesey, who reminds us (for example) that Lovecraft uses the moon and sun for the same symbolic purpose—implacable witness of the explorer's revelation—in "The Nameless City" and *At the Mountains of Madness*. Because, of course, exploring Kadath at night in Antarctica still happens under the midnight sun.

Lovecraft goes farther than standard horror atmospherics in some of his tales. Most notably, Randolph Carter's *Dream-Quest of Unknown Kadath* leads him to the Moon itself, and the beings of Ib filter down from the Moon to the plain of Mnar in "The Doom That Came to Sarnath." The Moon as a physical body acts as a foil to the titular Mountains of Madness despite never appearing in the sky of that novel. The moon takes an active hand in the events of "Nyarlathotep" and arguably (at least given the title) "What the Moon Brings," and in the persona of Artemis she draws Denys Barry up to her from "The Moon-Bog."

Another moon-goddess unleashes "The Horror at Red Hook," and a less fatal moon-bridge glimmers athwart "The White Ship." The dark of the moon (or moonset) unleashes the Mi-Go in "The Whisperer in

Darkness," the Thing in "The Unnamable," and Yig in "The Curse of Yig." Adding the pro forma werewolf moon in "The Ghost Eater" and the titular moon from the fragment "The Thing in the Moonlight" gives us nine stories, two revisions, and two prose poems in which the moon (or even the Moon)[6] plays a notable story role.

> *"Moonlight! Good God, what cheap sentimentality! For a supposedly sophisticated person you surely do hang on to some of the crudest claptrap that ever escaped from the dime novels! With art at your elbow, you have to think of the moon—cheap as a spotlight at the varieties! Or perhaps it makes you think of the Roodmas dance around the stone pillars at Auteuil."*

> — H.P. LOVECRAFT AND ZEALIA BISHOP, "MEDUSA'S COIL"

In just about twice that many stories, Lovecraft specifically provides the phase of the moon.[7] In an author's note to "Transition of Juan Romero" he mentions looking up the phases of the moon, and changing the story to fit—Lovecraft inserts his lunations deliberately. By far the most common Lovecraftian moon is full, appearing nine times, followed by the crescent (both waxing and waning) and gibbous (likewise) with five appearances apiece. (This counts the moon in "Celephaïs" twice, as it appears in a waning crescent over Earth and full over Celephaïs in Dreamland.) Twice he merely describes the moon as "waning," a half moon shines over "The Colour Out of Space" and "The Mound," and surprisingly the mystic new moon appears alone only once, in "The Very Old Folk." That said, in both "The Quest of Iranon" and "Whisperer in Darkness," the moon bats for the cycle, appearing as new and full and often other phases in between.

In ten stories and four revisions, the moon provides a strong thematic element. (And in the prose poem "Memory," which features the "Genie who haunts the moonbeams.") Often its phase signals the state of the pro-

---

6. In this Stop, I capitalize the actual astronomical body ("the Moon") and leave lowercase the optical and symbolic element in the sky ("the moon").

7. For details of this and other assertions in this section, see The Table in the Moonlight, at the end of this Stop on p. 34.

tagonist: e.g., as a waning crescent in "Polaris," first tender then full then without phase in "Quest of Iranon," eclipsed at the fatal climax of "The Other Gods." Sometimes it glares malevolently at blasphemous excavations, as in "The Nameless City" and "The Shadow Out of Time." In both, the moon seems eerily connected to the alien city, explicitly so in the earlier story. As in werewolf movies, the moon sometimes heralds or points up the approach of danger ("The Horror at Martin's Beach," "Medusa's Coil") or reveals the terror ("The Crawling Chaos," "He"). However, in at least four tales (five if you count the explicit lunar discouragement of the Outer Ones in "Whisperer") the natural moon acts as foil for the Outside: "The Unnamable," "The Colour Out of Space," "The Music of Erich Zann," and "The Festival," where its absence allows the cavern witch-light of the Kingsport cult to glitter evilly.

Finally, Lovecraft at least mentions the moon as a scenic element in another twenty tales and six revisions. In some cases, he does so quite evocatively: the white moonlight on the reanimated black boxer Buck Robinson in "Herbert West" may be his single strongest explicitly racist image, while the "gold-green" light of the moon on "Hypnos" provides a less problematic but more tantalizing mystery. The "Year of the Red Moon" in "Out of the Aeons" is just good fun. Lovecraft's near-cinematic (and rigorously astronomically accurate) use of the moon and its shadows in "The Shadow Over Innsmouth" helps bring that hideous town to unforgettable life. Since HPL didn't simply shine descriptive moonlight by rote—the moon barely appears twice in "The Dunwich Horror," and only once in any scene of *Charles Dexter Ward,* for example—when he does provide lunar luminescence, he probably means something by it.

"Their original place of advent to the planet was the Antarctic Ocean, and it is likely that they came not long after the matter forming the moon was wrenched from the neighbouring South Pacific. ... With the upheaval of new land in the South Pacific tremendous events began."

— H.P. LOVECRAFT, *AT THE MOUNTAINS OF MADNESS*

Even when the moon doesn't appear in the story's sky, Lovecraft means something by it. In *At the Mountains of Madness,* the Moon provides an ironic foil to Kadath throughout. Dyer begins by reporting the Elder Things' arrival on Earth in the void (the South Pacific and Antarctic Oceans) left behind by the Moon's ejection from our planet. Both R'lyeh and the Mountains of Madness themselves ("the first part that ever rose from the waters") rise from that void, twin peaks of (anti-lunar) evil boiled up from the hellish Underground. To underline this contrast, Dyer describes his discoveries as radically differentiating (separating) Antarctica from "the sterile disc of the moon." The Moon is pale, pure, and dead—the ideal Lovecraftian protagonist. What's left behind is evil, tainted, and maddening—the true Lovecraftian Earth.

Lovecraft didn't just pull the Moon being pulled out of the Earth out of nowhere. In 1878, George H. Darwin (the son of Charles) did the math and retraced the Moon's expanding orbit back to the point (he calculated 54 million years ago) when it overlapped with the Earth as a "molten viscous mass." In 1882, the geologist Osmond Fisher proposed that the Pacific Ocean basin represented the scar left behind when the Sun's tides wrenched the Moon out of the cooling Earth. Lovecraft probably came across Fisher's theory when Harvard astronomer William H. Pickering recapitulated it in popular works in 1903 and 1907.[8] The Pacific origin hypothesis continued intact into the 1930s, and only when the geology of the Pacific disproved it (the Pacific floor is only 200 million years old, and the Moon is billions of years young) did it finally pass from view.

> *"The close aspect of the moon as the galley drew near proved very disturbing to Carter, and he did not like the size and shape of the ruins which crumbled here and there. The dead temples on the mountains were so placed that they could have glorified no wholesome or suitable gods, and*

---

8. Lovecraft followed Pickering's work assiduously, calling him "the greatest living selenographer" in an article for the *Pawtuxet Valley Gleaner* in 1906. That article, "Is There Life on the Moon?" approvingly cites Pickering's theory that the lunar rays represent hoarfrost emitted by lunar volcanoes.

*in the symmetries of the broken columns there seemed to lurk some dark
and inner meaning which did not invite solution."*

— H.P. LOVECRAFT, *THE DREAM-QUEST OF UNKNOWN KADATH*

The Moon in the Dreamlands has its own connections with the Earth, or
at least with the Dreamlands of Earth. Three-banked black galleys crewed
by the satyr-like men of Leng carry gold and rubies from the Moon to
Dylath-Leen and other cities, taking slaves in return. This casts the Moon
as a sort of satanic or fairy realm, offering treasure in exchange for life. The
"crawling chaos Nyarlathotep" dwells "in a black cave on a far unhallowed
summit of the moon-mountains," the Satan, Pluto, or Oberon of this do-
main. The zoogs ferment their moon-tree wine—a fairy draught?—from
the sap of a tree grown from "a seed dropt down by someone" on the Moon,
and it befuddles even the wisest men into sleep or into sharing mystic
knowledge. The cats, graceful creatures of witchcraft and mystery, leap from
Earth to Moon at night, "to leap and gambol on the hills and converse
with ancient shadows." Like Dreamland itself, Dreamland's Moon appears
as both Fairyland and the land of the dead. When indeed Carter reaches the
Moon to discover that the toad-like moon-beasts actually enslave (and eat)
their own merchants, the satanic parallel seems definite.

Even in the Dreamlands, however, Lovecraft makes sure to put his cats
(and his toad-aliens) on the dark side of the Moon, maintaining astronomical accuracy with a disk of the Earth thirteen times larger than the moon
in Earth's sky. The Dream-Moon exists in a sort of halfway place between
astronomy and myth: the stars (astronomically accurately) still shine during the day on the Moon, although the Dreamlands Moon has an atmosphere that should scatter the sun's light. It also has accurate craters and
sharp mountains, along with moon-tree forests, fields of white fungi,[9] and

---

9. Lovecraft sowed the moon-fungi as a tribute to Clark Ashton Smith's poem "The Hashish-Eater, or,
the Apocalypse of Evil" (1920), which includes the lines: "I know the blooms / of bluish fungus, freak'd
with mercury / That bloat within the craters of the moon."

oily seas. While the moon-beasts show preternatural strength, their cousins the green, jelly-soft men of Ib who came down to Mnar from the Moon in primordial times prove weak in Earth's heavier gravity.

> *"O friend and companion of night, thou who rejoicest in the baying of dogs and spilt blood, who wanderest in the midst of shades among the tombs, who longest for blood and bringest terror to mortals, Gorgo, Mormo, thousand-faced moon, look favourably on our sacrifices!"*

> — H.P. LOVECRAFT, "THE HORROR AT RED HOOK,"
> quoting Edward B. Tylor, "Magic" in *Encyclopaedia Britannica* (9th ed.),
> quoting Hippolytus of Rome, *Refutation of All Heresies*, IV:35 (c. 225 A.D.)

Lovecraft's connection of cats with the Moon also occurred to the ancient Egyptians, who called their cat-goddess Bast "the Eye of the Moon" among other titles. The classical Greeks identified Bast with their moon-goddess Artemis, implying an even closer relationship than the odd epithet. But Lovecraft's relationships with other moon goddesses involve fewer skritches. In "The Horror at Red Hook," the chant of the Red Hook cultists above invokes the "naked phosphorescent" Lilith. Many Edwardian mythological compendia contain confident ascriptions of the Jewish murder-demoness Lilith to the moon, which seem to have originated with Dom Augustin Calmet's *Dictionary of the Bible* (1728) although he cites unnamed "Jewish doctors" as his source.

Lovecraft took that chant from the *Britannica*, which took it from the Christian theologian Hippolytus of Rome, who first wrote it down. According to Hippolytus, charlatans used this chant while invoking Hecate, who by his era was a three-headed goddess of witchcraft worshipped (or placated) at the new moon. The Romans tied Hecate to Diana (Greek Artemis) and Luna (Selene) herself. To the Greeks even as late as Apollonius (3rd century B.C.) Selene and Hecate seemed at odds given Hecate's preference for moonless nights for her witchcraft. In "Medusa's Coil," Lovecraft describes the titular lamia as "Hecate-born snaky strands of hair," and this brings us briefly past Gorgo, or as we usually know her, the

Gorgon.[10] Mormo, meanwhile, began as a Greek murder-demoness very similar to Lilith in legend.

The other moon-goddess active in Lovecraft, Artemis, has an appropriate dark side. In "The Moon-Bog" she and her priestess-avatar Cleis (also the name of a nymph who guards Dionysos, and of Sappho's mother) call up naiads and draw Denys Barry up to "the waning moon." This tracks with Artemis as a virgin goddess objecting to pollution and exposure. But Lovecraft well knew that the very un-virginal Artemis of Ephesus was in fact an aspect of Cybele, the Magna Mater he reviles in "Rats in the Walls" and "Red Hook" (where "headless moon-calves" bleat to her) as a vector of unwholesome rites. Lovecraft also wrote an "Ode to Selene" in 1902; in his poem "Revelation" (1919), he evokes the Phoenician goddess Astarte as a synonym for the moon: "While Astarte, calm and queenly / Floods of fairy radiance shed."

> "Stretching directly from the strange olden ruin on the far islet to the waning moon, my eyes seemed to trace a beam of faint quivering radiance having no reflection in the waters of the bog. And upward along that pallid path my fevered fancy pictured a thin shadow slowly writhing; a vague contorted shadow struggling as if drawn by unseen daemons."
>
> — H.P. LOVECRAFT, "THE MOON-BOG"

The moon as ambivalent (to say the least) fairyland, and the moon-goddess as dangerous (or worse) bring us back into "The Moon-Bog." The moon appears at the end, at one end of the "pallid path" that Gavin Callaghan, among others, identifies with the otherwise cryptic "moon-ladder" from Danforth's glossolalia at the end of *Mountains of Madness*. (A novel, remember, in which the moon never appears in the sky.) Callaghan notes the volcanic mists of those mountains, and the tale's brief mention of "gas-

---

10. Stephen Wilk notes the parallels between Homer's description of the Gorgon head on Achilles' shield and Lovecraft's descriptions of Cthulhu, where snake hair = tentacles, and notes that the Gorgons were marine monsters and daughters of the sea-god Phorcys. In addition to the "Medusa's Coil" lamia, Gavin Callaghan also cites the petrifying gaze of tentacled Ghatanothoa, and Lovecraft's explicit description of Rhan-Tegoth with the "serpentine locks of the Medusa."

eous wraiths" in the upper atmosphere, in this connection. He identifies the moon-ladder as an inversion of Jacob's Ladder to Heaven in Genesis, a bridge connecting vaporous monstrosities from the abyss to the ethereal demons (or aliens) of the air.

Since the moon-ladder most often appears at sea (or over a watery bog), Callaghan connects it with Lovecraft's repeated, often feminized, drowning imagery, apotheosized at the end of "Shadow Over Innsmouth." He further casts it as a metaphor for "the primal sexual act," noting the feminine aspect of the moon, the erectile nature of the "ladder," and the repeated motions up and down it by Lovecraft's various protagonists. One doesn't have to follow Callaghan into full Freudianism to note that the image nevertheless visibly extends (ahem) through Lovecraft's work from his earliest poetry to his last novel.

In the poem "Unda; or, The Bride of the Sea" (1916) Lovecraft describes a poet who sees that: "Straight from the moon to the shore where I'm sighing / Grows a bright bridge, made of wavelets and beams." He walks out "on the moon-path" led by Unda, and drowns. In another poem, "Revelation" (1919), he writes: "Madly on a moonbeam ladder / Heav'n's abyss I sought to scale," while in "To Mr. Galpin" (1921) "Adown the moonbeams' misty road / The nymphs celestial dance their way." He continues the motif in prose: in "The White Ship" (1919) Elton walks to the ship "on a bridge of moonbeams," and as noted in "The Doom That Came to Sarnath" (1919) the mists reach up from the lake of Mnar "to meet the moon" as "shadows descended from the gibbous moon into the lake."

The moon over Kilderry's "Moon-Bog" forces a dance on the workers before drowning them in the bog, while the moon brings on a mass hypnotic movement in "Nyarlathotep" as the god's power comes "down from the greenish moon." In "The Horror at Martin's Beach" a "shimmering lane of reflected moonbeams" serves as the guide wire for the monster's telepathy to hypnotize and drown the would-be rescuers. On an architectural level, the "impious pyramids flung savagely to the moon" in the future

New York of "He" recall the ziggurats of Babylon, actual towers to heaven that inspired the original "impious pyramid": the Tower of Babel. Thus the moon-ladder draws up blasphemy and confusion of language, bringing us to Cthulhu, and the "unpronounceable jumble of letters" that heralds him. Seeing him in the greenish flesh drives Johansen to visualize "hysterical plunges from the pit to the moon and from the moon back again to the pit." Finally, as we've noted, *At the Mountains of Madness* not only names the moon-ladder but creates a physical connection between the Pacific abyss and the Moon.

> *"The moon, slightly past full, shone from a clear sky and drenched the ancient sands with a white, leprous radiance which seemed to me somehow infinitely evil."*

> — H.P. LOVECRAFT, "THE SHADOW OUT OF TIME"

Lovecraft makes the final role of his moon explicit in "What the Moon Brings": the moon as omen, as harbinger, as the bringer of hateful true knowledge in its insane light. The moon reveals that "The Outsider" has dwelt underground; the "Congo moon" in "Arthur Jermyn" sees the sordid truth of his ancestry; the moon signals that Kalos' spirit still animates "The Tree." The reptile-beings of "The Nameless City" go so far as to depict their city under an eternal moonlight, depicting their new abyssal dwelling as a world of "eternal day."

But their propaganda lies; as the moon reveals, they are truly dead. The "evil" and "sardonic" moon in "The Shadow Out of Time" reveals the city of the Great Race in its "leprous radiance." In the seeming exception "He," sunlit New York City shows its true hideous face, while "the moon had hinted of loveliness and elder magic"—but then the full moon opens the way for the personal apocalypse of the magus and the urban apocalypse of future New York. The moon brings terror and doom, to Sarnath, to Danforth, and especially to Lovecraft.

THE TABLE IN THE MOONLIGHT:
LOVECRAFT'S USES OF THE MOON IN FICTION

MOON USED AS STORY ELEMENT		
"The Whisperer in Darkness"	new ("dark of the moon") at climax; entire phase cycles reported	Mi-Go come out on moonless nights
The Dream-Quest of Unknown Kadath	crescent	source of moon-beast pirates; Carter kidnapped to Moon; cat battle scene
"The Doom That Came to Sarnath"	gibbous	city and beings of Ib "descended one night from the moon in a mist"
"The Ghost Eater"	full	werewolf story
"The White Ship"	full	bridge of moonbeams
"The Moon-Bog"	waning	pulls Barry up to aerial torment
"The Thing in the Moonlight"	no phase, "faint"	Thing howls at moon
"The Curse of Yig"	no phase	moonset brings Yig; two mentions
"The Horror at Red Hook"	no phase	thousand-faced goddess
"Nyarlathotep"	no phase	source of taint and mass hypnosis
"What the Moon Brings"	no phase	brings fatal final tide
At the Mountains of Madness	midnight sun	removal leaves evil Mountains; ironic contrast of "sterile disc of the moon" with Antarctica; "moon-ladder"
"The Unnamable"	moonless	the Thing attacks on moonless nights

MOON USED AS STRONG THEMATIC ELEMENT		
"The Quest of Iranon"	begins as new ("tender"), middle full, ends no phase	"square of moonlight … that wasn't like any other light" "visions that danced in the moonbeams"
"The Colour Out of Space"	waxing half	acts as foil to the Colour
"The Shadow Out of Time"	waxing gibbous (Jul 11), slightly past full (Jul 17)	described as "evil," "leprous," "bloated, fungoid" "evil, burning," and "sardonic"; different markings reveal Triassic 'dream'
"He"	full	reveals apocalyptic future
"The Horror at Martin's Beach"	full or near-full ("fairly round")	"what they saw seemed subtly connected with" the moon
"The Other Gods"	full, then eclipsed	reflects Barzai's life

Moon Used as Strong Thematic Element

"Celephaïs"	waning crescent on Earth, full moon in Dream over Celephaïs	reflects Kuranes' life
"Memory"	waning crescent ("feeble horns")	"Genie that haunts the moonbeams"
"Polaris"	waning crescent ("horned, waning")	reflects narrator and city
"The Nameless City"	no phase, "bright" "gleaming vividly" etc.	"cold moon" connected to city "seemed to quiver as though mirrored in unquiet waters"
"The Night Ocean"	no phase, "bright"	illuminates and outlasts narrator; "moon's waxen corpse"
"The Crawling Chaos"	no phase, "ghastly"	reveals apocalypse
"Facts Concerning the Late Arthur Jermyn and His Family"	no phase	Rational 18th century contrasted with "strange scenes under a Congo moon"
"Medusa's Coil"	no phase	both Marceline and Sophy danced by moonlight, Frank despises moonlight
"The Music of Erich Zann"	no phase	return of moon signals returned normality; one mention
"The Festival"	moonless	unnatural earth-light

Moon Used as Scenic Element

"The Very Old Folk"	new moon	one mention
"Dagon"	gibbous	
"The Transition of Juan Romero"	gibbous	one mention
"The Lurking Fear"	nearly full	
"The Outsider"	full	
"The Shadow Over Innsmouth"	not much past full	twenty-eight mentions!
"The Tomb"	waning	two mentions
"The Mound"	waning half	
"The Statement of Randolph Carter"	waning crescent	
"Herbert West—Reanimator"	no phase, "bright"	reveals (and contrasts with?) reanimated black boxer Buck Robinson
"The Hound"	no phase, "pale," "weak"	
"Under the Pyramids"	no phase, "wan," "spectral"	

MOON USED AS SCENIC ELEMENT

"The Call of Cthulhu"	no phase	"hysterical plunges from the pit to the moon and from the moon back again to the pit"
The Case of Charles Dexter Ward	no phase	"the pale moon of Britain," one other mention
"The Dunwich Horror"	no phase	two mentions
"Hypnos"	no phase	sheds "gold-green" light over Hypnos; one mention
"In the Vault"	no phase	
"In the Walls of Eryx"	no phase	Stanfield can see it from Venus; one mention
"Out of the Aeons"	no phase	"Year of the Red Moon"
"Pickman's Model"	no phase	"moonlit sky"; one mention
"The Picture in the House"	no phase	"moonlit towers of Rhine castles"; no moon in story itself
"The Silver Key"	no phase	Dreamlands "sleep lovely and unbroken under the moon"
"The Terrible Old Man"	no phase	one mention
"The Tree"	no phase	one mention
"Through the Gates of the Silver Key"	no phase	Dreamlands "sleep lovely and unbroken under the moon"; recalls "waning moon" in Big Cypress Swamp incident
"Till A' the Seas"	no phase	dead Earth parallels dead Moon; one mention

This table only includes the thirty-nine stories and eleven major revisions in which Lovecraft mentions the moon, plus the two fragments with "moon" in the title ("What the Moon Brings" and "The Thing in the Moonlight"), "Memory," and the werewolf story "The Ghost Eater" by C.M. Eddy and HPL.

For me to consider it a "story element," the tale must feature the moon (or Moon) as a setting or an actor driving events, including lycanthropy and explicit moon-ladders. A "strong thematic element" reflects or signals the plot or characters of the story, and one can obviously parse those details differently. (If the moon in "The Horror at Martin's Beach" weren't "subtly connected" but overtly connected, I might have moved it up to a "story element," for example.) Likewise, one reader's "scenic element" (any mention of the moon in the story) might be another's "strong thematic element," as in "The Shadow Over Innsmouth," which mentions the moon something like 28 times. One could certainly argue that a moon Lovecraft connects elsewhere with duality, drowning, sex, secret evil, and hideous revelation strongly resonates with the themes of that story.

THE PACIFIC OCEAN

"It was in one of the most open and least frequented parts of the broad Pacific that the packet of which I was supercargo fell a victim to the German sea-raider."

— H.P. LOVECRAFT, "DAGON"

For a New Englander, Lovecraft gives surprisingly short shrift to the Atlantic. "The Temple" and a few minor pieces aside, almost all of Lovecraft's oceanic brooding concerns the vast Pacific. The Pacific swells in "Dagon," HPL's first story in *Weird Tales,* and if we take Australia as a Pacific nation, its waves echo in "The Shadow Out of Time," his penultimate story. What surfaces in Lovecraft, in the "least frequented parts" of the ocean?

"With the upheaval of new land in the South Pacific tremendous events began."

— H.P. LOVECRAFT, *AT THE MOUNTAINS OF MADNESS*

As befits our subject, let's broaden the scope somewhat. To Americans, and even to New Englanders, the Pacific has long been the next frontier. When America's westward expansion hits the shores of California and Oregon, it keeps going: to Hawaii and Samoa and Guam and the Philippines in Lovecraft's youth. Lovecraft's fellow Yankees started "the China trade" in 1790, furs and then whale oil and sandalwood across the Pacific to Canton, and it made them rich. Like the "amber waves of grain" in the West, the Pacific is a treasure-house. Melville, for example, repeatedly equates Pacific whales and gold in *Moby-Dick* (1851), reinforcing the parallel to the agrarian West with "harvest" metaphors. Lovecraft intriguingly recasts the image: in "The Shadow Over Innsmouth," Obed Marsh finds actual gold in the Pacific and brings it back to Innsmouth—along with the Pacific's Deep One taint.

> *"He was the only one as kep' on with the East-Injy an' Pacific trade, though Esdras Martin's barkentine* Malay Bride[11] *made a venter as late as twenty-eight."*

— H.P. Lovecraft, "The Shadow Over Innsmouth"

Here Lovecraft and Innsmouth wash up against the other great American motif of the Pacific: as a lure for Americans, a prelapsarian paradise of indolent lotus-eating. Melville's *Typee* (1846) and *Omoo* (1847) portray castaways or marooned victims worrying about being absorbed by the Pacific, or rather by the Pacific islanders' alien culture. James Fenimore Cooper's *The Crater* (1847) mirrors this metaphor; an idyllic Pacific island actually sinks under the weight of too many modern Americans. Jack London's South Seas tales likewise present the Pacific as an all-too-seductive beauty spot, remote from the modern world. Outside America, Paul Gaugin and Robert Louis Stevenson, among others, do their best to reinforce this vision.

While Lovecraft writes no paeans to the glories of Tahiti, note the siren calls in his Innsmouth ship names: *Malay Bride* and *Sumatra Queen*. Arch hints at the nature of the "Innsmouth taint" to be sure, but also evidence of the Pacific's powers of seduction. In *Moby-Dick,* Melville sets it out: "Lifted by those eternal swells, you needs must own the seductive god, bowing your head to Pan," and his story is of a man driven mad by a seductive god, a sea-monster from the Pacific.

---

11. Although most modern editions of this story follow HPL's original hand-written draft and name the ship *Malay Pride*, Lovecraft changed it to *Bride* in his typescript and reiterated the change in an errata sheet for the story's botched book publication. Since that change clearly echoes the theme of the story, I follow Lovecraft's typescript here.

"I talked with the mind of Yiang-Li, a philosopher from the cruel empire of
Tsan-Chan, which is to come in 5,000 A.D. … with that of an archimage
of vanished Yhe in the Pacific …"

— H.P. LOVECRAFT, "THE SHADOW OUT OF TIME"

If the Pacific washes away the rational and modern, it does so not least
because the Pacific is ancient, its people seen as still the "noble savages" of
Enlightenment prehistory, each of its islands an antediluvian Eden. But in
keeping with our earlier frontier topos, the Pacific is also the future. Even
now, one can hear that the 21st will be the "Pacific Century," as history
zooms westward around the globe. So, better yet, the Pacific is not merely
ancient, but timeless. Again in *Moby-Dick,* Melville notes that the Pacific
waves wash "the new-built Californian towns, but yesterday planted by
the recentest race of men, and lave the faded but still gorgeous skirts of
Asiatic lands, older than Abraham."

Lovecraft finds this metaphor of timelessness far more congenial than
the "island Eden" trope. The Pacific is simultaneously unthinkably ancient
and looming in the future, both long-dead and stirring to be born. Lovecraft's cosmic sensibilities thrill to the duality. His "Dagon" is both an ancient god and a modern threat. The "Kanakys" wiped out the Deep Ones
off Otaheite, but the batrachian race plans its resurgence—"the reel horror
… ain't what them fish devils hez done, but what they're a-goin' to do!"—in
Pacific-tainted Innsmouth. In "The Shadow Out of Time," the catalogue
of entities met by Nathaniel Peaslee includes representatives of both distant past and future Pacifics: Yhe and Tsan-Chan. Lovecraft's ultimate
blending of the timeless, the primordial, the apocalyptic, and the Pacific
looms over them all: Great Cthulhu.

"Remains of Them, he said the deathless Chinamen had told him, were
still to be found as Cyclopean stones on islands in the Pacific."

— H.P. LOVECRAFT, "THE CALL OF CTHULHU"

Cthulhu is very much *of* the Pacific, even of a specific spot therein, somewhere between Pitcairn Island (where the *Bounty* mutineers succumbed to the Pacific's seductions) and Easter Island (with its "ancient" statues). Even Cthulhu has perhaps bowed his head to Pan; his Pacific "deep waters" are "full of the one primal mystery through which not even thought can pass." But Cthulhu also *is* Pan, "the madness from the sea." Cthulhu is a prehistoric memory and the inevitable future all in one, both old and new, as Wilcox notes of his bas-relief at the beginning of the story: "It is new, indeed, for I made it last night in a dream of strange cities; and dreams are older than brooding Tyre, or the contemplative Sphinx." Cthulhu once ruled the Earth, then fell in a cataclysm, but "when the stars come right" he will emerge again in a kind of parodic Last Judgment, "a glorious resurrection ... a holocaust of ecstasy."

This rhythm, of ancient greatness, catastrophic destruction, current desuetude, and future ascension at the end of the age, is the rhythm of Theosophy. So Lovecraft slyly acknowledges in the introduction to "The Call of Cthulhu": "Theosophists have guessed at the awesome grandeur of the cosmic cycle ... [and] have hinted at strange survival in terms which would freeze the blood if not masked by a bland optimism." Lovecraft wrote "Cthulhu" shortly after reading a Theosophical omnibus, *The Story of Atlantis and the Lost Lemuria* (1925) by William Scott-Elliot, and specifically mentions that tome in the tale as one of Angell's "Cthulhu Cult" file sources. No one will be surprised to see Pacific mega-continents, sunken islands, and prehuman survivals prominently featured in Scott-Elliot's pages, albeit "masked by a bland optimism." Lovecraft further "demythologizes" Theosophy, recasting it as paleontology in *At the Mountains of Madness,* as the bas-reliefs in Kadath tell the epoch-spanning tale of prehuman races and sunken lands in the Pacific.

"Centuries hence ... China may yet form a titanic world force to be reckoned with. It would be curious if the oldest of all civilisations of today were to survive its younger rivals in the end."

— H.P. LOVECRAFT, LETTER TO HENRY GEORGE WEISS (FEB. 3, 1937)

Shrinking our scope down a bit from prehuman ecologies to mere lost civilizations, another beat of the Theosophist rhythm is that India, or "Asia," was great before the West was born, and would rise again to reduce Europe to irrelevance. (Lovecraft's fellow New Englander Ralph Waldo Emerson said much the same thing.) This theme not only fed Indian nationalism, but paradoxically fueled Western racism. The generally hopeful message of Theosophy is essentially identical to the generally fearful message of "the Yellow Peril": the dreaming, even sessile "Asiatics" (for Lovecraft and Americans, on the other side of the Pacific) will awaken from their slumber and destroy the (white) world. Sound familiar?

Lovecraft invokes the Yellow Peril even before he reads Theosophy: in "Polaris," "He," and "Nyarlathotep," the future is yellow, and (white) civilization is overthrown. When he adds Theosophy to the mixture, things get even weirder: in the cosmic time-cycles of "Through the Gates of the Silver Key," HPL takes time to note that Pickman Carter "in the year 2169 would use strange means in repelling the Mongol hordes from Australia," and we've already met "the cruel empire of Tsan-Chan" of 5000 A.D. Lovecraft doesn't leave the Yellow Peril in his fiction, either. In a 1919 letter to Alfred Galpin and Maurice Moe, he predicts that the Chinese "are a menace of the still more distant future" who "will probably be the exterminators of Caucasian civilization." And in a 1934 letter to Natalie Wooley, only the specific Peril changes: "In the end—as we grow weak & decadent … Japan will probably dominate the world," but HPL hopes "that period will be thousands of years in the future." It's not just Theosophy, then, that leads Lovecraft to put "the deathless Chinamen" in charge of the Cthulhu cult.

> *"The West, however, was never favourable to [the Ghatanothoa cult's] growth … In the end it became a hunted, doubly furtive underground affair—yet never could its nucleus be quite exterminated. It always survived somehow, chiefly in the Far East and on the Pacific Islands, where its teachings became merged into the esoteric lore of the Polynesian Areoi."*

> — H.P. LOVECRAFT AND HAZEL HEALD, "OUT OF THE AEONS"

Is "Call of Cthulhu" just a strange Yellow Peril story, Fu Manchu with tentacles? No, it's far vaster than that; it partakes not just of Theosophy's Pacific apocalypses, but the iconic Pacifics of Jack London and Herman Melville: forgetfulness and timelessness, madness and obsession. But for Lovecraft, at least, the Pacific is inextricable from the shores it washes. He demonstrates this in "Out of the Aeons," as the survivors of the lost continent of Mu (Lemuria renamed by a different Theosophist crackpot, James Churchward) gather in pilgrimage before the mummy of T'yog.

By the time the story is done, the litany of "swarthy Asiatics" and "eccentric foreigners" has included Hawaiians, "Cingalese" (Sri Lankans), Filipinos, Peruvian Indians, East Indians, Burmese, and Fijians—and Lovecraft's own authorial stand-in, Randolph Carter, in his "Swami Chandraputra" garb from "Through the Gates of the Silver Key." The Pacific swallows Lovecraft, too; he has bowed his head before the seductive god Pan. Or Dagon. Or Cthulhu.

NEW YORK CITY

"One of them had wagered him a heavy sum that he could not—despite many poignant things to his credit in the Dublin Review—*even write a truly interesting story of New York low life; and now, looking back, he perceived that cosmic irony had justified the prophet's words while secretly confuting their flippant meaning."*

— H.P. LOVECRAFT, "THE HORROR AT RED HOOK"

Lovecraft famously set three stories—"The Horror at Red Hook," "He," and "Cool Air"—in New York City. He wrote all three while living there, between the spring of 1924 and the spring of 1926. (Technically, HPL wrote "He" in Scott Park in Elizabeth, New Jersey, just across the river from Staten Island.) The "location-minded" Lovecraft resolved, as he wrote to Frank Belknap Long in August of 1925, to "attempt to extract horror from an atmosphere to which you deny any qualities save vulgar commonplaceness." The attempt was at best an indifferent success: in April of 1926, revolted and frustrated beyond measure, Lovecraft fled the deadly lights of New York for the peace and safety of his ancestral Providence. But … just perhaps … New York pursued him to Rhode Island, just as it did Thomas Malone, all the way from Red Hook.

"My coming to New York had been a mistake; for whereas I had looked for poignant wonder and inspiration in the teeming labyrinths of ancient streets that twist endlessly from forgotten courts and squares and waterfronts to courts and squares and waterfronts equally forgotten, and in the Cyclopean modern towers and pinnacles that rise blackly Babylonian

under waning moons, I had found instead only a sense of horror and
oppression which threatened to master, paralyze, and annihilate me."

— H.P. LOVECRAFT, "HE"

"If you want to know what I think of New York," Lovecraft wrote to
Donald Wandrei in 1927, "read 'He'." Michel Houellebecq has aptly described "He" as Lovecraft's "rejection letter to New York," and since it begins with a writer coming to New York in hope, and fleeing to New England in terror, the autobiographical element seems unmistakable. "Cool
Air" notably pits its shabby-genteel "magazine work" narrator ("unable to
pay any substantial rent") against foreign madness. Even Thomas Malone,
the detective in "Red Hook," is a literary man, and Malone, too, leaves
New York for Rhode Island at the end of his ordeal. Rounding off this line
of country, Lovecraft lived in Brooklyn Heights when he wrote the tale, a
mile and a half from the Red Hook neighborhood it literally demonizes.[12]

It's interesting to note, however, that the trend in Lovecraft's fictional
New York runs the other direction from his life experience: "Red Hook"
(written first) is horrified and disgusted, "He" is elegiac if not bittersweet,
and "Cool Air" (written only six weeks before Lovecraft left for Providence) is sardonic, knowing, and not a little romantic. The stories run generally northward: "Red Hook" desecrates and decorates Brooklyn, while
"He" burrows into the West Village[13] and "Cool Air" breathes on the border of Chelsea on West Fourteenth Street. They run on different levels,
too: "Red Hook" delves into cellars and sewers; "He" wanders through
courtyards and a second-floor room; "Cool Air" lurks higher yet, on the
fourth floor of a brownstone. Unexpectedly, we go further up as we go
further in, not deeper into the Pickmaniacal depths. Lovecraft's New York
is not merely a simple setting for a disguised autobiography.

---

12. In the story, Robert Suydam lives on Martense Street in Flatbush, five short blocks south of where
Lovecraft lived in 1924 with his wife Sonia.

13. Lovecraft based the "little black court off Perry Street" on an actual antiquarian ramble he made to
93 Perry Street in the Village.

"It is a mistake to fancy that horror is associated inextricably with darkness, silence, and solitude. I found it in the glare of mid-afternoon, in the clangour of a metropolis, and in the teeming midst of a shabby and commonplace rooming-house ..."

— H.P. LOVECRAFT, "COOL AIR"

If the nested tales of Arthur Machen's *Three Impostors* (1895) were, in Lin Carter's crystalline phrase, set in "Baghdad-on-the-Thames," then "Cool Air" posits New York as "Baghdad-on-the-Hudson." Machen took his idea from Robert Louis Stevenson's *New Arabian Nights* (1882); Lovecraft took the idea for "Cool Air" from Arthur Machen's *Three Impostors* tale "Novel of the White Powder"—and, of course, from Poe's "Facts in the Case of M. Valdemar," which as it happens is set in New York City as well. (In Harlem, rather than the Chelsea of "Cool Air".) The idea of the modern city—anonymous, bustling, crowded with mysterious foreigners—as a secret garden of wonders and terrors may well originate (like so much else) with Poe.

For Lovecraft, New York was Baghdad in more than just metaphor: he had a Syrian neighbor in Brooklyn, and his New York fiction and letters swarm with Near Eastern references. Suydam's cultists are Kurds who worship Hebrew demons in a "Babylonish court" and write in "Chaldee letters." "He" begins by comparing New York (of the "blackly Babylonian pinnacles") to, among other legendary cities, "Samarcand," and ends (less specifically) predicting its decadence under "yellow, squint-eyed" swarms. And in a 1930 letter to James F. Morton, HPL populates New York with "pouring tides" from two dozen Middle Eastern sources ranging from Antioch to Ophir, including Babylon, Ur, and Irem of the Pillars!

"[T]he gracious, glamorous elder New York of dignity & poise, which lies stark & horrible & ghoul-gnawed today beneath the foul claws of the mongrel & misshapen foreign colossus that gibbers & howls vulgarly & dreamlessly on its site."

— H.P. LOVECRAFT, LETTER TO DONALD WANDREI (FEBRUARY 10, 1927)

All those Syrians and such, of course, were "squat, swarthy strangers ... without kinship to the scenes about them," as Lovecraft writes in "He." His own near-neighborhood, Red Hook, he castigates as a "maze of hybrid squalor." His letters are even more fraught, howling with fear of the "monstrous and nebulous adumbrations of the pithecanthropoid and amoebal" throngs "slithering and oozing ... in and out of windows and doorways in a fashion suggestive of nothing but infesting worms or deepsea unnamabilities," as he ranted to Frank Belknap Long in 1924.

This "foreign corruption" besieged, eroded, and doomed what little of New York Lovecraft found to love: the "relics of this former happiness" as he says in "Red Hook," the "unexpected bits of square and court" the narrator seeks out in "He." Both are once-separate Georgian towns from Lovecraft's prized eighteenth century—Flatbush and Greenwich—swallowed by the city. Once, to Lovecraft, New York was a congeries of simple Georgian "Arkhams." But like Arkham (or worse, Dunwich), it has fallen to degeneration and invasion from Outside. The siege is over, and the "infesting worms" have won.

"I saw at last a fearful truth which no one had ever dared to breathe before— the unwhisperable secret of secrets—the fact that this city of stone and stridor is not a sentient perpetuation of Old New York ... but that it is in fact quite dead, its sprawling body imperfectly embalmed and infested with queer animate things which have nothing to do with it as it was in life."

— H.P. LOVECRAFT, "HE"

New York is no city for men, but a necropolis, as foreign and as dead as the Nameless City or the Pyramids. In "Cool Air," good old Dr. Muñoz blends our New York topoi of the necropolis and the Near East, pumping "exotic spices and Egyptian incense till his room smelled like the vault of a sepulchred Pharaoh in the Valley of Kings." All three New York stories are tales of unnatural survival: Suydam is reanimated in "Red Hook," the Georgian magus lives in the time-bubble of Perry Court in "He," and Dr. Muñoz is as "imperfectly embalmed" as the city itself.

Suydam and the magus in "He" are both representatives of Old New York, of the Dutch and English aristocracies respectively, and both have fallen into madness and succumbed to the foreign, the Outside. Both learn their magics from foreigners (the Kurds and the "half-breed red Indians"), and Dr. Muñoz is himself a foreigner, even if a cultivated one. Not even such cultivation, or ancestry, or (in the final analysis) the "will of mankind" (as we learn in "He") can stave off New York's inevitable demise.

> *"There are really two New-Yorks: the increasingly Georgian New-York of the ground, which passengers on the streets see ... and the elfin, heav'n-scaling New-York of the air—the New York which rears Babylonian pinnacles for admiration afar off ..."*
>
> — H.P. LOVECRAFT, LETTER TO FRANK BELKNAP LONG (FEBRUARY, 1924)

Lovecraft casts New York as another of his "double cities" (in Robert H. Waugh's apt phrase), with an "elfin" (or Georgian) ideal and a "hellish" (or foreign) shadow. It is both Arkham and Dunwich, both Sarnath and Ib: its glory contains its own doom. David Haden argues convincingly that for Lovecraft, New York's highly colored psychogeography hovered between dream and nightmare, fuelled by his endless walks up and down the city. In the letter above, written to Frank Belknap Long before his move and prefiguring the "sunset city"-Boston duality of the *Dream-Quest*, Lovecraft cites two cities in New York, both magical.

Then, once he grew to hate the place, both New Yorks became monstrous: the "too white" squire in "He" and the "swarthy, sin-pitted faces" of "Red Hook." Of all Lovecraft's cities, not even Innsmouth evokes the darkest tones of the shadow city that HPL reserves for Gotham. But even in "He," the double city still lingers: "at night ... darkness calls forth what little of the past still hovers wraith-like about." The "teeming labyrinths" of alien immigrants reflect the "inexhaustible maze of unknown antiquity" of old white and Native magic. New York, "in fact quite dead," thus becomes rather the opposite: an Arkham cemetery, infested by the unnamable perhaps, but still bearing the spirit of its past.

> *"I conceived the idea that the great brownstone house was a malignly sentient thing—a dead, vampire creature which sucked something out of those within it and implanted in them the seeds of some horrible and immaterial psychic growth."*

— H.P. Lovecraft, letter to Bernard Austin Dwyer (March 26, 1927)

Lovecraft didn't just write three tales in New York. He also wrote two New England stories: the thrilling and curious "The Shunned House" and the formulaic "In the Vault." On October 11, 1924, he walked all over Elizabeth, New Jersey, drawing succor and inspiration from the colonial-era houses along the river. On the corner of Elizabeth and Bridge Streets he discovered "a terrible old house" from the early 18th century that reminded him of a similar house on Benefit Street in Providence. He wrote "The Shunned House" the next week, about a house containing a vampiric spirit that drained its inhabitants.

So imagine his shock the next year when he discovered (or decided) he'd moved into just such a house, a brownstone on 169 Clinton Street in Brooklyn Heights. According to Lovecraft's admittedly highly colored recollection two years later to Bernard Austin Dwyer, the building followed the neighborhood into squalor, driving the geographically sensitive (and racially hypochondriac) Lovecraft to despair. ("In the Vault," written nine months after his move, perhaps speaks to how increasingly trapped HPL felt in the building.) To put a recursive bow on this topic, as Lovecraft felt his own fiction recapitulating itself in his life, he was reading (around July 1925) the autobiography of Arthur Machen. In *Things Near And Far* (1923), Machen recounts his own experience in 1900 of meeting "the young man in spectacles," a character from his 1895 novel *The Three Impostors*. Although Lovecraft never overtly used this specific concept, the motif of artistic creations suddenly becoming retroactively real repeatedly appears in his work over the next year, notably in "Pickman's Model," *Charles Dexter Ward,* and "The Call of Cthulhu."

> *"Without knowing what futurism is like, Johansen achieved something very close to it when he spoke of the city; for instead of describing any definite structure or building, he dwells only on broad impressions of vast angles and stone surfaces—surfaces too great to belong to anything right or proper for this earth, and impious with horrible images …"*

> — H.P. LOVECRAFT, "THE CALL OF CTHULHU"

It was in fact in New York, in that building, that Lovecraft plotted, in detail, "The Call of Cthulhu," as we learn from his diary for August 12-13, 1925—immediately after writing "Red Hook" and "He." So is there a fourth "New York tale," of an unnatural survival in an "imperfectly embalmed" necropolis, a scion of the dead past attended by Oriental cultists, a magus dwelling outside time and history? True, all of Lovecraft's necropoleis—the Nameless City, Kadath, Pnakotus—are "imperfectly embalmed and infested with queer animate things." But read Johansen's description of R'lyeh again, and tell me that's not Manhattan, busy drowning Lovecraft's Georgian fantasies beneath Modernist monstrosities. Even Wilcox's "Cyclopean [city] of Titan blocks and sky-flung monoliths" sounds mighty like the New York of "He," with its "Cyclopean modern towers and pinnacles."

R'lyeh becomes the New York that Lovecraft hated, with "vast angles" and "improper surfaces." Massimo Berruti notes that the geometry—and perhaps the actual physicality—of R'lyeh is always changing; that nothing is ever as it was. Is this not Lovecraft's great indictment of New York? Nothing is as it was, and it throngs with "deep-sea unnamabilities" to boot. There's even a connection between R'lyeh and Red Hook in the story itself: Angell's clipping file reveals that "New York policemen are mobbed by hysterical Levantines" when Cthulhu's citadel surfaces. *Ph'nglui mglw'nafh Cthulhu New York wgah'nagl fhtagn?* It *is* the city that never sleeps, after all.

UPSTATE

"In many parts the open country is astonishingly near, and most of the street vistas west and northwest have dim tracings of the violet Catskill foothills at their far, mysterious ends. I can well imagine Rip Van Winkle as flourishing in such a place—in fact, it is still a perfect part of the old America …"

— H.P. LOVECRAFT, "TRAVELS IN THE PROVINCES OF AMERICA" (1929)

Lovecraft visited Upstate New York at least five times between September of 1925 and May of 1930, usually in the company of Frank Belknap Long. The rustic charms of the Hudson Valley were easily accessible to urban New Yorkers by train, vacation launch, or automobile, and not beyond even Lovecraft's modest means. In May of 1929 he stayed with his friend and literary sounding board Bernard Austin Dwyer in West Shokan, in the foothills of the Catskill Mountains, and apparently enjoyed himself mightily. As we read in the above description, Lovecraft gave West Shokan, and Upstate, his stamp of approval—which, as in the cases of Vermont and Marblehead, should prepare us to find it populated with hideous decadent monsters. And weirdly, just as HPL wrote his first Kingsport story before seeing Marblehead, he wrote his first two Catskills stories years before he ventured up the Hudson.

Temporal hiccups notwithstanding, degenerate squatters and astral dybbuks in "Beyond the Wall of Sleep" yield to slithering inbred burrowers and "The Lurking Fear" itself. The revision tales "The Man of Stone" and "The Diary of Alonzo Typer" both introduce Lovecraftian magi to the region. On the technical border of Upstate, we can also include "Two

Black Bottles," which Lovecraft's collaborator Wilfred Branch Talman set not in the Catskills area but in his own native Ramapo Mountains, in Rockland County in southern New York.

> *"From the listless repose of the place, and the peculiar character of its inhabitants, who are descendants from the original Dutch settlers, this sequestered glen has long been known by the name of Sleepy Hollow ... A drowsy, dreamy influence seems to hang over the land, and to pervade the very atmosphere. Some say that the place was bewitched by a High German doctor, during the early days of the settlement; others, that an old Indian chief, the prophet or wizard of his tribe, held his powwows there before the country was discovered by Master Hendrick Hudson. Certain it is, the place still continues under the sway of some witching power, that holds a spell over the minds of the good people, causing them to walk in a continual reverie. They are given to all kinds of marvellous beliefs, are subject to trances and visions, and frequently see strange sights, and hear music and voices in the air. The whole neighborhood abounds with local tales, haunted spots, and twilight superstitions; stars shoot and meteors glare oftener across the valley than in any other part of the country, and the nightmare, with her whole ninefold, seems to make it the favorite scene of her gambols."*

— WASHINGTON IRVING, "THE LEGEND OF SLEEPY HOLLOW" (1820)

So what might make Lovecraft look up the Hudson for his early horrors? Could it be America's early horrorist, Washington Irving, wry historian of Upstate follies and fairy tales? Although it's hard to see any real Irving influence on these specific stories, his description of Sleepy Hollow above does sound like a waltz-time arrangement of Lovecraft's "witch-haunted Arkham." Irving further describes Sleepy Hollow as a "little Dutch valley" like a "little nook of still water" isolated from "the passing current." Here "population, manners, and customs remain fixed" and unchanged by "the great torrent of migration and improvement," a quality Lovecraft of course valued in life while anathematizing it in his fiction.

Lovecraft admired Irving, writing as early as 1918 to Rheinhart Kleiner: "Him I do admire vastly, both in themes and style." By 1927, he writes in *Supernatural Horror in Literature:* "most of his ghosts are too whimsical and humorous to form genuinely spectral literature, a distinct inclination in this direction is to be noted in many of his productions." He sums up Irving's "The German Student" (1824) as "a slyly concise and effective presentation of the old legend of the dead bride," which serves as a worthy critical judgement on all of Irving's spectral stories. Lovecraft visited Sleepy Hollow in May 1928 with Wilfred Branch Talman, from whom he later borrowed a massive tome by Helen Wilkinson Reynolds, *Dutch Houses in the Hudson Valley Before 1776 (1929),* taking extensive notes before returning it in early 1931.

Lovecraft first absorbed the historical atmosphere and folklore of Upstate not from Reynolds' architectural-genealogical compendium, or even from Irving at an arch remove. He got a strong dose of the stuff from his copy of Charles M. Skinner's *Myths and Legends of Our Own Land* (1896), which covers "The Hudson and its Hills" extensively in its first ninety pages. David Haden notes the echo of "The Catskill Gnomes" (who bloated the heads of their enemies with their moonshine) in Lovecraft's image of "dead men's skulls swelled to gigantic proportions." I might also point out Skinner's anecdote of the bulbous imps of the "Dunderberg" ("Thunder Mountain"), not unlike the bloated crawlers of his Tempest Mountain in "Lurking Fear."[14]

> *"The place is a remote, lonely elevation in that part of the Catskills where Dutch civilisation once feebly and transiently penetrated, leaving behind as it receded only a few ruined mansions and a degenerate squatter population inhabiting pitiful hamlets on isolated slopes. Normal beings seldom visited the locality till the state police were formed, and even now only infrequent troopers patrol it."*

> — H.P. LOVECRAFT, "THE LURKING FEAR"

---

14. HPL moves a different degenerate Dutch legend, of a man-shaped fungus in a basement in Schenectady ("The Green Picture") to Providence as the monster in "The Shunned House."

Lovecraft barely sketches the Catskills setting, or rather, backdrop, of "Wall of Sleep," which mostly occurs in the "state psychopathic institution." Although the New York State Pathological Institute in upper Manhattan dates back to 1895, the state's criminal asylum at the time of the story was the Matteawan State Hospital, on the Hudson south of Poughkeepsie. However, even that vaguely Upstate location goes unremarked by Lovecraft's narrator, who mostly invokes the Catskills as a signifier for the lowest possible degeneracy.

By contrast, the degenerate squatters in "The Lurking Fear" remain sympathetic: "curiously likeable ... simple animals" who eventually help the narrator "vastly" in his campaign against the Fear and the even-more-degenerate Martenses. Dubious eugenic ethnology aside, the color and detail Lovecraft invests in "The Lurking Fear" indicate a degree of fascination, and perhaps specific research. Trees, hills, cabins, and thunderstorms could perhaps be generic American Gothicisms, but Lovecraft layers on local history and a good dose of his burgeoning ability to evoke a specific terroir amidst the terror. He may have acquired what seed material he needed from his amateur journalism contact and fellow poet Jonathan E. Hoag, who lived in Troy, New York in the heart of the Upstate Dutch country.

> "*They ought to know better, for they know I am a Van Kauran on my mother's side, and anybody this side of the Hudson can tell what the Van Kaurans have handed down. We come from Nicholas Van Kauran, the wizard ... The soldiers never got his* Book of Eibon *when they burned his house, and his grandson, William Van Kauran, brought it over when he came to Rensselaerwyck and later crossed the river to Esopus. Ask anybody in Kingston or Hurley about what the William Van Kauran line could do to people that got in their way.*"
>
> — H.P. LOVECRAFT AND HAZEL HEALD, "THE MAN OF STONE"

By 1932 and "The Man of Stone" Lovecraft has visited the edge of the Catskills in the southern half of the Hudson Valley. He thus removes the evil farther north, to the fictitious town of Mountain Top in the Adirondacks,[15] replacing specific local color and topography with a thicker slab of historical and occult detail. He does locate something untoward in the Catskills in this story, though, mentioning "the Great Sabbat on Sugar-Loaf in the Catskills. Queer things used to go on there." But the evil comes to the Adirondacks in the seventeenth century as one of HPL's dangerously educated aristocrats, specifically "a Van Kauran." The tale's "barefoot old mountain decadent" simply delivers cornpone exposition, and the scenery is "breathlessly exquisite." The local villagers, far from being vectors for contamination, actively prevent "Mad Dan" from "doing the Great Rite."

Also by 1932, Lovecraft has read Robert W. Chambers' story "Maker of Moons" (1896), featuring hideous monsters spawned by an Oriental mastermind from a lake in Upstate New York. As we shall see, he happily lifted Chambers' Yian from that tale, and I suspect he also borrowed Chambers' hairy crab-creatures from that story for his own Mi-Go. Even more than a creature or a name, Chambers elsewhere provides Lovecraft with a model for "The Man of Stone." The basic love-triangle plot of "Man of Stone" seems entirely un-Lovecraftian, and given the uncommon combination of a very similar romantic situation and a mysterious alchemical petrification in Chambers' tale "The Mask" (1895) I think the case is made.

"Around the dreaded house a straggling village arose, populated by Indians and later by renegades from the surrounding country, which bore the dubious name of Chorazin. Of the singular hereditary strains which afterward appeared in the mixed Chorazin villagers, several monographs have been written by ethnologists. Just behind the village, and in sight of the van der Heyl house, is a steep hill crowned with a peculiar ring of ancient standing stones which the Iroquois always regarded with fear

---

15. There is no town called Mountain Top in New York, although there is a "Mountain Top View" near Binghamton in the southern part of the state nowhere near the Adirondacks.

and loathing. The origin and nature of the stones, whose date, according
to archaeological and climatological evidence, must be fabulously early, is
a problem still unsolved."

— H.P. LOVECRAFT AND WILLIAM LUMLEY, "THE DIARY OF ALONZO TYPER"

By 1935 and "The Diary of Alonzo Typer," the local folk go back to
being hateful mongrels, such as "John Eagle, the swarthy, simian-faced,
Indian-like villager." This despite the fact that he places the van der Heyl
house "near Attica," a town far outside any actual mountain range or isolated population. Lovecraft also brings those terrible thunderstorms back
for an encore, and some ancient standing stones for good measure. All
these features, however, do not arise organically from the Upstate soil,
but magnetically accumulate around another decayed house of wizardly
lineage, the van der Heyls of Chorazin.

The original town of Chorazin (the Aramaic name of the Hebrew
Korazim) in Galilee appears in the Bible, cursed by Jesus for rejecting his
ministry (Matthew 11:20-24; Luke 10:13-15). This curse gave rise to the
prophecy, first mentioned in the Apocalypse of Pseudo-Methodius (c. 690
A.D.), that the Antichrist would be born in Chorazin. The 14th-century
knight John Mandeville mentions this legend in his (mostly spurious)
Travels, which Lovecraft knew of and might have even read. However,
Chorazin and its legend also appear in a work we know Lovecraft read:
the story "Count Magnus" by M.R. James.

In that tale, the hideously ugly sorcerer Count Magnus de la Gardie
makes the "Black Pilgrimage to Chorazin" some time in the seventeenth
century to "salute the prince of the air" and gain prolonged life. Decipher-
ing Typer's garbled mission to Upstate's Chorazin, he seems to settle on
transfiguring "that Forgotten One who is Guardian of the Ancient Gateway" (Yog-Sothoth?) after discovering some "Aklo formulae" straight out
of Machen. (Lovecraft also borrows Chambers' Yian for "Alonzo Typer,"
as "Yian-Ho.") It's tempting to also identify Chorazin, New York with the

"small village in the Adirondacks whence reports of certain odd ceremonial practices had come" sought by Charles Dexter Ward, but Chorazin is
not in the Adirondacks.[16]

> *"Whether we were mad, dreaming, or in our senses, we did not try to
> determine. We only realised, with the blackest of apprehensions, that
> the apparently disembodied chatter was beyond a doubt* in the Dutch
> language."

— H.P. Lovecraft, "The Hound"

So, you may be asking, what does Lovecraft have against the Dutch?
These seemingly respectable, if bourgeois, Teutons signify horror time
and again. Dutch New York breeds three villainous dynasties (Martense,
Van Kauran, and van der Hyl), plus Robert Suydam from "Horror at Red
Hook," and hosts the involuntarily murderous parson Vanderhoof and the
black magician Dominie Slott from "Two Black Bottles."[17] To that we can
add the murderous doctor Thomas Slauenwite from "Winged Death" (a
Boer, but still Dutch), and the undead necromancer buried in "that terrible Holland churchyard" (inspired by HPL's visit to the Dutch Reformed
churchyard in Flatbush) in "The Hound."

So ridiculously recurrent is this weird prejudicial tic that Ruthanna
Emrys and Anne M. Pillsworth make "the degenerate Dutch" a running gag (and synecdoche for all of Lovecraft's racist constructions) in
their "Lovecraft Reread" series on Tor.com. Searching for Batavipho-
bic precursors, David Haden digs up Herman Melville's description of
the Dutch landholders in *Pierre* (1852) as both worms ("unimaginable
audacity of a worm that but crawls through the soil he so imperially
claims") and as uncanny survivals: "we may wonder at their thus surviving, like Indian mounds, the Revolutionary flood; yet survive and exist

---

16. Possibly Charles Dexter Ward sought Mountain Top from "Man of Stone", although the rituals were
restricted to the Van Kaurans and not practiced in the village at large.

17. The Dutch name Slott originated as Slot or Sloet, an occupational name for a locksmith, from the
Dutch *sloet* or *slot*, "lock" or "clasp."

they do." Thus, perhaps the Dutch represent to Melville's fellow New Englander Lovecraft a substratum or undercurrent of history in New York (and by extension America) beneath good, solid English settlement. We should also note that the Dutch settlement in New York happens during Lovecraft's "dark, witch-haunted" seventeenth century, not his beloved "enlightened" eighteenth.

> *"His name, as given on the records, was Joe Slater, or Slaader, and his appearance was that of the typical denizen of the Catskill Mountain region; one of those strange, repellent scions of a primitive colonial peasant stock whose isolation for nearly three centuries in the hilly fastnesses of a little-travelled countryside has caused them to sink to a kind of barbaric degeneracy ... "*

— H.P. LOVECRAFT, "BEYOND THE WALL OF SLEEP"

The Upstate Dutch thus embody one of Lovecraft's great archetypes: unnatural survivals, left over (or most often left *under*) from a shadowy past. Where does he see such survivals congregating? Among isolated populations, or groups exiled from civilization, or both. In short: in the hinterland, outside the city. Just as every city in Lovecraft has its own dark opposite or shadow city, it also casts its shadow deep into the countryside. The city-bred Lovecraft casts the hinterland—Upstate New York, or western Massachusetts, or Vermont—as what we might call "the abject rural." He first clearly evokes the abject rural, and even defends it as a general proposition, in "The Picture in the House," and perfects it in "The Dunwich Horror," but he plants it all across Upstate over his whole career.

Lovecraft's first abject rurals appear Upstate in "Beyond the Wall of Sleep," inspired by his reading of an article in the April 27, 1919 *New York Tribune* about the newly founded New York State Police. The author of that piece, one F.F. Van de Water, waxed proto-Lovecraftian himself on the topic of the Slahters or Slaters of the Catskills, painting them as degenerate habitual criminals sunk into ignorant savagery. He describes the town of Polly Hollow as almost literally frozen in time, claiming that the inhabitants resisted the World War I draft because they believed it to be the Civil War draft returned, and refused to "fight for [black people]." Other period writers described the Catskill Slaters as not just inbred but multi-racial: "a mixture of colored, white, and aborigine" in one 1893 text. Such descriptors also applied to the "Jackson Whites" (now called the Ramapough Lenape) of the Ramapo Mountains, who supposedly mixed black, Hessian, and Dutch blood with Lenape strains. Lovecraft curiously goes out of his way to remove the racial angle from Joe Slater, emphasizing his blue eyes and blond beard.

> *"History had led me to this archaic grave. History, indeed, was all I had after everything else ended in mocking Satanism. I now believed that the lurking fear was no material thing, but a wolf-fanged ghost that rode the midnight lightning. And I believed, because of the masses of local tradition I had unearthed in my search with Arthur Munroe, that the ghost was that of Jan Martense, who died in 1762. That is why I was digging idiotically in his grave."*
>
> — H.P. LOVECRAFT, "THE LURKING FEAR"

Like many of his "degenerate whites" from Delapore to Dunwich, the Slaters and their Upstate mountains represented a specific fear to Lovecraft, one not just racial or civilizational but local, and perhaps even personal. After all, he had personally slid backward from wealth to poverty in his own lifetime, and had other reasons to doubt the soundness of his blood—both his parents died insane, for starters. The name "Slater" perhaps caught his eye in 1919 because Lovecraft attended the Slater Avenue School in Providence intermittently between the ages of eight and twelve. The school's namesake Samuel Slater was no relation to the Catskill settlers, but seeing it in that unexpected context must have given him a turn and perhaps set him thinking about the secret bloodlines that recur again and again in his fiction.

"Lurking Fear" and "Alonzo Typer" both turn on genealogy, and both feature pure "occult investigator" protagonists, among the very few such in Lovecraft's oeuvre. (Ben Hayden in "Man of Stone" is another.) Lovecraft first introduces historical research as a vector for horror in "The Lurking Fear," lovingly tracing the Martense line as he eventually would the Suydam, Van Kauran, and van der Hyl stocks. Typer discovers his own cursed blood, and the monster repeatedly spares the investigator narrator in "Lurking Fear," hinting at an occult (familial?) immunity. Much of "Man of Stone" appears in the first-person form of the diary of Daniel Morris, who boasts of his own Van Kauran occult taint, including "my great-grandfather Bareut Picterse Van Kauran—the one who disappeared from New Paltz in 1839."

Lovecraft wrote to Maurice Moe in 1931 that his own great-grandfather, Joseph S. Lovecraft, died "on an experimental farm" in Upstate New York near Rochester. Joseph Lovecraft emigrated from England to Rochester via Ontario, arriving around 1831. His son George Lovecraft moved to Mt. Vernon, New York (just north of the Bronx, but rural at the time) in the 1860s. David Haden makes the very interesting observation that the first of Lovecraft's degenerate bloodlines, the Martense clan, takes exactly a Biblical four generations, or 140 years (1670-1810) to decay from country squires to inbred burrowers.

I further observe that in the opening Upstate chapter of Skinner's *Myths*, Lovecraft would have read the account of "The Deformed of Zoar," which mentions a curse on that town of round hoof-like feet and crab-claw hands: "he asked that they should wear the mark of crime even to the fourth generation." Joseph begat George, who begat Winfield, who begat Howard. H.P. Lovecraft thus recognized himself as being of the fourth generation after his great-grandfather arrived in the Dutch-haunted, degenerate land of Upstate New York.

DUNWICH

"It is always a relief to get clear of the place, and to follow the narrow road around the base of the hills and across the level country beyond till it rejoins the Aylesbury pike. Afterwards one sometimes learns that one has been through Dunwich."

—H.P. LOVECRAFT, "THE DUNWICH HORROR"

Lovecraftian critical opinion, in the persons of S.T. Joshi and his school, are as relieved as Lovecraft's narrator to "get clear of" Dunwich. Here, worse than any invisible monster, lie the seeds of August Derleth's "Derlethifying" of the Lovecraft Mythos: a battle between good and evil fought for the lives of humanity. But Lovecraft went through Dunwich for a reason, little as his soi-disant acolytes may like it. Even if "The Dunwich Horror" is, as its great introductory line has it, "the wrong fork at the junction," Lovecraft didn't take it by accident. He was led there by the call of Pan.

"'Inbreeding?' Armitage muttered half-aloud to himself. 'Great God, what simpletons! Shew them Arthur Machen's Great God Pan and they'll think it a common Dunwich scandal!'"

—H.P. LOVECRAFT, "THE DUNWICH HORROR"

Lovecraft first read the British horrorist Arthur Machen in 1923, and was smitten. Over the next few years, he worked Machen's territory of hidden races, underground decadence, and invisible monsters as sedulously as he had previously explored Poe's hysterics or Dunsany's daydreams. HPL wrote "The Rats in the Walls," "The Unnamable," and "The Festival" in 1923, and Machen's motifs echo through "The Horror at Red Hook"

(1925), "Cool Air" (1926), and "Pickman's Model" (1926). "The Colour Out of Space" (1927) is a Lovecraftian nihilist negative of Machen's "The Great Return," while sharing the indirectness of Machen's "The White People" and the strange wasting death from Machen's "Novel of the White Powder."

But with "The Dunwich Horror" (1928) Lovecraft went all in, composing a fugue on Machen's 1894 masterpiece "The Great God Pan." "Pan" concerns an invisible god breeding with a human woman, and the defeat of the dangerous, soulless offspring therefrom. But Lovecraft builds Dunwich with more than one Machen blueprint. Machen's "Novel of the Black Seal" also features inhuman miscegenation, and the grotesque death of its spawn (complete with "slimy, wavering tentacle"!) who, like Wilbur Whateley, is "goatish." Finally, "The White People" features the diary of a child-initiate into the Aklo letters and the Voor, as well as offering that meditation on the unnatural as "sinful" that uncharacteristically animates Lovecraft's inverted Gospel story. (But reparse Machen's "attempt to penetrate into another and higher sphere in a forbidden manner" through Lovecraft's fears of contamination, and the distance closes somewhat.) Robert M. Price's thesis convinces: with "The Dunwich Horror," Lovecraft was "Derlethifying" Arthur Machen—taking a mélange of great works by a senior horrorist and blending them into something shadowed by his own concerns.

> *"Some say they've seen the gas. I heard a man living in Dunwich saw it one night like a black cloud with sparks of fire in it floating over the tops of the trees by Dunwich Common."*

> —ARTHUR MACHEN, *THE TERROR*

Lovecraft likely got the name "Dunwich" from Machen, who used it (and "Dunwich Common")[18] in *The Terror*, a 1917 novel of Nature going

---

18. Robert Marten suggests that "Dunwich Common" might have reminded Lovecraft of the abandoned village of Dogtown Common near Gloucester on Cape Ann. Left bereft by the late 18th-century expansion of Gloucester, the population of Dogtown Common dwindled (and according to report, took to witchcraft) until 1830, when it lay empty.

mad and taking its revenge upon decadent mankind (sound familiar?). Machen may have borrowed the name from the actual town of Dunwich, in Suffolk, which more resembles Lovecraft's Innsmouth: following a century's worth of great storms, much of the town subsided into the sea in 1362. By the mid-19th century its picturesque ruins attracted tourists like H. Rider Haggard, Edward Fitzgerald, and Lovecraft's favorite modern poet, Algernon Swinburne. Lovecraft's copy of Swinburne included his poem about Dunwich, "By the North Sea."

However, Swinburne forbears to mention Dunwich by name in the poem, and Lovecraft may instead have created the name by back-formation from "Greenwich" or the like. The "dun" town would be the dreary, faded town—a more than adequate description, with echoes of the monstrous, portentous "dun cow" of Shropshire folklore.[19] Robert Marten suggests that Dunwich's standing stones inspired the name of Dunwich's county seat, Aylesbury: a name "halfway between" Avebury and Salisbury, two megalithic sites (Stonehenge stands on Salisbury Plain) in Wiltshire, England.

> *"Similarly, there is no 'Dunwich'—the place being a vague echo of the decadent Massachusetts countryside around Springfield—say Wilbraham, Monson, and Hampden."*
>
> —H.P. LOVECRAFT, LETTER TO AUGUST DERLETH (NOVEMBER 6, 1931)

Lovecraft clearly based his fictional Dunwich on a congeries of real towns in south-central Massachusetts: Wilbraham, Monson, and Hampden, as he mentions above.[20] He visited them for ten days (June 29-July 7, 1928) before writing the story, and soaked up local topography and

---

19. Lovecraft might have taken the "Dun-" from Sarah Orne Jewett's fictitious town Dunnet Landing, Maine, as an ironic tweak to his fellow New England regionalist. Portrayed in Jewett's *The Country of the Pointed Firs* (1896) as a fading fishing port with a hint of the numinous and supernatural, Dunnet Landing more closely prefigures Kingsport than Dunwich. Jewett was a best-selling author, but HPL doesn't seem to mention her in his letters; Jessica Amanda Salmonson nonetheless believes he must have been influenced by her work.

20. Andrew Rothovius advanced various arguments for the Leverett-Shutesbury-Pelham area to the north, including the prevalence of round-domed hills (and supposed megaliths) in that region.

folklore (including legends about spooky whippoorwills) to be reused.[21] He moved Wilbraham north and east, into his north-Massachusetts Miskatonic Valley, to the region of Athol. Lovecraft spent a week in Athol (June 23-28, 1928) picking up names like Bishop and Frye, as well as the Bear's Den and Sentinel Elm Farm. Near here, as Will Murray points out, sat the town of (a-ha!) Greenwich, Massachusetts, doomed to drown like the Suffolk Dunwich, under the Quabbin Reservoir.[22]

A drowning under the reservoir sends us on a quick detour through the blasted heath of "The Colour Out of Space," which scars the hills "west of Arkham." Lovecraftian scholarship argues whether the Quabbin Reservoir in western Massachusetts, flooded between 1935 and 1939 to supply water for Boston, is "the reservoir" in question. Construction on the reservoir began in 1926, a year before HPL wrote "Colour." Lovecraft likely heard of the soon-to-be-drowned towns of Dana and Greenwich (Dana-wich?) from his Wilbraham correspondent Edith Miniter. Lovecraft himself suggested another candidate in a 1935 letter to Richard Ely Morse: the Scituate Reservoir in Rhode Island, built (and visited by HPL) in 1926. This would seem conclusive, were it not in an entirely different state.

"It was like its father—and most of it has gone back to him in some vague realm or dimension outside our material universe; some vague abyss out of which only the most accursed rites of human blasphemy could ever have called him for a moment on the hills."

—H.P. LOVECRAFT, "THE DUNWICH HORROR"

21. David Goudsward labors valiantly to demonstrate the possibility that Lovecraft took the standing stones on Sentinel Hill in Dunwich from "Mystery Hill" in New Hampshire. The colonial ruin at Mystery Hill in North Salem, New Hampshire, now operates under the name "America's Stonehenge" thanks to the similarity between collapsed colonial cider presses and druidic menhirs. Lovecraft may have visited Mystery Hill (then called Pattee's Caves) in June 1921 with fellow amateur writer Myrta Little, or possibly in June 1930 with Athol fantasy writer H. Warner Munn. Munn claimed in later life that he and Lovecraft had toured Mystery Hill, though his account has a number of anachronistic details in it. The case, as Goudsward admits, is circumstantial and not proven.

22. Murray also draws attention to the hamlet of Cold Brook Springs to the east, a possible name source for Lovecraft's Cold Spring Glen.

But more importantly than where, *what* is Lovecraft's Dunwich? Since, unlike Arkham, the town only appears in one tale, we can't separate the setting from the story, which Lovecraft structures as a parodic Gospel. Both Wilbur and the Horror are Christ-figures. Indeed, like the Castor and Pollux of Greek myth or the divine and material Christs of Gnostic heresy, both Wilbur and the Horror are, as Donald Burleson points out, twin halves of the same hero, with two natures: visible and invisible, man and god.

The Horror-hero is explicitly and parodically Christological—conceived by an infinite god, born of a virgin on a corner of the year, prodigiously learned at a young age, prophesied over, emerged from a backwater to challenge the priests of the Old Law. Where Jesus goes out into the open desert to seek wisdom, Wilbur retreats into a book-lined chamber. The Horror lurks in Cold Spring Glen, a hellish Gethsemane where it too seeks to evade its destiny. He dies like Dionysus or Osiris (torn to shreds by wild beasts) and like Christ (on a hilltop calling for his Father)—and like them both, he will return when the End Times come. "After summer is winter and after winter summer."

This makes the town of Dunwich, in turn, a parody of Bethlehem, Nazareth, and Jerusalem. Like Bethlehem, Dunwich is the ancestral seat of the (un)holy lineage both of the Whateleys (fled from Salem in 1692) and of Yog-Sothoth. Here, too, the birth of the man-god is heralded by portents, though Lovecraft inverts the Star in the sky to noises under the earth. The Nazareth parallel is mostly one of common rustication, although Nathanael's query in John 1:46—"Can anything good come out of Nazareth?"—seems apropos, and Wilbur does a lot of carpentry while rebuilding the barn for his twin. Finally, the Horror dies on the hill outside Dunwich, just as Christ died on the hill outside Jerusalem—reminding us that witch-cult refugees from Salem founded Dunwich, making the town a kind of "New Salem"[23] or "New Jerusalem."

---

23. New Salem, Massachusetts, founded by (non-witch) settlers from Salem, lies just over nine miles from Athol.

"Straight on I walked, while all the night
Grew pale with phosphorescent light,
And wall and farmhouse gable glowed
Unearthly by the climbing road.
There was the milestone that I knew –
'Two miles to Dunwich'—now the view ... "

—H.P. LOVECRAFT, "THE ANCIENT TRACK" (1929)

One final Biblical parallel, sanctified by another great horrorist: Dunwich is Chorazin, the hamlet cursed by Christ, the future birthplace of the Antichrist. M.R. James' "Count Magnus" makes the "Black Pilgrimage to Chorazin," at which Lovecraft's ears must have twitched. Lovecraft gets it both ways: Christ cursed Chorazin for rejecting him just as the Dunwich folk rejected the Horror, while casting the Horror as explicit Antichrist works on the "Machen level" of sin and retribution so strangely prominent in this tale.

But where Chorazin births the coming apocalypse, Dunwich is but a symptom, or better yet a preview. Dunwich is degeneration before the apocalypse; it is indeed the degeneration before the degeneration. Lovecraft uses it in much that way in his 1929 poem "The Ancient Track," the only other place where Dunwich appears in his works. That narrator, anticipating a joyous homecoming, sees the signpost for Dunwich; immediately thereafter he finds himself in "a valley of the lost and dead." Note that in the tale, the signs to Dunwich have all been taken down, and one finds Dunwich only by taking "the wrong fork at the junction of Aylesbury Pike."

The signs are redundant; Dunwich is, itself, the sign that you're on the wrong fork. Dunwich is prophecy, a role again signified by the prophetic elements in the tale. Not just the predictions in the *Necronomicon* ("Man rules now where They ruled once; They shall soon rule where man rules now.") but Old Whateley's ironic (even tragic) oracle ("some day yew folks'll hear a child o' Lavinny's a-callin' its father's name on the top o' Sentinel Hill!")

prefigure Dunwich's role. The story is itself a prophecy of the End Times, which are recapitulated in Dunwich. Dunwich begins with good Anglo-Saxon stock, and even a few "armigerous families" to lead it, but falls into decay, at which point Yog-Sothoth emerges and nearly destroys the world. This is the apocalypse from "Call of Cthulhu" all over again: *first* mankind is "beyond good and evil, with laws and morals set aside" and only *then* do the Old Ones return. First degeneration, then apocalypse.

> *"[T]he natives are now repellently decadent, having gone far along that path of retrogression so common in many New England backwaters. They have come to form a race by themselves, with the well-defined mental and physical stigmata of degeneracy and inbreeding. The average of their intelligence is woefully low, whilst their annals reek of overt viciousness and of half-hidden murders, incests, and deeds of almost unnameable violence and perversity."*

> —H.P. Lovecraft, "The Dunwich Horror"

All of Lovecraft's cities are apocalyptic, at least potentially. From the destroyed necropoleis of Kadath, the Nameless City, and Pnakotus to the looming New Jerusalem of R'lyeh, his alien cities all recapitulate the horror of the end. On a human scale, likewise: Innsmouth is economic devastation, leading to miscegenation and decay; New York is the "elfin" city polluted from without, transformed into the pit of Babylon by alien alchemy and immigration; Arkham is genetically doomed, "witch-haunted" and cursed at its founding. The story of Dunwich encompasses all of these (Babylon is the other bruited birthplace of the Antichrist), but is essentially the story of mankind writ small. Everywhere, all mankind—even the best of Anglo-Saxon New Englanders—will degenerate, because everywhere is tainted with entropy and evolution, with the Great Old Ones: *"Their hand is at your throats, yet ye see Them not; and Their habitation is even one with your guarded threshold."* Doom is everywhere. Especially, at first, in Dunwich.

ARABIA

> *"Remote in the desert of Araby lies the nameless city, crumbling and inarticulate, its low walls nearly hidden by the sands of uncounted ages. … It was of this place that Abdul Alhazred the mad poet dreamed on the night before he sang his unexplained couplet…"*

> — H.P. LOVECRAFT, "THE NAMELESS CITY"

It is not Lovecraft who first associates Arabia with horror. Poe famously entitled his masterpiece collection *Tales of the Grotesque and Arabesque* (1840), implying not just fantasy, but a sort of occult, obscurantist Orientalism that carried with it a specific dark frisson. Where the "grotesques" were satires and gargoyles, the "arabesques" were pure pattern, retraced lines of obsession and madness.

Lovecraft was of course a fervent disciple of Poe, but admired Shelley as well—and is there a hint of Shelley's "colossal wreck" from "Ozymandias" (1818) in the "crumbling and inarticulate" ruin of the Nameless City? Even before Shelley, Robert Southey transposed the Gothic to Araby in *Thalaba the Destroyer* (1801), and William Beckford's lurid Arabian nightmare *The History of the Caliph Vathek* (1786) casts its shadows across them all. Lovecraft read *Vathek* in July of 1921 (six months or so after writing "The Nameless City"), and fell as hard for it as he had for the *Arabian Nights* themselves.

> *"… how many dream-Arabs have the Arabian Nights bred! I ought to know, since at the age of 5 I was one of them! I had not then encountered Graeco-Roman myth, but found in Lang's Arabian Nights a gateway to*

glittering vistas of wonder and freedom. It was then that I invented for myself the name of Abdul Alhazred, and made my mother take me to all the Oriental curio shops and fit me up an Arabian corner in my room."

— H.P. LOVECRAFT, LETTER TO ROBERT E. HOWARD (JAN. 16, 1932)

Reading *Vathek* also reinforced Lovecraft's childhood image of Arabia as a fountain of wonders and eldritch knowledge, an image that his later work hints at. In "The Silver Key," we learn that Harley Warren had "prehistoric books and clay tablets smuggled from India and Arabia." Of course, rather than settle for what knowledge merchants and smugglers bring out of Arabia, truly dedicated pilgrims and prophets seek out the source. Moses, Elijah, John the Baptist, Jesus, St. Anthony, St. Benedict— all of them went into the desert to find … Something. As does, of course, Lovecraft's own prophet, the "mad Arab" Abdul Alhazred, who (as we learn in "The History of the *Necronomicon*") "spent ten years alone in the great southern desert of Arabia." And when he returned to the cities, to Damascus, he wrote the *Necronomicon* in answer to Jesus' question in Luke 7:24: "What did you go into the desert to see?"

"That antique Silver Key, he said, would unlock the successive doors that bar our free march down the mighty corridors of space and time to the very Border which no man has crossed since Shaddad with his terrific genius built and concealed in the sands of Arabia Petraea the prodigious domes and uncounted minarets of thousand-pillared Irem. Half-starved dervishes—wrote Carter—and thirst-crazed nomads have returned to tell of that monumental portal, and of the Hand that is sculptured above the keystone of the arch, but no man has passed and returned to say that his footprints on the garnet-strown sands within bear witness. The key, he surmised, was that for which the Cyclopean sculptured Hand vainly grasps."

— H.P. LOVECRAFT AND E. HOFFMANN PRICE,
"THROUGH THE GATES OF THE SILVER KEY"

Randolph Carter tells us what Alhazred went into the desert to see, and answers the minor conundrum of where he saw it. In "The History of the *Necronomicon*," Lovecraft tells us that Alhazred "claimed … to have found beneath the ruins of a certain nameless desert town the shocking annals and secrets of a race older than mankind." In other words, the Nameless City. But in that earlier tale, the nameless narrator tells us that Alhazred merely "dreamed" of the Nameless City and did not penetrate it. I like to think that our nameless narrator is the bold Lord Northam from Lovecraft's fragment "The Descendant," who "once went into the desert of Araby to seek a Nameless City of faint report, which no man has ever beheld." This meshes well with our narrator's comment, that the Nameless City has been "seen by no living man" until his own misadventure. If true, this would imply that not only Alhazred's journey, but the Yithian-ridden Nathaniel Wingate Peaslee's 1911 attempt (which "roused much attention through a camel trip into the unknown deserts of Arabia") and the similar trip to "the Arabian desert" by the museum-keeper Rogers (of "The Horror in the Museum") all came to nothing.

But Carter gives us the answer. Although the Nameless City holds its own "shocking secrets and annals," the true quest is for "the very Border" of space and time. Hence, Alhazred can approach that Border as Randolph Carter does, by dreaming of it. (Randolph Carter, like Alhazred, is also searching for a nameless city in dreams, in a novel with more than a taste of *Vathek*-esque Arabian nightmarishness.) The Nameless City *is* the Border, half-buried in the sand, between life and death, city and desert, anciently on the border between sea and land. It is both and neither, counterpart and reflection. Thus the grotesque Nameless City has a fanciful arabesque twin across the Border, Carter's (and the *Koran*'s) "thousand-pillared Irem."

Also called Irâm, Aram, Ubar, Wabar, Omanum Emporium, or Civitas Iboritae, it approaches, paradoxically, namelessness in its own right. Named or nameless, it is likewise a pilgrimage destination for Lovecraftian magi. Not only Alhazred and Carter, but Alfred Clarendon (in "The Last Test") seemed satisfied with seeking the blasphemies and riches of Irem. Clarendon went not only to the "Hoggar country" (in the Algerian desert) but at least as far as Yemen on the Arabian peninsula as well. There, he met another pilgrim, "an old man who had come back alive from the Crimson Desert—he had seen Irem, the City of Pillars, and had worshipped at the underground shrines of Nug and Yeb…" Nug and Yeb, twin deities for twin cities?

> *"Very gorgeous are the descriptions given of Irem, the City of Pillars (as the Koran styles it) supposed to have been erected by Shedad, the latest despot of Ad, in the regions of Hudramaut, and which yet, after the annihilation of its tenants, remains entire, so Arabs say, invisible to ordinary eyes, but occasionally, and at rare intervals, revealed to some heaven-favoured traveller."*
>
> — FROM "ARABIA," IN THE *ENCYCLOPAEDIA BRITANNICA* (9TH ED.)
> AS COPIED INTO H.P. LOVECRAFT'S COMMONPLACE BOOK

It seems that Lovecraft consciously built the Nameless City as a vaster, deeper, more ancient version—or iteration—of Irem. In the *Arabian Nights,* Irem is a treasure-house city built by the proud King Shaddad determined to create Paradise (in Arabic, *iram*) on Earth. Having spent 70 years in the construction of Irem, Shaddad is killed by Allah before he sets foot in it. The city remains a pristine treasure-house out in the desert sands, with gems lying around for anyone to pick up; a symbolic expression, perhaps, of the eldritch lore available to the diligent seeker. In the *Koran,* Irem is similar to Sodom and Gomorrah—destroyed by Allah for its sinful ways. Pious legend elaborates thusly: The dissolute A'adites of Irem reject the words of Allah's prophet Hud, who invokes Allah's wrath, plaguing Irem with infertility and drought. The A'adite delegation to Mecca gets drunk instead of praying for deliverance, and that's the last straw for Allah, who destroys Irem in the sight of the returning pilgrims.

Lovecraft builds his own triple parallels to the Koranic legend into the story. Overtly, the Nameless City seemingly spawns the human imitation city Irem: Irem appears as the Nameless City dries out, and the debased remnants of the Nameless City tear "a pioneer of ancient Irem" to pieces before descending into the hollow earth. Historically, the two cities' stories run in tandem: Irem is riding for a fall as Mecca rises, the debased A'adites drive off Hud (the lone "pioneer" from Mecca), and Irem sinks into the sands. What Irem is to Mecca, the Nameless City is to Irem. And symbolically, the various legendary dooms of Irem recur as mirror-image, or black grotesque parody, in "The Nameless City." Irem is destroyed by a Shout from Heaven: the narrator is lured in by "a crash of musical metal" from "some remote depth." Or Irem is destroyed by a powerful wind: the narrator is hurled along by a "shrieking, moaning night wind." Is Irem destroyed by celestial fire, as with Sodom? The Nameless City is forever lit by "some unknown subterranean phosphorescence." Does Irem sink into the sand? The reptile-things dig their own sunken city beneath their temple.

> *"Of the cult, he said that he thought the centre lay amid the pathless desert of Arabia, where Irem, the City of Pillars, dreams hidden and untouched. It was not allied to the European witch-cult, and was virtually unknown beyond its members."*

> — H.P. LOVECRAFT, "THE CALL OF CTHULHU"

This parallel between the Nameless City and Irem, the "Atlantis of the Sands," can bear further extension. If the central feature of both is the "city sunken beneath the waste," with strong echoes of prehistory (in the case of Irem) and prehumanity (in the case of the Nameless City), what other sunken city can we look at in this light? Lovecraft gives us the pointer when he has Old Castro locate the center of the Cthulhu cult in (or near) Irem. (Castro's mention of dreams in this context also reinforces our theory about Randolph Carter's Border, as well.) Does the Nameless City "amid the pathless desert of Arabia" seem an odd place for such a thing? Perhaps not so much: "the nightmare corpse-city of R'lyeh" lies on the lifeless floor of the Pacific Ocean, beneath the lone and level waves. A city sunk in a "pathless desert," in other words. The coupling of ocean and desert becomes even more apparent when we remember that the Nameless City was "a mighty seacoast metropolis" slowly engulfed by the sands.

From magical symbolism, we can turn back to literary symbolism. Thus, like "Dagon" and "The Temple" and "The Festival" and "Celephaïs" and the Johansen narrative in "Call of Cthulhu" and *The Dream-Quest of Unknown Kadath* and "Shadow Over Innsmouth," "The Nameless City" is one of HPL's "Oceanic Underworld/Otherworld" motif stories. Again, Lovecraft piles on the parallels. The Nameless City's reptile-things are an aquatic blend of crocodile and seal, the Moore poem quoted mentions the "Sea of Death," and the narrator fights "swirling currents" and a "torrent." Lovecraft repeatedly plays with words like "abyss" and "gulf," which can apply to caverns and ocean deeps alike. The inner world of the reptiles—"a sea of sunlit mist"—resembles both the Dreamlands and Y'ha-nthlei: "glorious cities and ethereal hills and valleys." Finally, Lovecraft took partial inspiration for this tale from a dream he had, in which (in the words of his later Commonplace Book entry) a man is trapped in a "subterranean chamber—seeks to force door of bronze—overwhelmed by influx of waters." Dreamland, Underworld, Ocean, Otherworld.

> *"For this place could be no ordinary city. It must have formed the primary nucleus and center of some archaic and unbelievable chapter of earth's history whose outward ramifications, recalled only dimly in the most obscure and distorted myths, had vanished utterly amidst the chaos of terrene convulsions long before any human race we know had shambled out of apedom. Here sprawled a Palaeogaean megalopolis ... ranking with such whispered prehuman blasphemies as Valusia, R'lyeh, Ib in the land of Mnar, and the Nameless City of Arabia Deserta."*

> — H.P. LOVECRAFT, *AT THE MOUNTAINS OF MADNESS*

In *At the Mountains of Madness*, Dyer compares the Old Ones' city to other "whispered prehuman blasphemies," metaphorically linking "the Nameless City of Arabia Deserta" with Valusia, R'lyeh, and "Ib in the land of Mnar." (Lovecraft's mirroring of Ib and Sarnath within "The Doom That Came to Sarnath" is very similar to his construction of the Nameless City-Irem dyad.) As the Nameless City is covalent with R'lyeh, it is also connected symbolically with Lovecraft's other great cities in the wasteland: the City of the Great Race in the Australian desert and (as Dyer notes) the City of the Old Ones in the "ice desert of the south," to quote Alhazred from "The Dunwich Horror." In all three of those nameless cities, as in R'lyeh, ancient survivors lurk in immense caverns or chambers beneath a lifeless waste.[24] And as Old Castro tells us, the center of them all is the Nameless City in Arabia, a word that literally means "the waste," deriving (in one reading) from the Hebrew *'arav*.

As the cities reflect each other, so do their deserts. The confusion between Kadath in the Cold Waste and "the cold desert plateau" of Leng in "the cold waste north of Inganok" is well known.[25] In "The Hound," Leng is in Central Asia, a perhaps fictionalized Tibet. In "The Last Test," Lovecraft makes the Tibet-Arabia connection explicit: the sight of the peculiarly silent and stiff Tibetans (of U-tsang) "gave Georgina a queer, awed feeling of having stumbled into the pages of *Vathek* or the *Arabian Nights*." The titular hound in the previous story is the "soul-symbol of the corpse-eating cult," reminding us that the lore Lovecraft brought back from Beckford's Arabia was that of the ghouls, who would haunt his fiction thereafter.

The ghouls are, again, emblematic of the waste. In the words (which Lovecraft almost certainly read) of Sir Richard Francis Burton in his

---

24. Despite the contemporary vogue for Mayan ruins, Lovecraft interestingly never treats us to an ancient city covered in a jungle; the closest we get is Sarnath, swallowed by a marshy lake. See our stop in The Swamp, pp. 213-220, for more on that mire.

25. Robert M. Price speculates that Lovecraft derived Kadath in the Cold Waste from the Biblical "wilderness of Kadesh" (Psalms 29:8).

(1885) notes to the *Arabian Nights*, the ghoul is "an embodiment of the natural fear and horror which a man feels when he faces a really dangerous desert." Lovecraft's (and Beckford's) ghouls haunt the "cities of the dead," the ancient burying grounds of Babylon or Boston. The Nameless City, Pnakotus, Kadath, R'lyeh: All of these cities are graveyards; necropoleis where the corpses don't stay dead. The ghoul, then, is the desert in the midst of the city in the midst of the desert, a recursive ouroborous symbol of Arabia and its nightmares living forever in the midst of death. Nothing, as Shelley says, beside remains.

ANTARCTICA

"[P]aradoxically, no spot on earth holds my terrified imagination more potently and breathlessly than the aeon-dead, unknown reaches of the great white antarctic."

— H.P. LOVECRAFT, LETTER TO ROBERT E. HOWARD (MAY 7, 1932)

Antarctica was H.P. Lovecraft's first alien world. When he was 10 years old, HPL fell hard for Antarctica and wrote "many fanciful tales about the Antarctic Continent," as he later told his friend Rheinhart Kleiner. What captured Lovecraft's fancy, characteristically enough, was a combination of actual geography (Borchgrevink's 1898-1900 expedition), dime novel (W. Clark Russell's *The Frozen Pirate* (1877), which HPL devoured at age 8), and, most likely, Edgar Allan Poe.

"Lost Arctic & Antarctic civilisations form a fascinating idea to me—I used it once in 'Polaris' and expect to use it again more than once."

— H.P. LOVECRAFT, LETTER TO
ELIZABETH TOLDRIDGE (OCTOBER 25, 1929)

Be that as it may, Lovecraft's first imaginary world was "No-Mans Land," a "vast continent composed of volcanic soil," located at the *North* Pole. In his juvenile work "The Mysterious Ship," No-Mans Land is the arctic headquarters of a gang of kidnappers, who imprison random individuals there. It is certainly a stretch—but as Lovecraft might say, it is nonetheless darkly suggestive—to connect the polar kidnappers of "The Mysterious Ship" with the Great Race of Yith, who also commit seemingly random kidnappings, likewise removing their victims to inaccessible imprisonment. More suggestive still, the Great Race has its own Arctic connections. For example, according to "The Challenge From Beyond," the cone-beings have "a great polar city" where they stashed the Cube of Yekub.[26] Furthermore, in Lovecraft's original version of "The Shadow Out of Time," the time-napping villains were the men of Lomar in the (not yet) frozen Arctic, the heroes of his early tale "Polaris."

Or so Lovecraft described that draft to Clark Ashton Smith, whose own tales of pre-glacial Hyperborea riffed on the Greek legends of the "land above the North Wind," the home of Apollo. Scholars in Lovecraft's Lomar studied the Pnakotic Manuscripts ... which re-emerge four times in *At the Mountains of Madness* amid discussions of Smith's toad-god Tsathoggua and the Antarctic city of the Old Ones. And what else appears like a mirage in HPL's Antarctic prose? The city of Olathoë, the ancient capital of Lomar, which Dyer describes as a city "of today" beside the "Palaeogaean metropolis" of Antarctica. (I note idly that the entire point of "Polaris" is the impossibility of determining just when, exactly, "today" is.) And Olathoë is very similar to the Old Ones' city: it lies "still and somnolent ... on a strange plateau ... betwixt strange peaks." It, too, suffers a race war and dies under the ice.

This polar switcheroo puts me in mind of the Theosophical notion of the "pole shift," in which the Earth (for murky reasons) tumbles on its axis, triggering global catastrophe and racial destruction. If such a pole shift happened some time in the last 26,000 years, Olathoë might well be in Antarctica now! Lovecraft could have discovered the pole shift while swotting up on things Theosophical, but he certainly read about it in Plato and Herodotus, who both mention it obliquely. HPL hints at pole shifting in his collaboration with Robert H. Barlow, "Till A' the Seas," in which the last survivors of the doomed (human) race gather at the South Pole. More polar confusion—or, more precisely, conflation—shows up in "The

---

26. Perhaps this is why the Yithian in Peaslee's body travels to "the Arctic north of Spitzbergen," to look for the city of the Cube. He "returns shewing signs of disappointment" because the Cube vanished (looted by Lomarians?) to eventually turn up at a campsite in Canada.

Dunwich Horror," where we learn of "the inner city at the 2 magnetic poles." Two poles: one city.

"Who can forget the terrible swollen ship poised on the billow-chasm's edge in 'MS. Found in a Bottle'—the dark intimations of her unhallowed age and monstrous growth, her sinister crew of unseeing greybeards, and her frightful southward rush under full sail through the ice of the Antarctic night, sucked onward by some resistless devil-current toward a vortex of eldritch enlightenment which must end in destruction?"

— H.P. LOVECRAFT, *SUPERNATURAL HORROR IN LITERATURE* (1927)

Lovecraft pole-shifts (and Poe-shifts) in *Mountains,* when he equates Poe's "Mount Yaanek in the realms of the boreal [north] pole" (from "Ulalume" (1847)) with Mount Erebus in Antarctica. In his own novel *The Narrative of Arthur Gordon Pym* (1838), Poe likewise shifts his poles, rotating the North Polar "Hyperborean" myth—of a warm land beyond the wind—south to Antarctica. But instead of literally Apollonian gods, Poe populates the black island of Tsalal (his anti-Hyperborea) with Dionysian savages, prone to panic and murder.

This attribution of malignity to the Antarctic seems original with Poe, for all that the medieval geographers populated the "Antipodes" and "Terra Incognita Australis" with grotesques. Before Poe, for example, Coleridge's castaway in "The Rime of the Ancient Mariner" (1798) discovers a benevolent Spirit in the far reaches of the southern sea. In *Moby-Dick,* Melville follows Poe, with a supernaturally white death-bringer from the Antarctic oceans. Regardless of how they charge their poles, though, Coleridge, Poe, and Melville all end their narratives in maelstrom.

"Danforth was a great reader of bizarre material, and had talked a good deal of Poe. I was interested myself because of the antarctic scene of Poe's only long story—the disturbing and enigmatical Arthur Gordon Pym."

— H.P. LOVECRAFT, *AT THE MOUNTAINS OF MADNESS*

Lovecraft's Antarctic voyage, his "remake" of *Pym*, also ends in a maelstrom, albeit an intellectual one. Both *Pym* and *Mountains* begin in dry, almost clinical terms: Poe's sea narrative and Lovecraft's scientific report. But soon enough, disaster strikes; race war tears apart Pym's ship, and the Old Ones kill Dyer's fellow scientists. Both Pym and Dyer pass through a series of descents to discover strange hieroglyphics and a mysterious half-seen figure of terror.

Both sets of hieroglyphics are disturbingly cosmic: Poe's are startlingly large, comprising entire passageways, while Lovecraft's are unthinkably ancient.[27] And, of course, Lovecraft explicitly tips his hat to Poe by transferring the cry of "Tekeli-li! Tekeli-li!" from the eerie white birds of Tsalal to the bubbling black shoggoth of Kadath.[28] But where Poe is writing a journey of the psyche, purified by horrors and exalted by the discovery of its Source at the end of the world, Lovecraft is telling a journey of the intellect, battered by discoveries and horrified by its Source at the beginning of the world.

> *"That the antarctic continent was once temperate and even tropical, with a teeming vegetable and animal life of which the lichens, marine fauna, arachnida, and penguins of the northern edge are the only survivals, is a matter of common information; and we hoped to expand that information in variety, accuracy, and detail."*
>
> — H.P. Lovecraft, *At the Mountains of Madness*

Robert M. Price famously pinpoints *Mountains* as the high-water mark of Lovecraft's "demythologization" of his own cosmos. In its pages, the *Necronomicon* stands revealed as medieval distortion and cultist raving, and the Pnakotic Manuscripts become simply random accretions around half-understood alien detritus. Mighty Cthulhu is but one member of a

---

27. Angela Carter detects this Poe-esque vastness and vastation in Lovecraft's Antarctic. In her poetic words: "Under a cryptic sky, the landscape itself becomes a vast cryptogram …"

28. One can distract oneself endlessly hunting for the original source of that cry: I find Poe scholar J.V. Ridgely's theory, deriving it from the Maori *tekelili*, "to shiver or shake," pretty convincing.

transient species of octopoid aliens, and Tsathoggua just a broken memory of the Old Ones.

Fabled Leng becomes a name attached by mystics to the Old Ones' plateau, and "Kadath in the Cold Waste," far from being the mountain of the gods it was in its eponymous *Dream-Quest*, is only the tumbled ruins of the Old Ones' slave pen. Mythology becomes paleontology; archaeology takes the place of mysticism. There is no blasphemous knowledge; there are no gods to be blasphemed. Antarctica is neither the fecund womb of Poe's Gnostic imagination nor the soul-erasing vortex of his Gothic fears, but merely an icy Petri dish left in untidy condition by vegetable-men from another world.

> *"In the whole spectacle there was a persistent, pervasive hint of stupendous secrecy and potential revelation. It was as if these stark, nightmare spires marked the pylons of a frightful gateway into forbidden spheres of dream, and complex gulfs of remote time, space, and ultra-dimensionality. I could not help feeling that they were evil things—mountains of madness whose farther slopes looked out over some accursed ultimate abyss. That seething, half-luminous cloud background held ineffable suggestions of a vague, ethereal beyondness far more than terrestrially spatial, and gave appalling reminders of the utter remoteness, separateness, desolation, and aeon-long death of this untrodden and unfathomed austral world."*

> — H.P. LOVECRAFT, *AT THE MOUNTAINS OF MADNESS*

Certainly Price is correct, on the surface, at least as far as Dyer knows and tells us. But for such a rigorous demythologizer, Dyer has a strong streak of Arthur Gordon Pym in him. His quote above certainly doesn't sound like a geologist's report. It sounds, rather, like the ravings of a mystic, or (Poe might suggest) of an initiate. Lovecraft doesn't "demythologize" his cosmos in *Mountains*; if anything, he remythologizes Antarctica—and by extension, our cosmos—in that novel. Antarctica—"the strangest, weirdest, and most terrible of all the corners of earth's globe"—becomes another world, a world of Lovecraftian phantasy. Lake's transmission compares Antarctica to a "land of mystery in a dream," or a "gateway" to a "forbidden world of untrodden wonder." Dyer goes even farther, calling it the "unknown antarctic world of disordered time and alien natural law." Those "mountains of madness," which are "a frightful gateway into forbidden spheres of dream," are nothing compared to the range beyond, which are "the focus of the world's evil," and seem like "the serrated edge of a monstrous alien planet," for example.

Having read Dyer's warning, we see Antarctica anew through Lovecraft's eyes. Every expedition's report becomes fodder for his new mythology. Just lately, for example, paleontologists have determined that all octopi share a single Antarctic ancestor, and geologists have discovered an unknown mountain range buried beneath the Antarctic ice sheet in defiance of all known rules of plate tectonics. We read such news from the bottom of the world, and shudder. Perhaps Lovecraft knew best, when he wrote in the sonnet "Antarktos": "the bird told of vaster parts, that under / The mile-deep ice-shroud crouch and brood and bide." Under the scientific mind, frozen in place by human hubris, bigger truths "crouch and brood and bide." A truth "very far larger in its proportions," as Arthur Gordon Pym says, "than any dweller among men." Tekeli-li! Tekeli-li!

UNDERGROUND

"Who can, with my knowledge, think of the earth's unknown caverns without a nightmare dread of future possibilities? I cannot see a well or a subway entrance without shuddering ...."

— H.P. LOVECRAFT, "THE LURKING FEAR"

In his pioneering work *Lovecraft: A Study in the Fantastic* (1972), French literary critic Maurice Lévy writes: "In Lovecraft [the Beyond] is almost always situated in the depths." Perhaps unbidden, Anthony Pearsall gives an excellent roundup of Lovecraft's "Caves, Caverns, Wells & Abysses" in his *Lovecraft Lexicon*. In my own survey of the topic, I count seventeen solo tales (out of 51)[29] and twelve revisions (out of 28 examined)[30] with little or no underground content, and even that category includes such works as "The Doom That Came to Sarnath," "The Horror at Martin's Beach," and "The Moon-Bog," featuring horrors from beneath a lake, the ocean, and a bog respectively. While a strict mathematical count might thus be closer to "two thirds of the time" than "almost always," it's certainly notable that "The Haunter of the Dark" is the *only* major Lovecraft tale containing no (or no important) underground scenes or elements. And even in that story, Blake breaks into the Starry Wisdom church through the cellar, and gazes into "an infinite gulf of darkness" within the Trapezohedron.

---

29. See note 5, in the "Dreamland" Stop on p. 19.

30. This number includes the revisions and collaborations I cover in *Tour de Lovecraft: The Tales*, plus the other two Hazel Heald revisions. It also includes the four revisions for C.M. Eddy, and one each for Henry S. Whitehead and Wilfred Blanch Talman. This selection, though covering every remotely worthwhile revision story and then some, is otherwise admittedly entirely arbitrary.

Of the remaining two-thirds of Lovecraft's fiction, I count about fourteen solo tales (and eleven revisions) with some underground component, from the "pit of the shoggoths" in "The Thing on the Doorstep" to the cavern-tomb of Cthulhu in "The Call of Cthulhu." My last category, stories with a major underground aspect, encompasses twenty solo tales and six revisions; everything from HPL's first primitive tales ("The Tomb," "The Statement of Randolph Carter," "The Lurking Fear") through mid-career masterpieces ("Pickman's Model," *The Case of Charles Dexter Ward*) to his late, great triumphs (*At the Mountains of Madness*, "The Shadow Out of Time"). If Lovecraft doesn't always find his horrors in the depths, he certainly never stops looking into the abyss.

"For the first time I began to attempt writing—the earliest piece I can recall being a tale of a hideous cave …."

— H.P. LOVECRAFT, "SOME NOTES ON A NONENTITY" (1933)

In a 1931 letter to J. Vernon Shea, Lovecraft expands on the above précis of his first ever story, "The Noble Eavesdropper," describing it as featuring "a boy who overheard some horrible conclave of subterranean entities in a cave." Heady stuff for a seven-year-old, it began four decades of dire delvings. Lovecraft followed it at age eight with "The Secret Cave, or John Lees Adventure" and then another story about a man kidnapped into a secret apartment beneath a tomb. In 1905, at fifteen, he wrote "The Beast in the Cave," set in Mammoth Cave, Kentucky. Some of this obsession, no doubt, sprang from Lovecraft's lifelong "distinct fear of very large enclosed spaces," as he wrote to Harry Fischer in 1937.

It wasn't until June of 1928 that Lovecraft set actual (as opposed to fictive) foot in a cave, one of the "alluring caves" in the Bear's Den gorge near Athol, Massachusetts. Later that summer he visited the Endless Caverns in New Market, Virginia, a genuine subterranean system of "illimitable gulfs and chasms of elfin beauty and daemonic mystery" that doubtless account for the "vast limestone cavern systems" that Peaslee explores in Virginia during his Yithian possession in "The Shadow Out of Time." From his very first story to almost his last, Lovecraft moves (as he describes the Endless Caverns) "[from deep] to deep, gallery to gallery, and chamber to chamber ... transported to the strangest regions of nocturnal fancy."

> *"I have said that the fury of the rushing blast was infernal—cacodaemoniacal—and that its voices were hideous with the pent-up viciousness of desolate eternities ... down there in the grave of unnumbered aeon-dead antiquities, leagues below the dawn-lit world of men, I heard the ghastly cursing and snarling of strange-tongued fiends."*

— H.P. LOVECRAFT, "THE NAMELESS CITY"

Let's start our trip downward with the above quote, a fairly standard early-Lovecraft adumbration on the abyss: "infernal," "cacodaemoniacal," "pent-up viciousness," "down there," "the grave," "below," and finally "fiends." Almost the only note it misses is the word "abyss" itself, which Lovecraft uses in at least 27 different stories, including elsewhere in this one. What pops to my notice is the very traditional, Christian imagery throughout this latter-day Arabian nightmare by the atheist Lovecraft. You can take the Baptist out of the boy, but you can't take the boy out of the Baptists.

Some of Lovecraft's preoccupation with the underground seems likely to have grown from his native New England's preoccupation with the Devil. Lovecraft loves the adjective "hellish" rather more than his casual readers remember: beginning with the "hellish black mire" in "Dagon" and the "hellish moon-glitter" in "Nyarlathotep" through the "hellish" light show in "Colour Out of Space" and the "hellish Himalayan Mi-Go" of "Whisperer in Darkness." In "The Dunwich Horror," he applies the adjective to the Whateley fires, rituals, spawn, and diary, and to the advance of Yog-Sothoth in general.

More directly downward-facing, he repeatedly refers to Hell itself, though decorously decapitalized: a "blasphemous abnormality from hell's nethermost craters" in "The Lurking Fear," and a "hell-born babel" in "The Nameless City." It gets even more local in the underground city of K'n-

yan, that "nitrous hell of inner earth." Even Lovecraft's imprisoned octopoid Satan rules in Hell: Steven Mariconda discovered that Lovecraft's
original version of "R'lyeh" was "L'yeh," which as Donald Burleson points
out, is just "Hell" backwards. And last but hardly least, the deep channel behind the appositely named *Devil* Reef in Innsmouth Harbor: "that
cursed place of all wickedness whar the deep water starts. Gate o' hell—
sheer drop daown to a bottom no saoundin'-line kin tech."

Lovecraft recoups a bit for his pagan side by mentioning Tartarus, the
Greek mythical cavern of punishment, in "Herbert West," "The Festival,"
"Call of Cthulhu," "The Horror at Red Hook," and *Charles Dexter Ward,*
and in generously ecumenical fashion refers to Exham Priory as both "an
antechamber of hell" and "this grisly Tartarus" in "The Rats in the Walls."
But even Lovecraft's beloved "abyss" carries a strong religious charge. Although *abyssos* is a perfectly normal Greek word meaning "bottomless" or
"unfathomable," the Bible uses it as a term for the primordial chaos (Genesis 1:2), the abode of the dead (Psalms 71:20), and the prison of demons
(Luke 8:31). Finally, Revelation 11:7 declares that the Beast will rise up,
Cthulhu-like, from the Abyss, "the bottomless pit."

> *"It was the eldritch scurrying of those fiend-born rats, always questing
> for new horrors, and determined to lead me on even unto those grinning
> caverns of earth's centre where Nyarlathotep, the mad faceless god, howls
> blindly to the piping of two amorphous idiot flute-players."*

> — H.P. Lovecraft, "The Rats in the Walls"

From sublimated theology we turn to subterranean geography. After
forty-odd stories, Lovecraft's Earth winds up resembling the bhole-rad-
dled planet Yaddith, honeycombed with "primal tunnels." Take the Martense warrens in "The Lurking Fear" as a fractal sign of Lovecraft's underground, long burrows radiating out from foul centers. In "Red Hook"
we hear of similar tunnels beneath New York, and from his cellar Richard
Pickman retails stories (and paints schematics) of such excavations, both

human and inhuman, throughout Boston. On this stratum we might also put the echoing chambers that produce those eerie underground noises in "The Dunwich Horror."

Below the tunnels and burrows come the crypts, vaults, and deepest sub-cellars: as Alhazred puts it in "The Festival," those "great holes secretly … digged" down by sorcerers or up by troglodytes. Examples among the many include Curwen's Pawtuxet laboratory (like its hellish model, both prison and torture-ground for the dead), Exham Priory, and the myriad temples "Under the Pyramids." Suydam's deepest cellar in Red Hook might count here, too, as it debouches on a literally Stygian underground river much like the one flowing beneath Kingsport in "The Festival."

I'm inclined to put whole buried cities on the next level down. I disregard hydrology to do this, as another underground river washes the Antarctic city of the Old Ones in *At the Mountains of Madness*, and a watery gulf lies beneath the Nameless City. The Yithian city in Australia has no river—though it once suffered a "bygone influx of water"—exchanging it for even deeper pits for the imprisoned "daemon winds." The blue-tinted city of Tsath in K'n-yan has its own river, and beneath it lie its own even deeper pits: "red-litten Yoth" and beneath it "the black realm of N'kai," the home of the amorphous god Tsathoggua. At the center of the Earth, at the bottom of this modern Inferno roils Nyarlathotep, echoing Azathoth's writhing at the center of the universe.

"Below me was a chaos of tumbled masonry, sloping roughly down toward the north at an angle of about forty-five degrees, and evidently the result of some bygone collapse from above. Between its surface and the ground level was a gulf of impenetrable blackness at whose upper edge were signs of gigantic, stress-heaved vaulting. At this point, it appeared, the desert's sands lay directly upon a floor of some titan structure of earth's youth— how preserved through aeons of geologic convulsion I could not then and cannot now even attempt to guess."

— H.P. LOVECRAFT, "THE SHADOW OUT OF TIME"

When we fall in Lovecraft, we don't only fall down spatially. As Delapore demonstrates in his descent of Exham Priory, we also fall backward, down the evolutionary ladder. The degenerate supermen of K'nyan rule above the reptilians of Yoth, whose realm lies atop the formless slime of N'kai. The pit of the abyss is also the pit of the past; Lévy maintains that Lovecraft's descent underground "coincides always with a regression to an anterior state of chronology." Exham Priory literally functions as a core sample of human historical horror, and the past doesn't end there. The psionic masters of Tsath beneath "The Mound" went to earth before Atlantis sank, the Great Race built its Pnakotic library-cities before the Triassic period, and the crinoid Old Ones spawned in the earliest Archaean.

Elder ruins beneath the Earth's crust are bad enough, but their survivors still haunt those deeps—as do those insensate things, shoggoths and wind-polyps, that destroyed them. The original "lurking fear" that Lovecraft expressed concerned such "primitive survivals" living underground. Lovecraft's great precursor in such delvings, Arthur Machen, depicted hideous races beneath Welsh hills and London thoroughfares, but Lovecraft had mined those depths long before he read Machen's surveys in mid-1923. The things under the tomb in "The Statement of Randolph Carter," the Atlantean haunter from the abyssal trench in "The Temple," the half-spectral reptile-things in the gulf beneath "The Nameless City," and even the decayed and inbred Martense brood in "The Lurking Fear" all spawned from Lovecraft's burrows before Machen inspired "The Rats in the Walls."

"'I'm sorry to have to ask you to stay on the surface,' he said, 'but it would be a crime to let anyone with your frail nerves go down there. You can't imagine, even from what you have read and from what I've told you, the things I shall have to see and do.'"

— H.P. LOVECRAFT, "THE STATEMENT OF RANDOLPH CARTER"

The scholar Barton Levi St. Armand used "Rats in the Walls" as a template for a Jungian reading of all of Lovecraft's fiction. Without going completely over that particular slippery edge we can certainly shine a light or two down the hole. "Rats" does indeed directly conflate spatial descent with atavistic retreat into "race memory," to note just one unsavory Jungian tidbit in that particular feast. Descents into the underground repeatedly become literal descents into madness, again in "Rats," but also in "The Festival," "Red Hook," *Charles Dexter Ward,* and "The Shadow Out of Time," to list only the most explicit examples. We can also highlight the somewhat more anodyne notion of the subconscious as "below" the regular conscious mind, echoed by Randolph Carter descending the seven hundred steps of Deeper Slumber to emerge in the archetype-laden Dreamlands. Specifically, in the Enchanted Wood, where we not coincidentally emerged at the start of this Tour.

The subconscious operates not by rationality but by coincidence and intuition, impulses sparking without structure or immediate cause. The notion of an inchoate, formless sensation beneath the ground floor of reason shows up most explicitly in Lovecraft's stories of … well, of inchoate, formless monsters beneath the ground. The unknown but threatening horrors of "The Statement of Randolph Carter" could embody the death-wish, while the "loathsome night-spawned flood of organic corruption" bred over generations under the Martense lands in "Lurking Fear" might point toward a lustier *lustmord,* if we're giving in to our debased Freudian instincts. The flood of rats scurrying ever downward through Exham Priory could embody Lovecraft's Faustian urge to explore the abject self; we can make the fungous horror below "The Shunned House" represent the hideous truths of colonial history, one recapitulated by the hideous part-revenants in the Pawtuxet cellar-pits of *Charles Dexter Ward.* Cthulhu and the shoggoths both ooze black-and-green from primordial pits that violate not just reason but geometry itself, and have half-a-dozen diagnoses attached to them already.

More significantly or at least more demonstrably, notice the number of times that going Underground reveals an actual archetype: a literal image, symbol, or glyph. From the giant piscine bas-relief of "Dagon" in a crevasse to the impossible English handwriting (below layers of Yithian hiero-glyphs) in "Shadow Out of Time," Lovecraft encodes himself inextricably in this topos. A Green Flame burns alchemically beneath Kingsport in "The Festival," and parades of symbolic monsters process past fainting heroes in "Red Hook" and "Under the Pyramids." Sweeping bas-reliefs depicting secret (sacred) history recur under "The Nameless City" and on the walls of the crinoid city of Kadath in Antarctica. Go down below reason, and you shall see the truth.

"Most daemoniacal of all shocks is that of the abysmally unexpected ..."

— H.P. LOVECRAFT, "THE OUTSIDER"

Or ... you could go up. The story most often pointed to as Lovecraft's on-the-nose psychological self-diagnosis, "The Outsider," features a sub-terranean dweller climbing up a shaft to a new revelation. Randolph Carter makes a similar climb through the tower of the gugs in *Dream-Quest*, but rather than emerging in the waking world merely returns to the Enchanted Wood of his regular subconscious Dreamland. Thomas Olney likewise climbs up to revelation in "The Strange High House in the Mist," although Nodens (Lord of the Great *Abyss*) brings Olney not the ghoul-ish joy of the Outsider but the bourgeois safety to which even Randolph Carter eventually aspires.

In search of ultimate hyperspatial truths Walter Gilman deliberately takes an attic room in the "Witch House," and Robert Blake climbs the Starry Wisdom church tower to discover "The Haunter of the Dark," both climbs that end in death and oblivion. Other attic revelations greet the narrators of "From Beyond" and "The Music of Erich Zann," which surely gives us enough for a sub-pattern, an epicycle within the downward gyre of Lovecraft's fictions. (For what it's worth, as a child Lovecraft discovered and devoured much of his grandfather Whipple Phillips' library "in a black, windowless *attic* room.") I sense a certain geometric similarity between this tower-shaft up to the attic-void and what Gavin Callaghan calls Lovecraft's "moon-ladder" image, which we climbed in our stop on the Moon earlier in our Tour.

> *"The other gods! The other gods! The gods of the outer hells that guard the feeble gods of earth! ... Look away! ... Go back! ... Do not see! ... Do not see! ... The vengeance of the infinite abysses ... That cursed, that damnable pit ... Merciful gods of earth,* I am falling into the sky!"

— H.P. Lovecraft, "The Other Gods"

The final type of Lovecraftian Underground turns out, therefore, to be the one Above. Barzai the Wise memorably falls into the sky at the climax of "The Other Gods," but note his reference to "that damnable pit" atop, or rather over, the mountain Hatheg-Kla. In "Celephaïs," Kuranes somewhat reverses the pattern by falling over the Devonshire cliff—"the precipice and the abyss"—into the sky above Celephaïs. Walter Gilman begins his hyperspatial dreams in "plunges through limitless abysses," and ends at least one of them lying on a "high, balustraded terrace" above a city of the crinoid Old Ones, implying a fall into/from the triple-sunned sky of that planet.

Lévy aptly says Lovecraft turns the world inside-out, exposing the gross buried parts to the open air and open eye. And as befits Lovecraft's noblest alter ego, nobody gets turned more inside-out than Randolph Carter. Not only does he become an alien in "Through the Gates of the Silver Key," he falls in all directions at once at the climax of the *Dream-Quest*. A shantak carries Carter into space toward Vega, "cleaving the uttermost rim and spanning the outermost abysses"—in a word, Up. Carter nearly reaches the center of infinity, Azathoth, but jumps off the shantak and falls "down through endless voids of sentient blackness." During that eternal fall, Carter sees the cosmos die and be reborn (as he does on a slightly lesser scale in "Through the Gates of the Silver Key"), and then "descend[s] at last" to Boston. Thus outer space, the Underground, and indeed the dizzying future and deepest of past times, become one and the same. Just as Nodens rules both the oceanic depths and the dizzying skies above Kingsport, any gulf in space or time becomes the Abyss. Up, Out, Back, Forward … it doesn't matter. In Lovecraft's cosmos, every direction is Down.

ANTIQUITY

"The year after I first beheld the tomb, I stumbled upon a worm-eaten translation of Plutarch's Lives *in the book-filled attic of my home."*

— H.P. LOVECRAFT, "THE TOMB"

Jervas Dudley, the protagonist of Lovecraft's very first piece of adult fiction, "The Tomb," models himself after the Greek hero Theseus and sees "dryads," outbreaks of Classicism spawned and energized by his chance discovery of Plutarch's *Lives of the Noble Greeks and Romans*. As Poe put it, "the glory that was Greece, and the grandeur that was Rome" together make up a stretch of Lovecraft country that we can call (in somewhat, er, antique fashion) Antiquity. It's a space somewhat surprisingly neglected by Lovecraft scholars—and even more surprisingly neglected, at least on the surface, by Lovecraft himself despite his declaration to Clark Ashton Smith: "Classical legend is full of fruitful themes."

"On a verdant slope of Mount Maenalus, in Arcadia, there stands an olive grove about the ruins of a villa. Close by is a tomb, once beautiful with the sublimest sculptures, but now fallen into as great decay as the house. At one end of that tomb, its curious roots displacing the time-stained blocks of Panhellic marble, grows an unnaturally large olive tree of oddly repellent shape..."

— H.P. LOVECRAFT, "THE TREE"

Lovecraft only wrote one tale set in Antiquity, after all, and "The Tree" is far from his strongest work. It's set during the 4th century B.C. on the sacred mountain of Pan, Mount Maenalus, although the narrative drive comes from a liminal space between Greece and Rome, Sicily under the "Tyrant of Syracuse." It's a simple quasi-Gothic shudder-story retold (not particularly compellingly) as a minor Classical fable, but it has an interestingly Lovecraftian trunk within its foliage. Even in this classical Arcadia (literally!) there is corruption and desolation, albeit in this case caused by human motives.

To this solitary fruit, we can add if we like "The Green Meadow," a collaboration with Winifred Virginia Jackson about a Greek savant of the Classical era who is abducted or stumbles into the titular Otherworldly vale. And for the Roman side of things, we might consider "The Very Old Folk," a story fragment about an official of the late Republic who (unwisely, as it turns out) orders a cohort of soldiers to break up a primitive barbarian rite in the Hispanian foothills. "The Very Old Folk" is actually a fixup of a dream Lovecraft had in 1927 and described to many of his correspondents, among them Frank Belknap Long, who eventually turned it into his own story, "The Horror From the Hills" (1931).[31]

> *"When about seven or eight I was a genuine pagan, so intoxicated with the beauty of Greece that I acquired a half-sincere belief in the old gods and Nature-sprits. I have in literal truth built altars to Pan, Apollo, Diana, and Athena, and have watched for dryads and satyrs in the woods and fields at dusk."*
>
> — H.P. LOVECRAFT, "A CONFESSION OF UNFAITH" (1922)

In his letters, Lovecraft makes plain his visceral, emotional connection to Antiquity. He mentions his childhood discovery of Hawthorne's *Wonder-Book* and Bulfinch's *Age of Fable*, his grandfather's tales of Roman travel, and other inspirations including a handful of genuine Roman coins, the memory of which still brought Lovecraft to the verge of ecstasy in a letter written decades later. Given what changes HPL's ecstasies later wrought on Marblehead, Salem, and Newburyport, perhaps it comes as

---

31. As a final gloss, Robert H. Waugh notes that Lovecraft directly quotes Virgil in "The Tomb" and (anachronistically) "The Tree," introduces "The Festival" with an epigraph from Lactantius, and references Catullus (on obscene anti-Roman rites) in "Rats in the Walls" and "Medusa's Coil."

no surprise to find the narrator in "The Lurking Fear" exclaim: "It was a peaceful Arcadian scene, but knowing what it hid, I hated it."

At the age of seven, he wrote his own version of the *Odyssey* in iambic trimeter. His second childish pseudonym (after "Abdul Alhazred") was "L. Valerius Messala," and while he loved the stories (and eventually the philosophies) of the Greeks, Lovecraft from an early age considered himself a Roman, and repeatedly identified himself as such in his letters. Picking two examples out of many, on November 24, 1927, Lovecraft wrote to Donald Wandrei, "Psychologically, I am either a Roman or an Englishman,"[32] and on December 13, 1933, HPL described to Clark Ashton Smith his "natural and unshakeable feeling of *being a Roman.*"

"Anchester had been the camp of the third Augustan legion, as many remains attest, and it was said that the temple of Cybele was splendid and thronged with worshippers who performed nameless ceremonies at the bidding of a Phrygian priest. Tales added that the fall of the old religion did not end the orgies at the temple, but that the priests lived on in the new faith without real change. Likewise was it said that the rites did not vanish with the Roman power..."

— H.P. LOVECRAFT, "THE RATS IN THE WALLS"

Thus Lovecraft's fiction generally presents Rome as a synecdoche for "civilization," regardless of the seemingly absurd juxtaposition of alien super-technologists with Iron Age humans. The inhuman nature of the aliens is even refuted by appeal to Rome: in both "The Nameless City" and *At the Mountains of Madness,* archaeologists in denial argue the aliens' horrific self-portraits to be nothing more than artistic conventions like the wolf-symbol of Rome. In the cities of the Great Race of Yith, we are told, "the principle of the arch was known as fully and used as extensively

---

32. Once at least, Lovecraft presents a "Roman Englishman" as the ultimate pinnacle from which to fall. Lord Northam, the titular scion in the story fragment "The Descendant" comes from decayed Roman stock. This aspect of Rome's fall—and of Lovecraft's imaginary landscape—repeatedly recurs in a New England context.

as by the Romans." Like the Romans, the Yithians have howling barbarians penned up—until the barriers fail and civilization is destroyed. In *Mountains of Madness* Lovecraft explicitly compares the stultification of the senescent crinoid Old One civilization in Antarctica (who also "relied on" the Roman arch) to the decadence of Constantine's late-Roman empire, and the crude, imitative bas-reliefs carved by the Old Ones' shoggoth subjects and successors to "ungainly Palmyrene sculptures fashioned in the Roman manner."

The shoggoths in *Mountains* are the cosmic version of the ante-Roman (and anti-Roman) survivals demonized in earlier Lovecraft tales. In "The Horror at Red Hook," the evil cult's lore (and ancestry) comprises a macedoine of Rome's enemies, from Carthage to Persia. In "The Rats in the Walls," the Roman bastion that will become Exham Priory merely covers the Cymric horrors below, and becomes further polluted by the Asiatic cult of Cybele, the Magna Mater. The un-Roman East brings forth more monsters: "Dagon" is a Syrian god, Nyarlathotep comes "out of Egypt" in his story as do the horrors "Under the Pyramids," and the false Rome of the "Nameless City" lurks beneath Arabia.

The horrors that subverted Antiquity—specifically the cults of Dionysos/Bacchus and Cybele—threaten Lovecraft's modernity. Shub-Niggurath, the Black Goat of the Woods, the Goat With a Thousand Young, becomes Lovecraft's Cybele. In *The Case of Charles Dexter Ward*, Joseph Curwen seeks knowledge of "the Sign of the Goat found on the ancient Roman altar" in a Limoges crypt. John Salonia notes that the piping flutes and throbbing drums of Lovecraft's cults and gods from "Nyarlathotep" on down derive from Euripides' *Bacchae*. Dennis Quinn points out that the global cult of Cthulhu very much resembles the subversive cult of Bacchus in Livy's Roman history, and that Lovecraft explicitly describes the Louisiana rites as a "Bacchanal." Lovecraft's horrors are, as he put it in "The Very Old Folk," "dooms which ought not to exist within the territories of the Roman People."

"I believe I did ridiculous things such as offering prayers to Artemis, Latona, Demeter, Persephone, and Plouton. All that I recalled of a classic youth came to my lips as the horrors of the situation roused my deepest superstitions."

— H.P. LOVECRAFT, "THE MOON-BOG"

Five other Lovecraft tales deal with what we might call hauntings from Antiquity: "The Strange High House in the Mist," "The Moon-Bog," "The Temple," "Hypnos," and "Medusa's Coil." Intriguingly, all five are set outside the normal boundaries of the Classical world: Massachusetts, Ireland, the mid-Atlantic, London (a borderline case), and Missouri. Lovecraft rescues the Atlantis of "The Temple" for Antiquity by assuring the reader that its art was "largely Hellenic in idea … the remotest ancestor" of Greece. No pre-human aliens here, unless you count the Dionysian dolphins that follow the *U-29*. But all five are clearly Greco-Roman in inspiration, form, or both. In the first four, the horror follows the faultless classical pattern of Nemesis, striking down the hubris of the various unfortunate protagonists. The fifth combines two Greek monsters, the Gorgon and the Lamia, though it doesn't follow the classical moral or narrative structure.

Even as a specter, Antiquity is not entirely grim: in "Strange High House," "golden flames" and "sportive tritons" herald Roman Neptune, while by contrast, Celtic Nodens is "gray and awful." The naiads in "Moon-Bog," both the boy and the idol in "Temple," and the avatar of "Hypnos" are all explicitly described as beautiful. (So, for that matter, is the lamia in "Medusa's Coil.") In other stories, Antiquity merits only a shout-out, a way for Lovecraft to touch his historical bases. Among the kidnap victims in "The Shadow Out of Time" we find a Roman quaestor ("of Sulla's time") and a Greco-Bactrian scribe; in "The Haunter of the Dark," Minoan fishermen rescue the Shining Trapezohedron from the deep.[33] The *Necronomicon* itself, with its Greek-derived name (clearly a Lovecraftian riff on the first-century Roman poet Manilius' *Astronomicon*) and its Byzantine provenance, invokes Antiquity despite its early-medieval origins.

> *"[E]ven now on Maenalus, Pan sighs and stretches in his sleep, wishful to wake ... In thy yearning hast thou divined what no mortal, saving only a few whom the world rejects, remembereth: that the Gods were never dead, but only sleeping the sleep and dreaming the dreams of Gods in lotos-filled Hesperian gardens beyond the golden sunset. And now draweth nigh the time of their awakening..."*

— H.P. Lovecraft and Anna Helen Crofts, "Poetry and the Gods"

Or perhaps Lovecraft's ultimate evocation of Antiquity is the Cthulhu Mythos itself, the body of imaginary lore and legend that HPL explicitly patterned on the chaotic, contradictory matter of Greek mythology. (This is because Greek mythology was the only mythos that Lovecraft knew in any detail, but still.) In his seminal (and unconscionably neglected) essay "The Cthulhu Mythos," George T. Wetzel pointed out the similarities between, for example, the Dreamlands and the classical Elysium and Tartarus. Lovecraft describes R'lyeh as "this monstrous Acropolis," and compares Cthulhu to Polyphemus the Cyclops. Perhaps following on this, Gavin Callaghan notes that the later Mythos tales cruelly invert the pastoral classical Arcadia, with the "fauns and dryads" of myth mere masks for the Mi-Go, the gardens of the gods becoming blasted heaths or Antarctic desolation, and the wild piping on the Dunwich hills evoking not Pan but Yog-Sothoth.

On the scale of a single story, "The Dunwich Horror" recapitulates and recasts the Greek myths of gods and mortals interbreeding to produce

---

33. For what it's worth, on the other end of the time scale, Italians keep the Haunter of the Dark at bay, although this is almost certainly stretching a point. Lovecraft saw little commonality between modern Italians (or Italian-Americans) and his beloved ancient Romans. That said, in a letter of November 23, 1923 to Maurice Moe, Lovecraft jocularly describes the replacement of the Irish on Providence's Federal Hill by the Italians as "the legions of Caesar victorious over the Celts."

monsters and heroes. Its demigod, Wilbur Whateley, is a twin (like Heracles or Castor), shows prodigious talent as an infant (like Hermes and Heracles), fulfills an oracular prophecy (like Theseus and Jason) and dies torn to pieces (like Dionysos and Orpheus). On a larger scale, Lovecraft's deities resemble the disinterested entities of Epicurus—except for Nyarlathotep, the mocking messenger (Hermes also had a thousand faces), whose vendetta against Randolph Carter might be that of an arbitrary Poseidon against Odysseus. Or look at Lovecraft's collaboration "Poetry and the Gods." The excerpt above lays it out: regardless of what Plutarch heard, the Great God Pan is not dead but sleeping. Dionysos, torn to pieces, will revive. And when he returns, the world will resound with Maenad piping and with his worshippers' ancient cry: "Iä! Iä!"[34]

---

34. Technically, Euripides writes the cry of the Maenads and Dionysiac cultists as "Evoë!" Lovecraft may have combined the umlaut from Euripides and the Ovidian ejaculation "Io!" with the late-antique Greek divine name IAO. He might have turned up IAO in Diodorus or other antique sources, or in Arthur Machen's *Chronicle of Clemendy*. Machen might have gotten it from the Gnostics via the Golden Dawn.

EGYPT

"The red sun sank low, bringing the relentless chill of Egyptian dusk; and as it stood poised on the world's rim like that ancient god of Heliopolis—Re-Harakhte, the Horizon-Sun—we saw silhouetted against its vermeil holocaust the black outlines of the Pyramids of Gizeh—the palaeogean tombs there were hoary with a thousand years when Tut-Ankh-Amen mounted his golden throne in distant Thebes. Then we knew that we were done with Saracen Cairo, and that we must taste the deeper mysteries of primal Egypt—the black Khem of Re and Amen, Isis and Osiris."

— H.P. LOVECRAFT AND HARRY HOUDINI, "UNDER THE PYRAMIDS"

Behind Antiquity, as every Lovecraftian knows, lurks something still more antique. In point of historical fact, and perhaps even of Lovecraft's personal development, that something—or rather, that somewhere—was Egypt. He discovered the *Arabian Nights* at age five, and by age six consumed Egyptian myths alongside those of Greece and Rome thanks to a felicitous appendix in Bulfinch's *Mythology*. At that age, he produced (along with an abridged *Odyssey* in Coleridge's meter) "An Old Egyptian Myth Prepared Especially For Small Children," which he had expanded by age 12 to a whole resumé of "Egyptian Myths." (Neither version of this work survives, unfortunately.) In his adult career, three of his stories depend on strong Egyptian elements: "Under the Pyramids" is the only Lovecraft tale set in Egypt, but both "The Haunter of the Dark" and "Nyarlathotep" come out of Egypt in an unforgettable sense.

"And when I stopped to reflect what the paw was, it seemed to me that it was Egypt. In the dream I looked back at the events of the preceding weeks, and saw myself lured and enmeshed little by little, subtly and insidiously, by some hellish ghoul-spirit of the elder Nile sorcery; some spirit that was in Egypt before ever man was, and that will be when man is no more."

— H.P. LOVECRAFT AND HARRY HOUDINI, "UNDER THE PYRAMIDS"

Egypt envelops Lovecraft's fiction in a way that few other countries do: more than England, more than Rome, more than many states in his own New England. His fascination both pre- and post-dates the 1923 wave of Tutankhamen-driven Egyptomania that drenched the pulps in natron.[35] Nyarlathotep, as mentioned before, comes "out of Egypt" not just in his titular story but also his titular sonnet in *Fungi From Yuggoth*. Speaking of poetry, the wind in "Poetry and the Gods," which also presages awakening deities, comes "blowing from far Egypt, where at night Aurora mourns by the Nile for her slain Memnon." "The Outsider" ends with its narrator in Egypt, at least poetically; "an Egyptian of the 14th Dynasty" speaks with the captive Peaslee in "The Shadow Out of Time." Egypt flavors Marceline's magic in "Medusa's Coil" and Muñoz' immortality in "Cool Air," Surama in "The Last Test" "resembles a pharaoh's mummy," and while "Out of the Aeons" concerns a much older Pacific mummy it too genuflects to "Egyptian embalming."

The Dream-Quest of Unknown Kadath features Egyptian cats in the army, refers to the Nile Delta city of Bubastis, and depicts the guardians of Dream, Nasht and Kaman-Thah, wearing the pshent or pharaonic crown. In *The Case of Charles Dexter Ward*, Joseph Curwen gets a cargo of

---

35. In a bravura "Cthulhu index" table in his book *Spooky Archaeology* (clearly written just for me), Jeb Card graphs the number of *New York Times* stories mentioning archaeologists (excluding obituaries and society pages) about sunken lands or dead archaeologists from 1910 to 1937. The graph shows its two strongest spikes in November 1922-June 1923 (HPL writes "Under the Pyramids" eight months later, in February 1924) and July 1934-February 1935 (HPL writes "Haunter of the Dark" nine months later, in November 1935).

mummies from "Grand Cairo, Egypt," and Simon Orne gets a Scar from "such a Thing in Aegypt." Knowledge and danger, that potent Lovecraftian alchemy—a word, by the way, that comes from *Khem*, the ancient name of Egypt. In "Tree on the Hill" Theunis is writing "a treatise on Egyptian mythology" and cites Hermes Trismegistus "the ancient Egyptian sorcerer," and in "The Green Meadow" the narrator has translated something "disquieting" out of "an Egyptian book."

Lovecraft name-checks Egypt as a symbol of ancient history in "Beyond the Wall of Sleep," "The Nameless City," "The Very Old Folk," and the 1917 poem "Nemesis"; as Memphis in "The Festival," as the Sphinx in "Call of Cthulhu," as the Nile in "The Temple," and as Cheops in "The Mound." Somehow cultures older and deader than the Pharaohs reflect Egypt; Dyer considers the Old Ones' art *At the Mountains of Madness* in the light of "the scarabaeus." Even on his way to establishing New England as the true locus of horror in "The Picture in the House," Lovecraft passes through "the catacombs of Ptolemaïs."

> *"For the cat is cryptic, and close to strange things which men cannot see. He is the soul of antique Aegyptus, and bearer of tales from forgotten cities in Meroë and Ophir…. The Sphinx is his cousin, and he speaks her language; but he is more ancient than the Sphinx, and remembers that which she hath forgotten."*

> — H.P. LOVECRAFT, "THE CATS OF ULTHAR"

And finally and fully, Egypt is present by implication and inspiration in "The Cats of Ulthar." The story name-checks Aegyptus and the Sphinx, and springs from a line in Diodorus on the law of Egypt: "Whoever kills … a cat or an ibis … he is certainly put to death." The travelling people paint their carts with "strange figures with human bodies and the heads of cats [Bast], hawks [Horus], rams [Khnum or Amun], and lions [Maahes or Sekhmet]." Their leader wears the head-dress of Hathor: "with two horns and a curious disc betwixt the horns," and of course the wonder-working boy Menes has an Egyptian name. I have previously argued he's fairly obviously supposed to grow up to be (or be the dream-self of) Menes, the historical first pharaoh of the united Two Lands.

Lovecraft also makes the cat-Egypt connection in his essay "Cats and Dogs," approvingly noting that this beautiful, dignified culture "bowed down to the cat" and built temples "to its goddess at Bubastis." Ancient Egyptians did, in fact, revere the cat-goddess Bast, to the point that the name "Bast" or its derivatives became the second most common divine given name in the country (after names derived from Osiris) by the time of the Ptolemies. The Egyptians domesticated the desert cat (*Felis sylvestris lybica*) in the millions, creating the common house cat (*Felis domestica*), although Lovecraft's 9th edition *Britannica* does not know or say this, instead presenting the theory that "felis domestica is the product of many species commingled."

"The East ... Egypt ... truly, this dark cradle of civilisation was ever the well-spring of horrors and marvels unspeakable!"

— H.P. Lovecraft and Harry Houdini, "Under the Pyramids"

Lovecraft loved cats, and by extension admired the culture that had the good taste to worship (and create) them. But that culture was also profoundly alien to him, and we all know what that means. It's probably impossible to tease out just what percentage of his literary Egyptophobia ("the dark Egypt which you call ancient") comes from conventional Gothic spookiness about mummies and necrolatry, what comes from Lovecraft's phobia of enclosed underground spaces such as pyramid tunnels and crypts, and what comes from the fact of Egypt's non-Western ... African-ness. That the Egyptians were ethnically distinct from sub-Saharan Africans only somewhat lessens the terror for him, as we can see by his repeated use of the word "swarthy" to describe their avatar, in "Nyarlathotep" (1920) and "Haunter of the Dark" (1935).

A phrase like "the black soul of Egypt" (in "Under the Pyramids") can't really be *excused* with the argument that you're "actually" referring to the

Egyptian propensity for black magic, after all.[36] For Lovecraft, as "Medusa's Coil" demonstrates, the two were essentially one and the same. He also obliquely indicts the Egyptians for "Arthur Jermyn"-style miscegenation, when "Houdini" remarks on "statues of the Pharaoh ... found in curious juxtaposition to statues of baboons." Some of his particular horror might stem from the historical coincidence that Egypt was the colonized conquest of all three of the nations of Lovecraft's imaginative selves: Rome, Arabia,[37] and England. As we see again and again on this Tour, Lovecraft's fear of colonial and slave rebellion provided a strong sample track for his horror fiction.

"I saw the horror and unwholesome antiquity of Egypt, and the grisly alliance it has always had with the tombs and temples of the dead."

— H.P. LOVECRAFT AND HARRY HOUDINI, "UNDER THE PYRAMIDS"

Duncan Norris adumbrates Lovecraft's "Egyptian Mythos" as a collection of overlapping geographical-architectural images, associated with vile rites and dark knowledge, from which emerge various pharaonic demon-figures: Nyarlathotep, Nephren-Ka, and Nitokris. Norris' structure essentially summarizes or recapitulates the Cthulhu Mythos on almost all levels, which makes me think he's on to something.[38] Thus, we can get a hint of how Lovecraft's mythopoetics work by examining this specific case. Plus, we can have good fun with Egyptian magic words.

Alongside knowing allusions to the Pyramids and Sphinx, Lovecraft introduces three Egyptian locations in "The Outsider": the catacombs of Nephren-Ka, the sealed and unknown valley of Hadoth by the Nile, and

---

36. The phrase in the same story, "primal Egypt, the black Khem of Re and Amen" gets a superficial pass, since the word *khem* actually means "black" in ancient Egyptian, referring to the black soil of the Nile valley. But with Lovecraft, as with most great writers, words don't only have one meaning at a time.

37. Upon reading the *Arabian Nights* at age five, Lovecraft considered himself a "dream-Arab," complete with "Oriental curios," an "Arabian corner" in his room, and the play-persona "Abdul Alhazred." The family lawyer Albert A. Baker apparently coined this magnificent if ungrammatical sobriquet, perhaps in collaboration with his precocious five-year-old ward.

38. The exception of course is the arcane tome. Lovecraft's Egyptian Mythos never produces its own *Necronomicon*, unless you count Lovecraft and Rimel's *Book of Nath* from "The Tree on the Hill," or Bloch's later Egyptianizing of his and HPL's *De Vermis Mysteriis*. In a way, the Shining Trapezohedron fulfills the function of a dread tome: revealing and confirming the secret, ancient truth.

the rock tombs of Neb. Note that all three of these locations share common markers: underground-ness (though a "sealed valley" might merely be sealed at both ends, it's still pretty claustrophobic), ritual nature (Curwen uses "Nephren-Ka nai Hadoth" as a ritual closing in his letters), and of course death. Rock tombs and sealed valleys both evoke the Valley of the Kings, the famous New Kingdom necropolis across the Nile from Thebes (modern Luxor). Nyarlathotep emerges not from any of those specific locations, instead coming "out of Egypt," but in his self-titled story recreates the catacombs in apocalyptic city subway tunnels.

The catacombs of Nephren-Ka clearly descend from the "catacombs of Ptolemaïs" Lovecraft name-checks in "Picture in the House," a place-image he borrowed from the Poe story "Shadow—A Parable" (1835). Poe describes the catacombs as "hard by" the underworld, to boot. Given five cities in Egypt named Ptolemaïs, none known for catacombs, it's dealer's choice which one you pick: Joshi identifies this Ptolemaïs as one with "a Hellenistic tower-tomb" in Cyrenica (very "Outsider"-y), Klinger stumps for the mortuary labyrinth-temple of Amenemhet III in Crocodilopolis (briefly renamed Ptolemaïs Euergetis), and Poe scholars generally go for Ptolemaïs Theron on the Red Sea where the sun casts no shadow at midsummer. Wisely evading the whole question, Lovecraft later has Alhazred study his "subterranean secrets" in the catacombs beneath Memphis,[39] the ancient Egyptian northern capital, near the site of modern Cairo.

What does Alhazred study down there? Lovecraft hints of vile rites and abominations: as "Houdini" says, "nor were all tombs inviolate, so that certain grotesque mistakes and fiendish abnormalities were to be looked for." He also horrifically expands on and extends Egypt's beast-headed gods into blasphemous mixing of human and animal forms, pointing the way to the protean, undying shoggoths of Alhazred's alkaloid nightmares. The rock tombs of Neb might refer to a similar entity, the Egyptian word *neb* meaning "lord" with con-

---

39. He only mentions "Memphis's catacombs" as such in a letter to Clark Ashton Smith (Nov. 27, 1927). By the time HPL recycles that letter into the final "History of the *Necronomicon*," Alhazred has merely "visited ... the subterranean secrets of Memphis."

notations of both obedience and unity. (Lovecraft could have taken the word from the Tomb of Perneb, which he saw exhibited at the Met in New York, or from the vulture goddess Nebthet, a.k.a. Nephthys.) As for Hadoth, saluted by Curwen and excavated by Enoch Bowen in 1844, Lovecraft likely took the name from Freemasonry via his grandfather Whipple Phillips' library. The Masonic "exposure" *Ecce Orienti* (1870) by Moses Wolcott Redding glosses "Hadoth" as "a place of secret meetings." Like, for example, the sort of meetings one has with Nephren-Ka.

> *"The Pharaoh Nephren-Ka built around it a temple with a windowless crypt, and did that which caused his name to be stricken from all monuments and records. Then it slept in the ruins of that evil fane which the priests and the new Pharaoh destroyed, till the delver's spade once more brought it forth to curse mankind."*

> — H.P. LOVECRAFT, "THE HAUNTER OF THE DARK"

Besides catacombs, and (probably) a tomb at Hadoth, what else do we associate with Nephren-Ka? In "Haunter of the Dark" we learn that Nephren-Ka was a Pharaoh who acquired the Shining Trapezohedron and "built around it a temple with a windowless crypt, and did that which caused his name to be stricken from all monuments and records."[40] Egyptian priests commonly applied this retroactive punishment, for instance to the monotheist 18th-dynasty Pharaoh Akhenaten, who Robert Bloch used as a model for his version of Nephren-Ka in "The Fane of the Black Pharaoh" (1937). Bloch may have consulted with Lovecraft on his version of Nephren-Ka, as he likely wrote this story during HPL's lifetime, though no letters to that effect survive. Bloch's Nephren-Ka, "of no known dynasty, a priestly usurper," exclusively worships the Blind Ape of Truth, Nyarlathotep.

Let's see if we can know the dynasty, at least. Nephren-Ka's reign, at the earliest, must be contemporaneous with the Minoan fishermen who haul

---

40. Speaking of Nephren-Ka's name, his name sort of works: *nefer* ("good, beautiful") *ren* ("true name") *ka* ("spirit"). The *ren* and *ka* are two parts of the five-part Egyptian soul. Norris argues for Nephren-Ka as a female pharaoh like Hatshepsut, preferring *neph* ("great lady") to *nefer*.

up the Trapezohedron: no earlier than 1800 B.C. or thereabouts, or during the Egyptian Middle Kingdom. Bloch also tells us "fables placed his reign in almost biblical times," which might mean just before the time of Joseph, conventionally dated to the Hyksos period, 1700 B.C. to 1550 B.C. Significantly, Peaslee speaks to one Khephnes of the Fourteenth Dynasty, who reveals "the hideous secret of Nyarlathotep"—and the Fourteenth Dynasty (a chaotic period with very few surviving records and very many unnamed pharaohs[41]) slots in neatly to our target zone: 1725-1650 B.C.

> "And it was then that Nyarlathotep came out of Egypt. Who he was, none could tell, but he was of the old native blood and looked like a Pharaoh. The fellahin knelt when they saw him, yet could not say why. He said he had risen up out of the blackness of twenty-seven centuries ... "
>
> — H.P. LOVECRAFT, "NYARLATHOTEP"

One thing we can't say about Nephren-Ka, or rather that Lovecraft never says, is that he was Nyarlathotep. Yes, in *Dream-Quest*, Nyarlathotep has "the young face of an antique Pharaoh," and wears the pharaonic pshent-crown. And in "Haunter" we hear that the Mighty Messenger did "in antique and shadowy Khem [take] the form of man," but no specifics. The specifics we do get, in "Nyarlathotep," point us to a time considerably later than our mooted Fourteenth Dynasty.

In that piece, the Crawling Chaos emerges from "twenty-seven centuries" ago into the presumed present day of 1920.[42] That would put his ap-

---

41. And at least one pharaoh named Apepi, after Apep the gigantic serpent of chaos who opposed the sun god Ra. Did the Fourteenth Dynasty spawn a devotee of Cthulhu or Yig after Nephren-Ka destabilized the country? Better still, in the Fifteenth Dynasty, *another* Pharaoh Apepi, with the intriguing regnal name Neb-Khepesh-Ra, exclusively worshipped the "evil god" Set, killer of Osiris.

42. For some reason, Joshi argues that Lovecraft means twenty-seven centuries before Christ, not 2,700 years before the story's present. That would at least place Nyarlathotep potentially within the Pyramid- and Sphinx-building Fourth Dynasty, dated in Lovecraft's time to 2900-2750 B.C., and by modern Egyptologists to 2613-2494 B.C. (Manetho gives Nepherkeres as the name of the 2nd-dynasty pharaoh we moderns might place at exactly 2700 B.C., and says he made the Nile flow with honey. Excitingly, nothing else is known about him.) Herodotus accuses the 4th-dynasty pharaohs Cheops and Chephren (Khufu and Khafre) of impiety, shutting the temples to concentrate the people on pyramid-building. He adds, "So much do the people hate the memory of these two kings that they do not greatly wish to name them."

pearance in Egypt in the seventh century B.C., or 780 B.C. at the earliest (2700 years-1920 = 780).[43] During that period, as in the Fourteenth Dynasty a millennium earlier, chaos overspread Egypt. Nyarlathotep could therefore potentially show up in the Twenty-Second Dynasty (c. 945-720 B.C.) or Twenty-Fourth Dynasty (732-720 B.C.) in the Delta or the concurrent Twenty-Third Dynasty (c. 837-728 B.C.) up the river.[44]

None of the pharaohs of those three dynasties remain nameless, or even have particularly promising names. (The common throne name Setepenra turns out to have nothing to do with Set, meaning "elect of Ra.") Nyarlathotep's name came to Lovecraft in a dream in 1920, probably echoing (as Price suggests) Dunsany's god Mynarthitep and prophet Alhireth-Hotep. William Hamblin delightfully back-forms the dread name from the Egyptian words *ni-har-rut-hotep,* construable as "no peace at the gate," but Lovecraft didn't get his copy of Wallis Budge's interlinear *Book of the Dead* until 1935.[45]

> *"I know that light is not for me, save that of the moon over the rock tombs of Neb, nor any gaiety save the unnamed feasts of Nitokris beneath the Great Pyramid; yet in my new wildness and freedom I almost welcome the bitterness of alienage."*

> — H.P. LOVECRAFT, "THE OUTSIDER"

The third figure in our alliterative Egyptian trinity, Nitokris, comes not from Lovecraft but from Herodotus. He retails the history of a female pharaoh who succeeded her brother after his assassination. Nitokris then

---

43. Bloch's "Fane of the Black Pharaoh" uses a similar calculation, although it posits Nephren-Ka's reign as concurrent with Nyarlathotep's incarnation. The walls of Nephren-Ka's tomb depict him as "dust for nearly two thousand years" when Ludwig Prinn enters the tomb around 1280. Bloch's date of ~720 B.C. thus meshes with Lovecraft's date from "Nyarlathotep."

44. I suppose Lovecraft could be archly referring to the Twenty-Fifth Dynasty (732-653 B.C.), which would cover the latter part of the "twenty-seventh century" in question. That dynasty, however, was not Egyptian but Nubian, conquering and ruling Egypt from Meroë in the Sudan. A Nubian Nyarlathotep would be an even Blacker Man, but not one "of the old native blood."

45. David Haden suggests a derivation from the Hebrew words *n'yar* ("letter, paper") and *lath* ("trust," specifically from the Hebraicized Akkadian name Tiglath-Pileser, which derivation HPL could have seen in his *Britannica*), thus meaning something like "trusted messenger."

invited "those Egyptians whom she knew to have had the most complicity in her brother's murder" to a banquet, held in a chamber beneath the level of the Nile—and opened the floodgates, drowning them all. She then supposedly committed suicide in a "room of hot ashes" to escape justice. The later historian Manetho also puts her in his history, but erroneously maintains that she built the Third Pyramid.

For many years, Egyptologists considered Nitokris pure bunkum, based on a misprint in the Turin King List for the 6th-dynasty Pharaoh Netjerkare Siptah. However, current thinking has begun to come around to Nitokris' actual existence, complete with a reign just after the deaths of her father Pepi II in 2185 B.C. and brother Merenre Nemtyensaf II the next year. Real or not, Lord Dunsany wrote a play about her, *The Queen's Enemies* (1916), in which he casts her revenge as human sacrifices to the Nile. Lovecraft heard Dunsany read that play in Boston in 1919, an imprimatur that doubtless sealed Nitokris into the Mythos with "The Outsider" in 1921. Lovecraft riffs on Dunsany to imply cannibal cuts at "the ghoul-queen" Nitokris' postmortem banquets. He likewise takes Manetho's mistake about the Pyramids (and some assonant lines from Thomas Moore)[46] as license to put her under the Great Pyramid as the consort of an undead Pharaoh Khephren.

> *"But the scene wasn't Egypt—it was behind Egypt; behind even Atlantis; behind fabled Mu, and myth-whispered Lemuria. It was the ultimate fountainhead of all horror on this earth ..."*

— H.P. LOVECRAFT AND ZEALIA BISHOP,
"MEDUSA'S COIL"

---

46. From "Alciphron" (1839): *"The subterranean nymph that dwells,'*
Mid sunless gems and glories hid—
The lady of the Pyramid!"

Moore identifies her as "fair Rhodope," meaning the legendary Greek courtesan Rhodopis, who supposedly enchanted a Pharaoh so much that he built the Third Pyramid (Nitokris' pyramid!) to house her body. (In Strabo's version, the Pharaoh fell in love with her sandal, so in a sense, Nitokris is the first Cinderella.) Classicists generally think that these overlapping Rhodopis and Nitokris stories come from a tangle of Greek legends originating in the first Greek colony in Egypt, Naucratis.

Note Lovecraft's description of "the beautiful Queen Nitokris ... the right half of her face was eaten away by rats or other ghouls." This remarkable incarnation of his double- and shadow- fixation reveals Egypt as the mask for antediluvian horror, a meaning reinforced by the shock ending of "Under the Pyramids." The gods are just puppets on the paw of a hideous monster, and the Sphinx wears Khephren's face to mask its "elder features."

Everywhere in Lovecraft, Egypt serves as mask and disguise. Even Menes' folk in Ulthar enter disguised as vagabonds, not magi. The Egyptian incense in Muñoz' room—"till his room smelled like the vault of a sepulchred Pharaoh in the Valley of the Kings"—covers up his living death, for example. Dyer deludes himself about Antarctic alien truths with prattle about Egyptian scarabs. The Egyptian ankh in the Starry Wisdom church covers up the worship of Nyarlathotep. The "Thing in Aegypt" that scarred Orne came from a mis-labeled tomb. Catacombs, whether of Nephren-Ka or Ptolemaïs, are literally secret tunnels hidden beneath the official Egyptian temples. The Egyptian Khephnes knows the secret of Nyarlathotep, who himself appears to be an Egyptian but is actually the Crawling Chaos from the Seven Suns. The received history of the past— even the fabulous history of nighted Khem—only covers the hideous reality of ancient gods and alien masters.

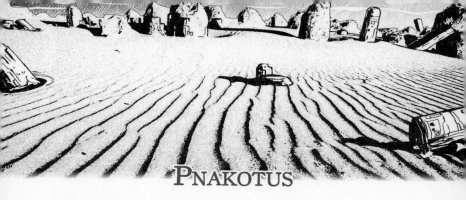

Pnakotus

"But my eyes were the keenest in the city, despite the long hours I gave each day to the study of the Pnakotic manuscripts..."

—H.P. Lovecraft, "Polaris"

Although our quote above starts us in "the city," we must first seek our next stop in the pages of the Pnakotic Manuscripts. Technically, of course, we must first seek it in the pages of Lovecraft's 1918 story "Polaris," where we first hear the name of that dread anthology. "Polaris" is also the story where Lovecraft tells us the name of his first primordial city, Olathoë in frozen Lomar. Is there a connection? Maybe, if only a fragmentary one.

"That kind of thing resembles my own (purely mythical) 'Pnakotic Manuscripts'; which are supposed to be the work of 'Elder Ones' preceding the human race on this planet, and handed down through an early human civilization which once existed around the north pole..."

—H.P. Lovecraft, letter to William Lumley (May 12, 1931)

Lovecraft mentions the Pnakotic Manuscripts in ten tales (three times as the "Pnakotic fragments") written or "revised" from 1918 to 1935. Over all that time, he reveals a remarkably consistent legend, especially when compared to the many uses to which he puts the *Necronomicon* over the years.

This legend begins, as we noted earlier, in the frozen Arctic land of Lomar. Elsewhere in "Polaris," we read that the Manuscripts hold "some lore of the skies," which could mean anything from astrology to the history of extraterrestrial contact. In "The Other Gods," the "Pnakotic Manuscripts of distant and frozen Lomar" tell the story of Sansu, a previous climber of Hatheg-Kla; later climbers saw a symbol "like to one that learned men have discerned in those frightful parts of the Pnakotic Manuscripts which were too ancient to be read." Even the "moldy" histories of Sansu are more recent than some parts of the Manuscripts, which are apparently an anthology of different texts.

In *At the Mountains of Madness,* we read that the Manuscripts (which "affrightedly hint" at "fiendish elder myths") may have a "pre-Pleistocene origin," which is to say, a pre-human origin. "The Horror in the Museum" ties that tail back to the Arctic and Lomar, where Rogers finds Rhan-Tegoth: "That long ritual in the eighth Pnakotic fragment ... could only have one meaning. There were things in the north before the land of Lomar—before mankind existed—and this was one of them." From *Mountains,* we know that the Manuscripts hint at the crinoids and their Antarctic city of Kadath; that tale also references Tsathoggua, himself Pnakotically name-checked in "The Whisperer in Darkness."

> *"The traditional account of the origins of the Manuscripts ... claims that the earliest chapters were reputedly set down before the first forms of life had come into existence on this Earth, the authors supposedly a mysterious race of mental entities from 'Yith' ... who dwelt somewhere in primordial Australia in a cyclopean stone city known to subsequent races as 'Pnakotus,' a name which was believed to mean something in the nature of 'The City of the Archives.'"*

> —LIN CARTER, "ZOTH-OMMOG" (1976)

Finally, in "The Shadow Out of Time," the Yithian-possessed Peaslee consults the Pnakotic Manuscripts, of which "part of the text" is a survival from the era of the Great Race. Thus, the Pnakotic Manuscripts are, as we suspected, an anthology: a core of alien pre-human "lore of the skies," at one point "too ancient to be read," and a "moldy" collection of rituals and histories assembled or codified by the human scribes of Lomar. Later editors or magi may have deciphered the earlier texts, or added their own fragments: there is Pnakotic material dealing with Tsathoggua, the crinoids, the Yithians, both the Antarctic and the Dreamland Kadath, Mu, and Lomar itself.

It could be for this reason that Lin Carter named the City of the Great Race "Pnakotus" in his story "Zoth-Ommog"—we know that the Great Race feverishly assembled just such material for its own archives. Indeed, among the Yithian prisoners we specifically read of crinoids, "furry pre-human Hyperborean worshipers of Tsathoggua," and "a king of Lomar." Thus, perhaps, the Pnakotic wisdom traveled from its crinoid origins in Kadath to the land of Lomar at the other pole: some Lomarian, like Peaslee, remembered his captivity and the Pnakotic wisdom he studied there. What better name for a library-prison for an anthology of minds than Pnakotus?

> *"The notion is that of a race in primal Lomar perhaps even before the founding of Olathoë & in the heyday of Hyperborean Commoriom—who gained a knowledge of all arts & sciences by ... angling in time, as it were."*

—H.P. LOVECRAFT, LETTER TO CLARK ASHTON SMITH (MARCH 2, 1932)

And as we see above, in Lovecraft's first notion of the story the time-traveling psychics were the men of Lomar! Suddenly, Lin Carter's wild leap seems even less wild. The Pnakotic Manuscripts enter human history (and Lovecraftian lore) in the Lomar of "Polaris," and the time-nappers and their "City of the Archives" began (in Lovecraft's mind) in the same place and time!

Indeed, Pnakotus and Olathoë have much in common, even without mind-switches. Both cities are devoted to the study of "Pnakotic" lore. Both face (and then suffer) destruction by racial enemies. Both save their knowledge at the end: the Yithians bury it in their invulnerable archive to be salvaged by their coleopterous future selves, while the *Dream-Quest* tells us that the men of Lomar carry "the last copy" of the Pnakotic Manuscripts into the Dreamlands. Both cities are somehow fluid in time: the

Great Race sends its minds across the eons, leaving only nightmares behind, and at least one inhabitant of Lomar may well "actually" dwell in the 20th century, or both times at once.

> *"When I came to the space I saw that the trap-door yawned widely open. Ahead, the shelves began again, and I glimpsed on the floor before one of them a heap very thinly covered with dust, where a number of cases had recently fallen. At the same moment a fresh wave of panic clutched me, though for some time I could not discover why."*
>
> — H.P. LOVECRAFT, "THE SHADOW OUT OF TIME"

Of course, all of Lovecraft's great cities of the dead, his necropoleis, have much in common. Like Pnakotus and Olathoë, Kadath and the Nameless City lie in deserts, as does R'lyeh, on the dead Pacific sea bottom. Further, they all have a common structure: information above a prison. In the Nameless City, the bas-reliefs lie above the glowing abyss where the prehuman inhabitants dwell; in R'lyeh, the ever-changing geometry roils around the doorway (which, like the Dreamlands' Kadath, bears a Sign or a Seal) beneath which Cthulhu dwells; the crinoids' Kadath holds its carven histories above the shoggoths' gulf; in Pnakotus, the buried archive room sits atop the vaults of the imprisoned polyps.

This same pattern occurs elsewhere in the stories, of course: in *Charles Dexter Ward*, magical spell graffiti line the walls of the cellar above the oubliettes of the "unfinished" ones. You can draw similar parallels in "The Festival" (vestry library above subterranean river) and "The Rats in the Walls" (inscriptions on the walls leading down to the charnel pens in the deepest cellars), even "The Horror at Red Hook" (with women and infants imprisoned below Suydam's Parker Place flat, its walls covered with paintings and inscriptions). Finally, this pattern undergoes a sinister reversal in "The Haunter of the Dark," with the books in the vestry—including the Pnakotic Manuscripts—below the prison-Trapezohedron—once handled by the crinoids of Kadath—in the steeple above.

"Of all things surviving physically and directly from that aeon-distant world, there remained only certain ruins of great stones in far places and under the sea, and parts of the text of the frightful Pnakotic Manuscripts."

—H.P. LOVECRAFT, "THE SHADOW OUT OF TIME"

Let's return to Pnakotus, then, or to the City of the Great Race, if you prefer, and examine the specific inscriptions therein and thereupon. First, we can note that Lovecraft describes it in the same way he does his other necropoleis: it is "paleogaean" and "Cyclopean," built of "basalt masonry" and "titan blocks." Like "labyrinthine" Kadath it is a "labyrinth of primordial stone," a maze containing and protecting ancient lore. But Pnakotus is "collapsed" and broken, indeed barely even discernible as a city to the other members of Peaslee's expedition. Without Peaslee's dreams, he might never have discovered the entrance to the library-vault he seeks. The blocks of the city are "tumbled and fragmentary." Sarnath/Ib vanishes entirely, to be sure, but Lovecraft's other great alien cities—R'lyeh, the Nameless City, Kadath in the Antarctic—are surprisingly intact, and immediately recognizable to the unfortunates who enter them, unlike Pnakotus.

But like those other cities, in Pnakotus "the exposed stonework held curious carvings," in this case "always in curvilinear ... designs, and ... chiselled inscriptions," as Peaslee discovers anew. Indeed, at least one wall holds inscriptions from Kadath: one of the crinoid Elder Things, imprisoned in a Yithian body, "had chiselled certain pictures on the blank space of the walls." Like the Pnakotic Manuscripts, the library of the Great Race holds Antarctic lore. And the closer Peaslee gets to that archive, the thicker come the words, both in Lovecraft's narration and in Peaslee's flashlight beam: "The walls ... were densely hieroglyphed and chiselled with typical curvilinear symbols—some added since the period of my dreams." Even before Peaslee gets to the library, he has passed document after document, manuscript after manuscript. Or rather, he has passed *through* those manuscripts, delving deeper into Pnakotus.

> *"From the very outset I realized that there was some utterly unprecedented*
> *quality about those stones. … The impression did not come when I looked at*
> *one block alone, but only when I ran my eye over several almost simultaneously.*
> *Then, at last, the truth dawned upon me. The curvilinear patterns on many*
> *of those blocks were closely related—parts of one vast decorative conception."*

—H.P. LOVECRAFT, "THE SHADOW OUT OF TIME"

Pnakotus is its own manuscript: "fragmentary, it is true, but none the less existing in a very definite sense," as Lovecraft's paragraph quoted above concludes. Like the hieroglyphic maze of Tsalal at the climax of Poe's *Arthur Gordon Pym,* the dead city in Lovecraft *is* the book. "Reading" the city unleashes horror, just as surely as does reading the *Necronomicon.* Peaslee's act of reading Pnakotus ends with terror and madness, as he flees from the invisible polyps, impelled by a prehuman instinct. What is the city but Peaslee's nightmares made visible and tangible? Peaslee's nightmare is but the same "chance joining of memories" that Lovecraft says give rise not just to human scriptures ("all legends of prophets") but to the *Necronomicon* itself: "hints of the forbidden past" brought "to future ages."

Not only is the city of Pnakotus a book, its archive is, like the Pnakotic Manuscripts, an anthology, assembled from the black wisdom of all races and times. Pnakotus itself *is* a collection of manuscripts. Indeed, carvings and "chiselled inscriptions" must, by definition, be literal manuscripts, since they can hardly be produced by machines, unlike print or pixels! The books in the Yithian archive are also manuscripts, hand-written (well, claw-written) by prisoners kept in rugose cone bodies and provided only with stylus and cellulose. Manuscripts inside a manuscript; books inside a book. And below the city, between the pages? Something invisible and amorphous, that does not speak but whistles—in other words, something that simply cannot be heard or read or written in words. No matter how many books, or cities, or city-books you pile on top of it, the horror will break out of the stone pages and leave them in … Pnakotic fragments.

KINGSPORT

"And because my fathers had called me to the old town beyond, I pushed on through the shallow, new-fallen snow along the road that soared lonely up to where Aldebaran twinkled among the trees; on toward the very ancient town I had never seen but often dreamed of."

—H.P. LOVECRAFT, "THE FESTIVAL"

Lovecraft archly alludes, perhaps, to a strange and suggestive fact: he wrote his first story about Kingsport, "The Terrible Old Man," while that "very ancient town" was indeed still a dream for him. It was only after seeing Kingsport (about which more in a bit) that HPL celebrated it—and explored its occult, cavernous depths—in "The Festival." Kingsport is the main setting of a third tale, "The Strange High House in the Mist," and of one scene in "The Silver Key." It appears briefly, in glimpse or rumor, in five or six more stories: *The Dream-Quest of Unknown Kadath*, "Through the Gates of the Silver Key," "Thing on the Doorstep," *The Case of Charles Dexter Ward*, and "The Shadow Over Innsmouth," which also mentions "Kingsport Head," as does *At the Mountains of Madness*. So what keeps Lovecraft coming back to Kingsport?

"Then beyond the hill's crest I saw Kingsport outspread frostily in the gloaming; snowy Kingsport with its ancient vanes and steeples, ridgepoles and chimney-pots, wharves and small bridges, willow-trees and graveyards; endless labyrinths of steep, narrow, crooked streets, and dizzy church-crowned central peak that time durst not touch; ceaseless mazes of colonial houses piled and scattered at all angles and levels like a child's disordered

blocks; antiquity hovering on grey wings over winter-whitened gables and
gambrel roofs; fanlights and small-paned windows one by one gleaming out
in the cold dusk to join Orion and the archaic stars."

—H.P. LOVECRAFT, "THE FESTIVAL"

Kingsport is beautiful, the ideal type of Lovecraft's "ideal city," as Waugh terms it. Only Providence summons up the same rapture for Lovecraft as "snowy Kingsport" does; Peter Cannon notes that HPL's luxuriant descriptions almost set Kingsport in his Dunsanian "Dreamland" rather than prosaic Massachusetts. Kingsport is not entirely of the earth; indeed, as we've already seen, the road to Kingsport "soared ... up to where Aldebaran twinkled," and the narrator of "The Festival" saw Kingsport in dreams before he did in reality.

Kingsport sits literally on the border between the real and the unreal, with impossible structures both below its streets and above its roofs. In "Strange High House" Lovecraft describes this liminal Kingsport a mystical three times: "as if the cliff's rim were the rim of all earth, and the solemn bells of buoys tolled free in the aether of faery." The titular House "journeyed betwixt earth and sky," and its seemingly solid crag is "one with the mists and the firmament." Indeed, in the *Dream-Quest*, Lovecraft retroactively makes Basil Elton, the protagonist of "The White Ship," a "lighthouse-keeper in ancient Kingsport," planting Kingsport firmly on the shores of the Dreamlands' ocean.

"Now north of archaic Kingsport the crags climb lofty and curious, terrace
on terrace, till the northernmost hangs in the sky like a gray frozen wind-
cloud. Alone it is, a bleak point jutting in limitless space, for there the
coast turns sharp where the great Miskatonic pours out of the plains past
Arkham, bringing woodland legends and little quaint memories of New
England's hills."

—H.P. LOVECRAFT, "THE STRANGE HIGH HOUSE IN THE MIST"

But Lovecraft's towns always have their double side, as Robert Waugh reminds us. Kingsport is both a city on the edge of Dream and a city where "the drains were impossibly bad." Kingsport, like Arkham and Innsmouth and Providence, has a solid, physical geography to it. Its most famous feature, the "sinister northern crag" fixes Kingsport to the Earth, an unmistakable landmark in all time and space: "Always over Kingsport it hung." Olney's sweaty, frustrating climb up to the crag in "High House" is, along with Olmstead's flight along the Rowley railway cut in "Shadow Over Innsmouth," one of Lovecraft's masterpieces of utterly naturalistic setting.

Kingsport's human geography is likewise determinative, with central features—the old Congregational Church, with its steeple clock and its hillside burying-ground—so fixed in history that both Randolph Carter and the narrator of "The Festival" recognize their alteration as a sign that something uncanny has occurred. "The old maps still held good," as Lovecraft's protagonist explains; even if the trolleys appear and vanish at random. Even when Kingsport seemingly shifts to "a sea of roofs in which only about one in five was ancient," with "the sound of trolleys and motors in the streets below," its identity, its reality, is absolute: "They insisted that this was Kingsport, and I could not deny it."

"Regarding the settings for the tales—I try to be as realistic as possible. The crumbling old towns with winding alleys & houses 100 to 250 or more years old are realities on the New England coast. ... My fabulous 'Kingsport' is a sort of idealised version of Marblehead, Mass. ..."

—H.P. LOVECRAFT, LETTER TO EMIL PETAJA (DECEMBER 29, 1934)

With similar certitude, Lovecraft scholars insist that Kingsport is "actually" Marblehead, Massachusetts. And indeed, as Donovan Loucks points out, Lovecraft seemingly agrees, not only in that letter to Emil Petaja, but in over 50 other letters, published and unpublished. In another letter (to Richard Ely Morse in 1933), Lovecraft wrote "'The Festival' ... formed a sincere attempt to capture the feeling that Marblehead gave me when I saw it for the first time." In a 1930 letter to James F. Morton, Lovecraft called that feeling "the most powerful single emotional climax" of his life. Here is the explanation for the power and longing in Lovecraft's description of Kingsport—and the explanation for a good bit of Kingsport's unusual geographical solidity.

Philip Shreffler, Donovan Loucks, and others have mapped Kingsport locations onto actual streets and buildings in Marblehead: Kingsport's Central Hill may well be Old Burial Hill in Marblehead, Kingsport's Back Street is Marblehead's Elm Street (called Back Street in colonial times), and the "old brick powder-house" that Olney passes still exists on Marblehead's Green Street (Lovecraft's Green Lane). The evil church in "The Festival" might be St. Michael's Episcopal Church in Frog Lane, which may have also been the inspiration for "St. Toad's cracked chimes" in Lovecraft's poem "St. Toad's." (St. Michael's also has an eerie crypt, though no pillar of green flame.) But for every identification, there are counters: Central Hill might be Training Field Hill instead, and how can St. Michael's be Kingsport's Congregational Church, when it was neither a Congregational Church, nor razed for a hospital? (Nor did it have a clock in its steeple.) Perhaps Lovecraft is thinking of two other churches: the Unitarian church (formerly the Second Congregational) had a steeple, and Marblehead's First Congregational was indeed razed and replaced with a hospital.

Or perhaps we're on the wrong road entirely. In a 1931 letter to August Derleth, Lovecraft makes the Marblehead-to-Kingsport identification, but adds that the "fabled seat of the Strange High House" was, if anywhere, "the headland near Gloucester called 'Mother Ann'" as "Marblehead has rocky cliffs—though of no great height." Will Murray argues that the actual geographic description of Kingsport in "Shadow Over Innsmouth" leads not to Marblehead but north to Rockport, "near Gloucester" as Lovecraft wrote to Derleth. In Kingsport, Lovecraft combines Marblehead and Rockport; putting the buildings and history of one beneath the cliff of the other.

> *"I knew we must have passed down through the mountain and beneath the earth of Kingsport itself, and I shivered that a town should be so aged and maggoty with subterraneous evil."*
>
> —H.P. LOVECRAFT, "THE FESTIVAL"

Robert Marten speculates that Lovecraft similarly combined two Rhode Island towns, Kingstown and Newport, to create the name "Kingsport," as the only other Kingsport is in Tennessee—Manly Wade Wellman country, not Lovecraft land. I think it's rather more likely that Lovecraft wanted to emphasize the antiquated nature of the town, still a colonial town, a "King's port," even in the twentieth century.

Because the one thing that's always true of Kingsport is this: it's very, very old. It has "antediluvian gables" and "narrow olden lanes" and "antiquity hovering on grey wings," and the telltale "gambrel roofs." It is "quaint" and "archaic" and "hoary," its leading citizen is a Terrible Old Man and its landmark High House is built of crumbled bricks and worm-eaten shingles. And like many old things and many old towns in Lovecraft's New England, Kingsport is polluted. Not just the worm-cult in "The Festival," but the practitioners of "nameless rites" in *Charles Dexter Ward*, go back centuries, perhaps to the town's founding. Kingsport also attracts a bad element from outside: foreign criminals plague "The Terrible Old Man," and the "dark furtive folk" infiltrating the land of "the blue-eyed fishers" are up to no good in "The Festival." Even "The Strange High House" has its "Portuguese sailors"—but here, Lovecraft pulls perhaps his greatest reversal.

> *"And they do not wish quaint Kingsport with its climbing lanes and archaic gables to drag listless down the years while voice by voice the laughing chorus grows stronger and wilder in that unknown and terrible eyrie where mists and the dreams of mists stop to rest on their way from the sea to the skies."*
>
> —H.P. LOVECRAFT, "THE STRANGE HIGH HOUSE IN THE MIST"

The great threat to Kingsport in "Strange High House" is not foreigners, or even worm-cultists, but presences that have lived there since the days of Atlantis, or even before. It is the "olden gods," perhaps even "the other gods" of whom the House-keeper speaks timidly. Thomas Olney merely reawakens the danger, from "fresh lights" and "fresh mists" from the North and from the sea, but the mists and lights herald the olden gods' return. Specifically, the gods who drink the light from Thomas Olney's eyes and send him down to prosaic Purgatory in Bristol Highlands are Nodens and Neptune: a British god of the hunt, and the Roman god of the sea.

In other words, the horrors are the gods of Britain and Rome, the two bulwarks of Lovecraft's rational, heroic self and his rational, heroic past. And why should we be surprised? Lovecraft laid it all out to James Morton in that 1930 epistolary description of Marblehead: "In a flash, all the past of New England—all the past of Old England—all the past of Anglo-Saxondom and the Western World—swept over me and identified me with the stupendous totality of things …"

> *"Matter of highest—I might say transcendent—importance.* Arkham *must relay to Kingsport Head Station at once. Strange barrel growth is the Archaean thing that left prints in rocks."*
>
> —H.P. LOVECRAFT, *AT THE MOUNTAINS OF MADNESS*

Kingsport is the dead past that, as Faulkner puts it, "isn't dead—isn't even past." Kingsport is the "musty and venerable abode" of the Terrible Old Man, keeping ghosts alive in a bottle, to unleash them on the unwary modern outsider, be he a Portuguese criminal or a bourgeois professor of philosophy. Kingsport sits on one more border: between past and present. In "The Festival," the protagonist apparently slips into the colonial past for his Yuletide ritual. The anomalous reappearance of the Congregational Church in Kingsport signals Randolph Carter's time-slip in "The Silver Key," and in *Mountains of Madness*, Kingsport

Head literally transmits the horror of revenant prehistory to the modern world of the *Arkham Advertiser*.

Kingsport, with its "dizzy, church-crowned central peak that time durst not touch," is a town afraid of Heaven—because it can see across the border, through a mist, darkly. Think about this: Lovecraft saw his own Heaven there in 1922 ... *and wrote a horror story about it.* For the traveler who comes to Kingsport, for Yuletide or for summer vacation, such revelation is likewise no unmixed delight. As Alhazred puts it: "Cursed the ground where dead thoughts live new." Even if they're Lovecraft's dead thoughts. Especially if they're Lovecraft's dead thoughts, perhaps.

BOSTON

> *"West's last quarters were in a venerable house of much elegance,*
> *overlooking one of the oldest burying-grounds in Boston. He had chosen*
> *the place for purely symbolic and fantastically aesthetic reasons, since most*
> *of the interments were of the colonial period and therefore of little use to a*
> *scientist seeking very fresh bodies."*
>
> —H.P. Lovecraft, "Herbert West—Reanimator"

Although Boston only stars in one Lovecraft tale ("Pickman's Model") and one revision ("Out of the Aeons"), and comes onstage in four others ("Herbert West—Reanimator," and three of the five Randolph Carter stories), HPL mentions Boston in thirteen other tales and three more collaborations. In total, Lovecraft uses or mentions Boston in more stories than Providence (six) and Arkham (fifteen) combined! Part of it, surely, is Boston's pre-eminence in urban New England—Lovecraft also mentions New York City fifteen times, despite setting relatively few tales there. But some of it must be Boston itself.

Like Herbert West, Lovecraft chose Boston for its "symbolic and aesthetic reasons." Two come to mind immediately, and echo repeatedly throughout Lovecraft's work. First, Boston's connection to Cotton Mather and the Puritan past, which Lovecraft deeply mined for horror, following Hawthorne's lead in limning a "witch-haunted" seventeenth century, prone to paranoia and secret sin. As does Hawthorne's *House of the Seven Gables,* Lovecraft's ancient monstrous sinners reach back in lineage (or in horrific immortality!) to the heyday of Puritan Boston and Salem. Even Herbert West fears to dig up tunnels and graves of such figures, and fittingly (and finally) the "dead past" catches up with him in Boston.

Second, Lovecraft exploits Boston's cultural centrality: Daniel Upton studies with a Boston architect, Charles Dexter Ward and Wilbur Whateley seek out Harvard's Widener library, and the "eminent Boston authority" Dr. Lyman examines Ward after such researches bear fruit. Moreover, both of Lovecraft's Boston tales ("Pickman's Model" and "Out of the Aeons") seemingly center not on Puritanism but on Bostonian artistic culture. But of course, "Out of the Aeons" includes a sly yet horrific indictment of a long-dead theocracy (of Mu rather than of Massachusetts-Bay), Richard Upton Pickman comes of "old Salem stock," and both tales involve the discovery that the dead past ... isn't.

> *"It's my business to catch the overtones of the soul, and you won't find those in a parvenu set of artificial streets on made land. ... The place for an artist to live is the North End. If any aesthete were sincere, he'd put up with the slums for the sake of the massed traditions. God, man! Don't you realize that places like that weren't merely made, but actually grew? Generation after generation lived and felt and died there, and in days when people weren't afraid to live and feel and die."*

> —H.P. LOVECRAFT, "PICKMAN'S MODEL"

Thus Boston's artistic culture grows in literally ghoul-haunted soil. Even Boston's intellectual greats—"Holmes, Lowell, and Longfellow"—no longer lie buried beneath her, but have been digested and distributed throughout. The nineteenth and twentieth centuries feed the seventeenth: Pickman boasts that eight of ten "surviving houses built before 1700 ... I can shew you something queer in the cellar." The "tangle of alleys" that Pickman nests within serve not just as our standard Lovecraftian labyrinth but as a circulatory system carrying unwholesome truths and nutrients into the city.

Boston lives on a foundation of the uncanny past: not just burial vaults but "bricked-up arches and wells leading nowhere." As we see in the story, Pickman believes that not all of Boston partakes of sufficient terror to fertilize his art, but he also believes that "the night-spirit of antique horror" is necessary to provide "overtones" to the soul. Pickman, even in this first tale, already collaborates with the ghouls of Boston. By *The Dream-Quest of Unknown Kadath*, he becomes a ghoul, a living tribute to his own art, sitting "on a tombstone of 1768 stolen from the Granary Burying Ground in Boston."

> *"I'm interested to know that you've visited the Boston North End section mentioned in 'Pickman's Model.' This region used to be a good deal more picturesque than it is now, and the sinister alley described in the story was more or less literally based on a real alley (Foster St., I think) which zigzagged peculiarly up from Commercial St. to Charter St. not so very far from Copp's Hill [Burying Ground]."*

> —H.P. LOVECRAFT, LETTER TO EARL PEIRCE (NOVEMBER 28, 1936)

Lovecraft apparently had a specific house in the North End in mind as Pickman's studio, saying as much to Duane Rimel in 1934. Having promised to show Donald Wandrei some "curious sights" of "sinister quaintness," they arrived in June of 1927 to find the whole section demolished. As Lovecraft tells Earl Peirce in the letter above, Pickman's haunt had been renovated into "a barren waste of exposed foundations … the whole damn tangle of alleys had been torn down in the few months between Dec. '26 and June '27, and I had nothing tangible to back up the glowing accounts …" A year later, he told Rimel, "the whole thing was covered up with a great brick building." The "antique horror" of Lovecraft's Boston was no more immune to the predations of modernity than was his "dead" New York.

> *"For know you, that your gold and marble city of wonder is only the sum of what you have seen and loved in youth. It is the glory of Boston's hillside roofs and western windows aflame with sunset, of the flower-fragrant Common and the great dome on the hill and the tangle of gables and chimneys in the violet valley where the many-bridged Charles flows drowsily. … So to the organ chords of morning's myriad whistles, and*

dawn's blaze thrown dazzling through purple panes by the great gold
dome of the State House on the hill, Randolph Carter leaped shoutingly
awake within his Boston room."

—H.P. LOVECRAFT, *THE DREAM-QUEST OF UNKNOWN KADATH*

But like all of Lovecraft's cities, as Robert Waugh reminds us, Boston is a "double city." Against every Pickmanian shadow in the cellar, there shines Randolph Carter's sunset vision on the hill. The above passage from *Dream-Quest* shows that Lovecraft's love of New England had two centers: his own native Providence, and the "glory of Boston" revealed at the heart of Miskatonic Country. Carter's rediscovery of Boston at the end of *Dream-Quest* echoes Lovecraft's own rediscovery of Providence after the disaster of New York, and prefigures Charles Dexter Ward's rediscovery of Providence after his European tour. Randolph Carter, as one of New England's intellectual and aristocratic elite, was a Bostonian. "The Silver Key" connects "his Boston home" with our artistic theme: "hung in appropriate colours, furnished with befitting books and objects, and provided with sources of the proper sensations of light, heat, sound, taste, and odour." Even, or perhaps especially, Pickman also sees the beauty of Boston: "these ancient places are dreaming gorgeously and overflowing with wonder and terror and escapes from the commonplace."

Like most of his urban loves, Boston appealed to Lovecraft visually and artistically, through architecture and literary and poetic experience. This appeal could only be stronger in a city so associated, symbolically and aesthetically, with the arts and letters.

Lovecraft repeatedly visited Boston's galleries and museums from his youth to his final illness; in Boston he heard Lord Dunsany read his own work, and met his future wife Sonia. Although some hint of "second city" resentment sneaks through on occasion, the son of Providence nonetheless willingly orbited the sun of Boston.

"With this friend, Joel Manton, I had often languidly disputed. He was principal of the East High School, born and bred in Boston and sharing New England's self-satisfied deafness to the delicate overtones of life. It was his view that only our normal, objective experiences possess any esthetic significance, and that it is the province of the artist not so much to rouse strong emotion by action, ecstasy, and astonishment, as to maintain a placid interest and appreciation by accurate, detailed transcripts of everyday affairs."

—H.P. LOVECRAFT, "THE UNNAMABLE"

But that "second city" resentment remains, channeled into arch mockery of Boston as unworthy of its own beauties and genius. Above, Lovecraft rebukes Henry James and the Boston social novelists of the previous century; with Thurber and Pickman, he casts Boston elites as ignorant and callow. The Boston Art Club is full of "fussy old women" unable to see Pickman's genius: it refuses to exhibit "Ghoul Feeding," and "the Museum of Art wouldn't accept it as a gift." To hear Pickman tell it, Boston features little but "pale-pink brains" and even "a club of supposed artists" shares "the feelings of a Beacon Street tea-table." Indeed, "nine-tenths of the homes and clubs of Boston" would ostracize Pickman if they saw his art.

If anything, Lovecraft is even more sly in "Out of the Aeons," repeatedly contrasting the stuffy elites and "austere neighbours" who patronise the Cabot Museum with the scruffy (but knowledgeable) hordes of proles and foreigners exercised by the "undesirable notoriety" of the mummy exhibit. His Boston is more than a little bit boring, in fact. Not only is it one of "the sections which modernity has touched," capital of a drab New England full of "foreigners and factory-smoke, bill-boards and concrete roads," it is ruthlessly, stiflingly conventional. The "eminent Boston authority" Dr. Lyman drastically fails to notice Ward's changed identity, "Boston naturalists" are baffled by the "Horror at Martin's Beach," and another "expert Boston analyst" sheds no light on "The Green Meadow."

"'South Station Under—Washington Under—Park Street Under—
Kendall—Central—Harvard –' The poor fellow was chanting the
familiar stations of the Boston-Cambridge tunnel that burrowed through
our peaceful native soil thousands of miles away in New England, yet to
me the ritual had neither irrelevance nor home feeling."

—H.P. LOVECRAFT, *AT THE MOUNTAINS OF MADNESS*

Boston also signifies mundanity by repeated appearances in contrast to horrors elsewhere in Miskatonic Country. The surveyor in "Colour Out of Space" flees back to Boston; the "capable Boston man" Zenas Low comes to work in "The Shunned House"; the Boston *Globe* trivializes the "Dunwich Horror"; and a "frank, prepossessing" clerk allows the theft of the black stone at Boston's North Station in "Whisperer in Darkness." Boston further emphasizes its mundanity in train-tables. An 8:20 p.m. night train runs to Boston from Arkham in "Thing on the Doorstep," and the entire episode of the lost package in "Whisperer" (which also introduces the 8:07 a.m. Arkham commuter train to Boston) turns railroad stops and routes into a prosaic labyrinth enmeshing the occult horror.

Lovecraft returns to that specific contrast in Danforth's manic mantra quoted above. Danforth seeks the safety of the familiar world in Boston, even though Boston is specifically where his doomed expedition stepped off the grid. In Danforth's litany of Boston subway stations, Dyer can detect "neither irrelevance nor home feeling," implying instead relevant alienation. Perhaps that key reconciles our two Bostons: neither purely horror nor entirely home, Boston instead signifies reality itself. Pickman, after all, is a "thorough, painstaking, and almost scientific realist," who paints "in stark objectivity" with "nothing ... blurred, distorted, or conventionalised." Randolph Carter leaves his dreams to find himself in Boston, the waking city behind his sunset vision. Both tales depict awakening to reality, the discovery that the seeming illusion—art or dream—was "a photograph from life!"

"I was glad that the first faint, fragmentary words were in a human voice—a mellow, educated voice which seemed vaguely Bostonian in accent, and which was certainly not that of any native of the Vermont hills. As I listened to the tantalisingly feeble rendering, I seemed to find the speech identical with Akeley's carefully prepared transcript. On it chanted, in that mellow Bostonian voice ... 'Iä! Shub-Niggurath! The Goat with a Thousand Young!'"

—H.P. LOVECRAFT, "THE WHISPERER IN DARKNESS"

But reality, for Lovecraft, is horror, agreeing with Eliot that "human kind cannot bear very much reality." When Randolph Carter returns again to Boston in "Through the Gates of the Silver Key" it is as a monster, "creat[ing] certain nightmare rumours ... [in] Boston's West End." Pickman's ghouls haunt not just Mather's seventeenth century but the modern Boston subways, which prove ineffective at soothing Danforth's mind even as they prey on Thurber's. Joseph Curwen's mummy-trading ship is "seen in Boston Harbour, though it never openly entered the Port of Boston," and Francis Wayland Thurston, "of Boston," discovers what happens when reality is allowed full reign. The "mellow Bostonian voice" on the cylinder in "Whisperer in Darkness" may well be that of Nyarlathotep himself—and was it not Nyarlathotep who revealed to Randolph Carter the reality of Boston behind the violet-and-gold dreams of sunset?

HYPERSPACE

"Even now I absolutely refused to believe what he implied about the constitution of ultimate infinity, the juxtaposition of dimensions, and the frightful position of our known cosmos of space and time in the unending chain of linked cosmos-atoms which makes up the immediate super-cosmos of curves, angles, and material and semi-material electronic organisation."

—H.P. LOVECRAFT, "THE WHISPERER IN DARKNESS"

Lovecraft never uses the word "hyperspace" at all, which is a trifle surprising at first blush. Ever since Fritz Leiber's 1963 essay "Through Hyperspace With Brown Jenkin," the term has been inextricably linked with Lovecraft's physics, and perhaps with his metaphysics as well. Leiber demonstrated that Lovecraft was not only a monumental horrorist, but a path-breaking harbinger of the new aeon of serious American science fiction. Indeed, Lovecraft wrote his hyperspatial magnum opus "The Dreams in the Witch House" in early 1932, less than a year after John W. Campbell imported the word "hyperspace" into speculative fiction (from mathematics) in his story "Islands of Space."

But Lovecraft had been exploring hyperspace, under a number of guises, his whole literary career. Indeed, that exploration might be seen as his fundamental artistic principle: as he wrote to Clark Ashton Smith in 1930, "my wish for freedom is not so much a wish to put all terrestrial things behind me & plunge forever into abysses beyond light, matter & energy [but rather] a wish for infinite visioning & voyaging power, yet without loss of the familiar background that gives all things significance." Those "abysses beyond light, matter & energy" are Lovecraft's Outside, his supersensible world, his ultra-violet. They are hyperspace, and once unlocked with the correct (silver?) key they grant "infinite visioning & voyaging power"— and danger to match.

> *"Men of broader intellect know that there is no sharp distinction betwixt the real and the unreal; that all things appear as they do only by virtue of the delicate individual physical and mental media through which we are made conscious of them; but the prosaic materialism of the majority condemns as madness the flashes of super-sight which penetrate the common veil of obvious empiricism."*
>
> —H.P. LOVECRAFT, "THE TOMB"

Lovecraft's hyperspace emerges from the straightforward Platonism of "The Tomb": there is another, more powerful, universe of which ours is but one facet or reflection. In both "The Tomb" and "Polaris," travel between perceptual universes is travel through time. This linkage between time, perception, and space recurs throughout Lovecraft's works, both his philosophical and scientific-minded pieces and the more mystical fantasies.

Relativity and time dilation appear under minimal disguise in both "Polaris" and "The Quest of Iranon," for example. In "Beyond the Wall of Sleep" Lovecraft establishes a "unity of all time and space," while telepathic communion with the light-being occurs in a "vaulted chamber" very similar to future Lovecraftian hyperspaces. And in "Celephaïs," not only does Kuranes travel back in time to Dreamland at the end, while searching for Ooth-Nargai he travels into its distant future, and then to "a part of space where form does not exist ... outside what he had called infinity." Perhaps significantly, Kuranes' informant there is "a violet-coloured gas."

> *"With five feeble senses we pretend to comprehend the boundlessly complex cosmos, yet other beings with wider, stronger, or different range of senses might not only see very differently the things we see,*

but might see and study whole worlds of matter, energy, and life which
lie close at hand yet can never be detected with the senses we have. I
have always believed that such strange, inaccessible worlds exist at our
very elbows, and now I believe I have found a way to break down the
barriers."

—H.P. LOVECRAFT, "FROM BEYOND"

That violet glow glimmers throughout Lovecraft's writing, a signal flare of approaching hyperspace. The "sinister violet luminosity" of "From Beyond" shines where Lovecraft lays out, in appropriately purple prose, his cosmic metaphysics. Hyperspace, the Outside, the "ultra-violet" realm, whatever you term it, is vast, dwarfing our purely local dimensionality. It interpenetrates our universe, but is independent of our concerns. Encountering hyperspace is horribly dangerous, as are its inhabitants, some of whom reflect or encompass seemingly conventional objects or beings. Perhaps most importantly, humans (and inhumans and prehumans) can access it, harness it, and use it to expand human ability and perception and "put all terrestrial things behind me." This metaphysics becomes common to the rest of Lovecraft's oeuvre. In "From Beyond," Tillinghast's resonator opens the querent to hyperspace; in other stories, it can be a chance encounter, an alien attack, or dreams that do the same thing. Hyperspace is not about mechanics, but about angles of perception.

In "From Beyond," hyperspace signals its approach "ears first," which provides an interesting link to Lovecraft's next brush with the Outside, "The Music of Erich Zann." Eerie music from Outside awakens our protagonist, who opens Zann's garret window onto "the blackness of space illimitable; unimagined space alive with motion and music, and having no semblance of anything on earth." Another window, this one in the fragment "Azathoth," includes our violet light alongside "vortices of dust and fire, swirling out of the ultimate spaces." Such language is not mere poetry, but specific lyrics tuned for specific meaning: the ultimate spaces.

"Of our studies it is impossible to speak, since they held so slight a connection with anything of the world as living men conceive it. They were of that vaster and more appalling universe of dim entity and consciousness which lies deeper than matter, time, and space, and whose existence we suspect only in certain forms of sleep—those rare dreams beyond dreams ..."

—H.P. LOVECRAFT, "HYPNOS"

Lovecraft uses the same sort of imagery, recast with increasing confidence, in "Hypnos" and "He," two encounters with magical hyperspace. In addition to the quote above, the questers in "Hypnos" perceive "unbelievable elements of time and space—things which at bottom possess no distinct and definite existence," whirling into "limitless vacuum beyond all thought and entity." The questers embark on a magical vision-quest or path-working, seeking to penetrate a series of barriers. But at the end, they realize "time had become to us the merest illusion," a revelation that unhinges the narrator of "He."

In that piece, a warlock opens a hyperspatial window onto all times at once, while reaffirming the Platonist insights of "The Tomb": "All the world," he says, "is the smoke of our intellects." The narrator gains his vision by a chance meeting (as in "Erich Zann"), but other narrators gain theirs by a physical ordeal ("Strange High House in the Mist") or, like Kuranes, in dreams. Lovecraft writes in "The Silver Key" that "there are twists of time and space, of vision and reality, which only a dreamer can divine; and from what I know of Carter I think he has merely found a way to traverse these mazes." That way is the "arabesque" of the Silver Key, the time loop of "Polaris" wound around another curve.

Lovecraft's sorcerous hyperspace has magic on one side, sf on the other: Yog-Sothoth joining universes equals folded space joining worlds. HPL first equates the two explicitly in "The Shunned House," in which young Whipple already knows that "the known universe of three dimensions embraces the merest fraction of the whole cosmos of substance and energy." In a vampire-haunted basement, he sees "a shadowy geometrical confusion" and "queerly disordered pictures superimposed one upon an other; an arrangement in which the essentials of time as well as of space seemed dissolved and mixed in the most illogical fashion." The spectral vampire "continued to function in some multiple-dimensioned space," and overlaps "more palpably living things into which it penetrates and with whose fabric it sometimes completely merges itself."

"Not in the spaces we know, but between them, they walk serene and primal, undimensioned and to us unseen. Yog-Sothoth knows the gate. Yog-Sothoth is the gate. Yog-Sothoth is the key and guardian of the gate. Past, present, future, all are one in Yog-Sothoth. ... Yog-Sothoth is the key to the gate, whereby the spheres meet."

—H.P. LOVECRAFT, "THE DUNWICH HORROR"

Lovecraft leaves the higher physics behind for a bit as he erects the dizzying temples of the Cthulhu Mythos on the foundation he has laid. In "The Call of Cthulhu," Henry Wilcox sees a hyperspace in dreams: "He said that the geometry of the dream-place he saw was abnormal, non-Euclidean, and loathsomely redolent of spheres and dimensions apart from ours." R'lyeh becomes a place tangent to hyperspace, where an obtuse angle can become an acute wormhole and translate unfortunate sailors into another sphere of being. Now the act of perceiving hyperspace becomes blasphemous worship and terrible punishment at once. In "The Whisperer in Darkness," the "monstrous nuclear chaos beyond angled space" is Azathoth, personifying hyperspace and horror simultaneously, and the Nyarlathotep-worshipping Mi-Go travel "outside the curved cosmos of space and time."

In the above excerpt from the *Necronomicon*, hyperspace lies between the spaces we know, where time has no meaning, undimensioned and (perception again) "to us unseen." Yog-Sothoth, not a silver artifact, is the real "key to the gate, whereby the spheres meet." Henry Armitage explains it as "a kind of force that doesn't belong in our part of space; a kind of force that acts and grows and shapes itself by other laws than those of our sort of Nature." These forces, just like those of Tillinghast's ultra-violet, "come out of places where aesthetic standards are—very different," or as Derby testifies in "The Thing on the Doorstep," from "complex angles that led through invisible walls to other regions of space and time."

> *"One afternoon there was a discussion of possible freakish curvatures in space, and of theoretical points of approach or even contact between our part of the cosmos and various other regions as distant as the farthest stars or the transgalactic gulfs themselves—or even as fabulously remote as the tentatively conceivable cosmic units beyond the whole Einsteinian space-time continuum."*

—H.P. Lovecraft, "The Dreams in the Witch House"

As Fritz Leiber explained in 1963, the gates to hyperspace swing wide open in "The Dreams in the Witch House." Walter Gilman's mathemagical themas approach hyperspace by solution and extrapolation, combining "non-Euclidean calculus" with "mystical formulae." Here is Lovecraft's "infinite visioning & voyaging power" with a vengeance: Gilman theorizes that "a man might—given mathematical knowledge admittedly beyond all likelihood of human acquirement—step deliberately from the earth to any other celestial body which might lie at one of an infinity of specific points in the cosmic pattern."

Gilman's explorations and deductions range across the entire field of hyperspace we've already mapped. His, or rather Keziah Mason's, use of "curves and angles" is well-known, but Gilman also gains Tillinghast's symptom of "excited hearing" and suffers a "stupendous sound intense beyond all human conception or endurance" reminiscent of Erich Zann. Brown Jenkin appears "in a violet mist" and bright violet light accompanies Keziah's translations into hyperspace from Gilman's garret. The mixture of "organic and inorgan-

ic" forms Gilman encounters—all "unspeakably menacing and horrible"—
recall the images in the ultra-violet and in the basement of "The Shunned
House." Even his visions of gazing down on an alien metropolis recall those
of Kuranes, Wilcox, Randolph Carter, and the narrator of "Beyond the Wall
of Sleep." In an inversion of the first three, his journey into hyperspace un-
locks his own dreaming talent; like the disciple in "Hypnos," Keziah can
step outside time. The hyperspace of "Dreams in the Witch House," appropriately, encompasses Lovecraft's whole Outside.

*"And beyond all else he glimpsed an infinite gulf of darkness, where solid
and semisolid forms were known only by their windy stirrings, and cloudy
patterns of force seemed to superimpose order on chaos and hold forth a key
to all the paradoxes and arcana of the worlds we know."*

—H.P. LOVECRAFT, "THE HAUNTER OF THE DARK"

Lovecraft recapitulates it all with brio in "Through the Gates of the
Silver Key," which updates the quests of Kuranes and Randolph Carter
alongside the path-working of "Hypnos." The impersonal barriers of that
earlier story become incarnate in 'Umr at-Tawil rather than Azathoth or
Yog-Sothoth; having passed them, Carter/Zkauba travels physically in
space and time in a "light-envelope" made of thin metal. In this story,
hyperspace evokes Theosophical mysticism, pure geometry, and science fiction almost at random. By now, however, even a silver key is not
enough: his human perspective gone, Carter fails to translate an ancient
parchment and collapses into alien mentation. Hyperspace can reject as
well as destroy.

Or it can embrace as it destroys. "The Haunter of the Dark" is Lovecraft's last look into hyperspace "at the Universe's outside rim." Like
Walter Gilman, Robert Blake feels a constant tugging, suffers som-
nambulistic episodes, experiences weird time slips, and has his dreams
awakened by a gaze into an alien geometry: this time, the Shining Trapezohedron. "Haunter" does for hyperspace what "Shadow Over Inns-

mouth" does for contamination: presents an eerily seductive vision of the Outside. In its "vortices of space where wisps of black mist floated before thin shimmerings of cold purple haze" Blake mystically joins the Haunter, unifying man and hyperspace in a way that even Keziah Mason and Randolph Carter cannot. Lovecraft comes to terms with hyperspace's cold equations: Blake plunges "forever into abysses beyond light, matter & energy" at the cost of annihilation. In the end, hyperspace is Heaven and Hell simultaneously, and we are all already there.

MISKATONIC UNIVERSITY

"West and I were doing post-graduate work in summer classes at the medical school of Miskatonic University, and my friend had attained a wide notoriety because of his experiments leading toward the revivification of the dead."

— H.P. LOVECRAFT, "HERBERT WEST—REANIMATOR"

Lovecraft introduces Arkham's signature school of higher lower learning with those words in 1921, aptly enough in a tale of scientific necromancy. That incongruous admixture becomes one of his great contributions to the horror genre, lying at the center of his oeuvre like a campus quadrangle. What better way to symbolize the scientifictioning of horror than by inventing a university for the study of the unknowable?

"Herbert West" is one of only two Lovecraft stories that set at least one major scene on the Old Misk' campus, the other being "The Dunwich Horror." In two more (as in "Reanimator") the main character is a student at Miskatonic, and thus the University obtrudes in greater ("Thing on the Doorstep") or lesser ("Dreams in the Witch House") detail. Three stories ("The Whisperer in Darkness," *At the Mountains of Madness,* and "The Shadow Out of Time") feature Miskatonic University professors as protagonists, though the action mostly happens on expeditions well off campus. Finally, Lovecraft mentions Miskatonic U. in passing in the "History of the *Necronomicon*" and in three more tales: "The Festival," "The Colour Out of Space," and "The Shadow Over Innsmouth."

"They are typical but imaginary places—like the river 'Miskatonic,' whose name is simply a jumble of Algonquin roots."

— H.P. Lovecraft, letter to August Derleth (November 6, 1931)

Internet legend claims (with zero substantiation) that Lovecraft based his tenebrous academy on Bradford College (then women-only) in Haverhill, Massachusetts, where "he dated a student." Although Lovecraft visited his amateur publisher "Tryout" Smith in Haverhill in June 1921 (four months before he invented M.U.), his putative co-ed romance is pure invention.[47] To the extent that Lovecraft modeled Miskatonic University on any particular college, it must have been on Brown University in Providence, the school he had once hoped to attend and had visited regularly as a teenager.[48] When he moved to 10 Barnes Street on College Hill in 1926, he lived a short walk from the Brown campus. After 1933, his last house (then at 66 College Street) stood in Brown's Fraternity Row a hundred yards from the University gates, but his only Miskatonic story from that period ("Shadow Out of Time," completed in 1935) barely sketches the school as a backdrop.

The name of the University, both fictively and actually, comes from Lovecraft's Miskatonic River, first mentioned in "The Picture in the House" (1920). The occultist and faux-*Necronomicon* author Simon posits that *-katonic* is a pun on the Greek word "chthonic," meaning underground, or underworld, often used by classicists (and by the ancient Greeks more or less) to describe a set of deities such as Hades and Persephone. Thus "mis-katonic" would imply (mis-) malign (-chthonic) underground deities, such as Nyarlathotep or Cthulhu. Whether Lovecraft intended such

---

47. Its thin, shadowy factual basis is Lovecraft's friendship with, and two (chaperoned) visits to, the writer Myrta Alice Little, who lived in Hampstead, New Hampshire, just over the border from Haverhill. Roughly two years Lovecraft's senior, she was considerably better educated than he was (B.A., Colby College 1908; M.A., Radcliffe 1912) and married the Reverend Arthur Davies in 1922.

48. In his graphic novel *Providence,* Alan Moore identifies St. Anselm College in Manchester, New Hampshire as the "real" Miskatonic. Apparently Moore read Lovecraft's note (in a 1934 letter to F. Lee Baldwin) that Arkham was "perhaps near Manchester" without realizing HPL referred to Manchester, Massachusetts, roughly halfway between Gloucester and Salem.

a play on words or not, he mentions nothing about it in his letters, calling "Miskatonic" a mere "jumble of Algonquin roots."

Enter the enterprising Will Murray, who has hunted down a number of promising Narragansett and Wampanoag words, settling on *misk-* or *misq-* as "red, blood-like." The *-atonic* ending, found in the Mohican name for the Housatonic River in western Massachusetts, turns out to be a likely compound of *adene-* "mountain" and *-uk* (also *-ak, -ok, -auk*) "place." Thus the adept Lovecraftian (although almost certainly not Lovecraft himself) constructs *misk-adene-uk,* "blood mountain place," only slightly slowed by the absence of any mountain, bloody or otherwise, in the Miskatonic valley. William Bright, an actual linguist, suggests *mishque-tunkw* ("red tidal stream") as a more economical derivation. Such post hoc fun aside, Lovecraft more likely combined Nathaniel Hawthorne's beloved Housatonic with the Rhode Island beach community Misquamicut.

> *"Some of the whispered rumours about the wild Miskatonic set were extremely singular. There was even talk of black magic and of happenings utterly beyond credibility."*
>
> — H.P. LOVECRAFT, "THE THING ON THE DOORSTEP"

From the signifier to the signified, then. In Lovecraft's ongoing project of modernizing the Gothic, Miskatonic University updates the folk legend of the "Devil's school." According to folklore gathered in Scotland, Germany, and the spaces between, the Devil operates a school of black magic for a significant few (seven, ten, thirteen) pupils, demanding the soul of the last (or first) as tuition. That student occasionally escapes with only the loss of his shadow—a motif used, for example, by Lord Dunsany in *The Charwoman's Shadow* (1926). Icelandic legend claims that Saemundr the Learned (a real 12th-century scholar) mastered his arts at the Svartaskóli or Black School, variously placed in Wittenberg or Paris or nowhere. The Scots version is the "Black Airt," sometimes located in Edinburgh and sometimes associated with the magician Michael Scot.

In "Lay of the Last Minstrel" (1805), Sir Walter Scott associated Michael Scot with the famous Cave of Salamanca, a sorcerous seminary supposedly established by Satan behind the university in that city, itself thought tainted by its connection with Moorish learning. The Protestant pamphleteers who introduced the Devil's bargain into the biography of the historical alchemist Johannes Faust implied he got his satanic start at the Catholic university in Krakow. Dracula himself studied magic at the Devil's School, the Scholomance "amongst the mountains over Lake Hermannstadt" according to Bram Stoker. Stoker borrowed authentic Transylvanian legends of the Solomonari ("students of Solomon") and their academy, which may have come from Dacian traditions of their undying god Zalmoxis' priests (who studied magic in caves) or from German settlers in the region bringing their own folklore with them. Whether from folklore, Scott, or Stoker, Lovecraft picked up the lesson and applied it.

"The professors at Miskatonic had urged him to slacken up, and had voluntarily cut down his course at several points. Moreover, they had stopped him from consulting the dubious old books on forbidden secrets that were kept under lock and key in a vault at the university library."

— H.P. LOVECRAFT, "THE DREAMS IN THE WITCH HOUSE"

But Miskatonic University doesn't teach black magic, classes in "medieval metaphysics" notwithstanding. It's respectable, consulted by the police and by eminent authorities. It has a Spa and a Club, and even its decadents don't approve of Aleister Crowley.[49] The closest it gets to the satanic arts is a political economy class that invokes sunspots to explain the business cycle. Although the Miskatonic library seems mighty reckless in "The Festival," lending its copy of the *Necronomicon* to a recovering mental patient, it clamps down under Henry Armitage's watchful eye by the time of "The

---

49. Crowley clearly serves as Lovecraft's model for "Doorstep"'s "notorious cult-leader, lately expelled from England, who had established headquarters in New York." Crowley established his headquarters in New York in October 1914, departing in December 1919. Crowley spent the 1929-1933 period of "Thing on the Doorstep" between London and Berlin.

Dunwich Horror." It must be admitted that Armitage himself commanded "wide linguistic learning and skill in the mystic formulae of antiquity and the Middle Ages," but he might have picked that up at Princeton.

Miskatonic academic culture, if anything, quashes Mythos research. Although in "Dreams in the Witch House" Professor Upham initially encourages Gilman's blend of higher mathematics with magical lore, he apparently soon reverses himself and signs on to restricting Gilman's coursework and library privileges. The same pattern holds across departments, and not just for undergraduates. Dean Halsey of the Medical School does everything he can to discourage and discredit Herbert West's experiments. The comparative anatomy department shows "singular reticence" to discuss the skeleton of Brown Jenkin. At least at first, the Miskatonic Antarctic Expedition survivors "kept certain doubts and guesses to [them]selves with splendid unity and faithfulness." Professors Wilmarth, Dyer, and Peaslee unanimously insist that nobody should follow in their academic footsteps—admittedly, just before launching into unwisely complete descriptions of their expeditions and experiences.

"The full story, so far as deciphered, will shortly appear in an official bulletin of Miskatonic University."

— H.P. LOVECRAFT, *AT THE MOUNTAINS OF MADNESS*

University policy and terrified hindsight aside, however, there may be something to the notion that Miskatonic itself encourages such behavior even if its faculty does not. Walter Gilman "began to connect his mathematics with the fantastic legends of elder magic" "only after he had entered college in Arkham." Something about the campus atmosphere, perhaps, first and foremost all those crumbling tomes of "subterranean magical lore, for which Miskatonic's library was and is famous." Everyone from Dunwich yokels to Vermont rustics knows that Miskatonic holds a copy of the *Necronomicon*. Edward Derby has the run of the rare book room in "The Thing on the Doorstep," although he attends Miskatonic around 1907-1910 in the pre-Armitage era. A geology grad student like Danforth can apparently read the *Necronomicon* on an optional syllabus for his classes on Poe. This seems only fair, given that three geology professors from Miskatonic accidentally unleashed the Colour Out of Space in 1882 by cracking open its meteorite.

More worrisomely, Asenath Waite and the "wild Miskatonic set" seem able to study those tomes even under Armitage in 1929, perhaps thanks to her hypnotic persuasions. Even in faculty circles, the bar on dangerous knowledge lowers repeatedly: Nathaniel Peaslee publishes a nearly complete description of his Pnakotic captivity in an academic journal, and Dyer promises "an official bulletin" will report his full findings from the walls of Kadath. Professor Dyer, especially, embodies the University's contradictory mindset. In the opening of *Mountains of Madness*, with one breath he demands respect for his findings, and with the next he urges their abandonment by academia. Then four years later in "Shadow Out of Time," he launches another expedition into prehuman lore with full knowledge beforehand.

"He and his wife had gone with the three professors from Miskatonic University who hastened out the next morning to see the weird visitor from unknown stellar space ..."

— H.P. LOVECRAFT, "THE COLOUR OUT OF SPACE"

But Walter Gilman isn't the only magus on the Miskatonic campus, and nor is Asenath Waite. Miskatonic also holds three wise men: Armitage, Rice, and Morgan, who come from the East to witness an unholy birth. They respond to prophecies and signs, and destroy the son of Yog-Sothoth with incantations and the powder of Ibn Ghazi rather than offering hymns and frankincense. They join their hideous epiphany with a righteous passion, both witnesses and unmakers of miracles. They redeem the sin of their forebears, the "three professors" 36 years earlier who also came from the East following a sign from the heavens and unwittingly brought death into the Gardner farm. Those wise men sought knowledge, while Armitage and his fellow magi sought to suppress knowledge.

"It is an unfortunate fact that relatively obscure men like myself and my associates, connected only with a small university, have little chance of making an impression where matters of a wildly bizarre or highly controversial nature are concerned."

— H.P. LOVECRAFT, *AT THE MOUNTAINS OF MADNESS*

For "a small university," Miskatonic seems to punch well above its weight in expeditions to far-flung corners of the world, bibliographic resources, and bespoke curriculum. Primarily, of course, this derives from Lovecraft's desire for unity in his legendry and minimization of invention aside from the central horrors throughout his tales. He doesn't need to create two or five universities when the same one can work in any given story. But also, it speaks to Miskatonic's role as a symbol. The university—especially this university, and even more especially this university's library—embodies the correlation of contents, the unification of the separate scientific disciplines into one body of knowledge that presages, and ushers in, mankind's doom.

Miskatonic thus, like so many of Lovecraft's great places, is a sign with two sides. In its duality, Miskatonic University combines respectability and wildness, reason and madness, secrets published in the name of secrecy, the tools to unseal the world held "behind lock and key." It is the Solomonic Temple of Lovecraft's blasphemous "Ark-enclosing" Ark-ham city, with an Unholy of Unholies inside its precincts: the locked library holding the *Necronomicon*. Miskatonic is not just the American Scholomance but an institutional Faust, seeking knowledge and tempted by its own Mephistophelean tomes. Its professors reflect and embody its Faustian core, regretting their bargain once its parameters become horribly visible.

OUTER SPACE

"Howard Phillips Lovecraft was the Copernicus of the horror story. He shifted the focus of supernatural dread from man and his little world and his gods, to the stars and the black and unplumbed gulfs of intergalactic space."

— FRITZ LEIBER, JR., "A LITERARY COPERNICUS" (1949)

Lovecraft presciently sums up this artistic goal in the early (1920) story "Nyarlathotep," where he writes, "everyone felt that the world and perhaps the universe had passed from the control of known gods or forces to that of gods or forces which were unknown." Two 1919 stories also look to the skies, featuring a meteorite opener ("The Green Meadow") and even space travel and aliens ("Beyond the Wall of Sleep"). Fascinated by astronomy from his earliest adolescence, HPL wrote two regular astronomy columns for the *Pawtuxet Valley Gleaner* and the Providence *Tribune* between 1906 and 1908, and contributed a monthly "Sky" column to the Providence *Evening News* from January 1914 to May of 1918.

Outer space remains a continuing motif in Lovecraft's fiction, as well. Stars haunt the narrators of "Polaris," "Hypnos," and "Dreams in the Witch House." After "Green Meadow," two more meteorites bring horror to the Earth, in "The Challenge From Beyond" and of course the utterly cosmic "The Colour Out of Space." Space travel occurs astrally in "Beyond the Wall of Sleep" and physically in "In the Walls of Eryx" and "The Whisperer in Darkness," and somewhere between the two in "Dreams in the Witch House," "Through the Gates of the Silver Key," and *The Dream-Quest of Unknown Kadath*. Not just the Dreamlands-Moon voyage but also Carter's final shantak excursion ventures into space. When Nyarlathotep tells Carter to steer for Vega, he implies that the stars (admittedly the visual stars, not the bodies) act as portals or wayfinders to the waking world.

Aliens seep or fall or fly to Earth[50] not just in "The Colour Out of Space" but in "The Call of Cthulhu," "The Mound," and "The Whisperer in Darkness," and teleport into our bodies in "Beyond the Wall of Sleep," "The Challenge From Beyond," and "The Shadow Out of Time." Aliens deploy three monsters or weapons to our planet (for those invasions?) from Yuggoth: Rhan-Tegoth in "The Horror in the Museum," Ghatanothoa in "Out of the Aeons," and the Haunter itself (in its trapezohedral capsule) in "The Haunter of the Dark."

> *"Some day his descent into the solar system may be told. He saw Kynarth and Yuggoth on the rim, passed close to Neptune and glimpsed the hellish white fungi that spot it, learned an untellable secret from the close-glimpsed mists of Jupiter and saw the horror on one of the satellites, and gazed at the Cyclopean ruins that sprawl over Mars' ruddy disc."*
>
> — H.P. LOVECRAFT AND E. HOFFMANN PRICE,
> "THROUGH THE GATES OF THE SILVER KEY"

Lovecraft's fiction touches, or at least flies past, every planet but one of our Solar system, and may even add a spare on the rim (the planet Kynarth, noted above).[51] Mercury hosts "bulbous vegetable entities," or at least it will when the Great Race of Yith settles there in the distant future.[52] Lovecraft's Venus has a Theosophical past in "Diary of Alonzo Typer" when its "lords … came through space to civilise our planet," presumably 18 million years ago per Blavatskyan belief.[53] It also has a distant future "incalculable ep-

---

50. And alien cats fly or jump from Saturn to the Moon, albeit in the Dreamlands, in *The Dream-Quest of Unknown Kadath.*

51. On the grounds that if Lovecraft had meant Yuggoth he would have said Yuggoth, Kynarth may be the "unknown trans-Neptunian planet" with a hollow interior with whose "half-plastic denizen" Peaslee speaks.

52. In his raisonné of the Lovecraftian Solar system, Fred Lubnow suggests the Yithians migrate into Mercury's distant past, as the Sun's expansion into a red giant will obliterate Mercury in about five billion years. However, Lovecraft followed the older astronomical model, which predicted that the "slow yet inevitable contraction of its bulk" (as HPL put it in a 1918 column for the Providence *Evening News*) would shrink and cool the Sun as the eons wore on.

53. Or possibly longer, given that the same story provides the mystical city of Shamballah in Asia a founding date of 50 million years ago.

ochs to come," from whence the Yithians snatch a captive mind who speaks with Peaslee in his Pnakotic captivity in "Shadow Out of Time." Whether the cunning lizard-folk of "In the Walls of Eryx" produce that mind, and whether they descended from the "lords of Venus," remain open questions.

Lovecraft kept a skeptical attitude toward Percival Lowell's canals on Mars, and even in fiction avoided the red planet save to note (in "Through the Gates of the Silver Key") the "Cyclopean ruins that sprawl over Mars' ruddy disc." Peaslee also recalls the "queerly pigmented" alphabet of an asteroid civilization, the relic of "the archaic life and lore of the primal planet whereof [the asteroid] formed a fragment." (In his astronomical writing, HPL cast mild doubt on such asteroidal origins, but you can't blame him for using the more exciting if antiquated theory in his fiction.) Peaslee also chatted with a mind "from an outer moon of Jupiter six million years in the past," possibly one of the "insect-philosophers that crawl proudly over the fourth moon of Jupiter" in "Beyond the Wall of Sleep." More intriguingly, Randolph Carter gleans "an untellable secret from the close-glimpsed mists of Jupiter" on his way past in "Through the Gates of the Silver Key," and your guess is as good as mine. A cousin to the "gaseous wraiths" above Antarctica? A surviving flying polyp?[54]

Although his creator Clark Ashton Smith pegged Saturn as Tsathoggua's planet of (at least recent) origin, to Lovecraft Saturn only serves as the home of the malevolent Dreamland cats that oppose earthly Felidae in the *Dream-Quest*. Astrologically, Saturn has a generally baleful effect, which might explain why its cats rub ours the wrong way. Lovecraft skips over Uranus entirely,[55] but for Neptune he provides two more captive minds (imprisoned by the Mi-Go this time, in jars in "Whisperer") and "hellish white fungi" spotting its surface (or upper atmosphere) in "Through the Gates of the Silver Key."

Yuggoth, or Pluto, almost deserves a whole Stop of its own on this Tour. Clyde Tombaugh announced his discovery of Pluto in March

54. After all, the polyps "dominated the earth and three other solar planets about six hundred million years ago." Being only semi-material, the absence of solid matter in Jupiter won't have fazed them.

55. Ramsey Campbell helpfully filled in this gap in "The Insects From Shaggai" (1964), in which he provides Uranus with cubical, metallic, many-legged inhabitants who call their world L'gy'hx.

1930 while Lovecraft was writing "The Whisperer in Darkness." HPL incorporated the discovery into the tale, implying that Tombaugh had received "thought-currents" from the Mi-Go revealing their world to him.[56] As originally described in *Fungi From Yuggoth*, that world (and its possible moon Nithon) lay "past the starry voids," but the gift of a whole new planet moved Yuggoth definitively onto the Outer Rim of our own Solar system. As described by the Mi-Go, an even earlier "elder race" built black, terraced, windowless towers on Yuggoth's rivers of pitch.[57] In just a few words, Lovecraft conjures a lightless world at the edge of existence, where even the Sun is powerless. Here, appropriately enough, the Haunter of the Dark was bound into the Shining Trapezohedron, perhaps by the Nyarlathotep-worshipping Mi-Go.

> *"I learned whence Cthulhu first came, and why half the great temporary stars of history had flared forth. I guessed—from hints which made even my informant pause timidly—the secret behind the Magellanic Clouds and globular nebulae …."*

> — H.P. LOVECRAFT, "THE WHISPERER IN DARKNESS"

Lovecraft's Copernican vision extends even past the rolling orbit of Yuggoth. Leaving aside the "stars of eternal night" as ornaments, navigation markers, or time-keepers in the stories' skies, Lovecraft utilizes extrasolar planets and stars throughout his fiction. Some of them—Shaggai, Thog, Kath, Mthura, Shonhi[58]—just provide distance and exoticism, exactly like the random syllables that spangle the map of the Dreamlands. However, many of Lovecraft's stellar landmarks come from his astronomical background.

---

56. Those "thought-currents" appear to be the scientistic version of the poetic "star-winds" that reveal "what fungi sprout in Yuggoth" in Sonnet XIV ("The Star-Winds") of the *Fungi From Yuggoth* cycle.

57. Whether that race or the Mi-Go are the "spawn of Yuggoth" who built or deployed Ghatanothoa in "Out of the Aeons" remains unclear.

58. This name (of a transgalactic planet in "Through the Gates of the Silver Key") may have begun as "Shalmali," the Theosophical "esoteric name" of Lemuria. According to Joshi, Price objected to Lovecraft recycling Theosophical terms willy-nilly in this story, and changed some of them while typing Lovecraft's manuscript. Some bad printings (and Lin Carter pastiches) spell it "Stronti."

Entirely comfortable in the actual night sky landscape, Lovecraft deploys this confidence to provide plausibility throughout the tales: the titular Colour out of Space launches itself toward Cygnus, Aldebaran and Fomalhaut may have their own Dreamlands, the planet Kythanil (home to "doubtfully shaped" entities who worship Tsathoggua) orbits Arcturus, the Pennacook in "Whisperer" claim the Mi-Go come from "the Great Bear," the star-being in "Beyond the Wall of Sleep" incarnates Nova Persei 1901 and hangs out in Orion's Sword, some hellish secret (feared even by the Mi-Go) lurks behind "the Magellanic Clouds and globular nebulae." Interfiling his cosmic horrors with orthodox astronomy, Lovecraft reaps the same dividends that he does by inserting Arkham and Innsmouth into the actual Essex County, Massachusetts.

Stars play another major role in Lovecraft's stories: evil influencers from afar. In short, the ultimate rational materialist repeatedly presents baneful astrology in his fiction! Algol, the Demon-Star, somehow lives and oppresses other astral beings in "Beyond the Wall of Sleep"; even insensitive humanity "unwittingly felt its distant presence." "Some monstrous thing" emanates from Corona Borealis, haunting the narrator's muse in "Hypnos" with both "droning, clamouring, mocking" tones and "a shaft of horrible red-gold light" collimated like a laser. In *Fungi From Yuggoth*, Fomalhaut emits "The Star-Winds" that blow in dreams from Outside and sweep ours away. In "Dreams in the Witch House," Walter Gilman suffers from fixation on and attention from the stars, following his hyperspatial travels to them: the first to a planet somewhere between Argo Navis and Hydra,[59] the second to a world orbiting three suns lying "infinitely north."[60] Finally,

---

59. Chris Perridas suggests a possible in-joke reference to Jerome Lalande's proposed (but now obsolete) constellation Felis, the Cat. Lalande's Felis sat between Hydra and Argo Navis, and Lovecraft could have seen it (among other places) in Alexander Jamieson's *Celestial Atlas* (1822), perhaps in the library of Ladd Observatory. I think the author of "The Call of Cthulhu" pulling his protagonist to a spot between the monster (Hydra) and the ship (Argo Navis) doesn't need any more explanation than that.

60. T.R. Livesey makes the very interesting observation that Lovecraft knew Polaris to be a trinary star system. Polaris, of course, lies "infinitely north" and had already been used by HPL in a tale of stellar obsession and mind transfer. Polaris may also be "the triple star Nython" that Randolph Carter pretends to depart for on his return to Earth in "Through the Gates of the Silver Key." In Lovecraft's time it was believed to lie fairly close to Earth (less than 100 parsecs), making the stratagem plausible.

of course, actual malevolent forces descend to Earth from the extragalactic stars hosting the planets Yekub and Yith.

> *"They will not hurt us if we let them alone, but no one can say what will happen if we get too curious about them. Of course a good army of men could wipe out their mining colony. That is what they are afraid of. But if that happened, more would come from* outside—*any number of them. They could easily conquer the earth, but have not tried so far because they have not needed to."*

> — H.P. LOVECRAFT, "THE WHISPERER IN DARKNESS"

Lovecraft didn't invent the alien invasion, of course. The Colour Out of Space and the Mi-Go both descend from H.G. Wells' Martians, from their rewriting of earthly ecology to their tentacles and telepathy. For all that, Lovecraft preferred *The Time Machine,* calling *War of the Worlds* a "semi-classic."[61] Lovecraft was hardly alone in shrugging off Wells' influence: between Wells' 1897 novel and Lovecraft's first definitive "alien invasion" tale ("The Colour Out of Space" (1927)) almost no science fiction stories described a contemporary alien invasion from a human viewpoint.[62]

After the spate of Wellsian near-plagiarism that followed *War of the Worlds,* the field seems to have settled out for a decade or two. Then in 1923, Edgar Rice Burroughs tried his hand with *The Moon Maid,* describing an invasion from the Moon in the 22nd century led by a Terran traitor. Bohun Lynch's *Menace from the Moon* (1925) features a contemporary attack by human Lunarians (descended from a 17th century lunar expedition) who attempt to boil the Earth. Two *Weird Tales* stories in

---

61. *War of the Worlds* first saw American publication in serialized newspaper stories in 1897-1898, often (badly) re-edited to set the action in the U.S. If Lovecraft only read the *Boston Post* version, as an eight-year-old no less, it might explain his uncharacteristic under-rating of the novel.

62. Lovecraft's apparent creation of the "alien infiltrators lurking among us" motif (in "Whisperer in Darkness" (1930)), although a natural sfnal progression from Arthur Machen's Little People paranoid fantasies "Novel of the Black Seal" and "The Red Hand" (both 1895) proved staggeringly original, but perhaps resonated even more in ufology than in fiction. Joseph J. Millard's *The Gods Hate Kansas* (1941) was the next work of fiction to take up the theme after HPL, although it blossomed during the Cold War with Robert Heinlein's *The Puppet Masters* (1951) and Jack Finney's *Invasion of the Body Snatchers* (1955).

1925 also feature pre-Lovecraftian Lovecraftesque alien invasions: Joseph Schlossel's "Invaders From Outside" features alien invaders who destroy a dinosaur civilization in the Cretaceous, while Nictzin Dyalhis' "When the Green Star Waned" features a far-future invasion of Earth by huge blobs and energy beings. (Neither story is told from a human viewpoint.) Still more Lovecraftian, and highly praised by HPL, G. McLeod Winsor's *Station X* (1919) features a Martian psychic invasion of contemporary Earth via radio, told from a human viewpoint. Lovecraft hadn't seen Winsor's novel before writing "Beyond the Wall of Sleep" in the spring of 1919, but read it in a 1926 *Amazing Stories* reprint just before writing "Colour Out of Space."

> *"This book is as much a factual accounting as possible. However, among its readers there will certainly be some science-fiction fans who would like to know what the connection is between the mysteries we have described in this chapter and the myths created by H. P. Lovecraft and linked to the same region. ... It is not impossible that at least a part of Lovecraft's myth may be verified when the Empty Quarter is opened to exploration."*
>
> — JACQUES BERGIER, *EXTRATERRESTRIAL VISITATIONS FROM PREHISTORIC TIMES TO THE PRESENT* (1970)

So much for invasion in the present and future: what about alien invasion in the past? *At the Mountains of Madness* and "Shadow Out of Time" chronicle endless alien arrivals on and invasions of our strangely interesting planet deep in paleontological prehistory.[63] Lovecraft, as I have said elsewhere, created the form of our post-scientific mythology by remythologizing the frontiers (or fringes) of the scientific world: paleontology, relativity, cosmology, astronomy, even anthropology became grist for

---

63. T.R. Livesey suggests that Lovecraft made Earth more important to his alien races after reading works by the astronomers Harlow Shapley (*Starlight* (1926)) and Arthur Eddington (*The Nature of the Physical World* (1928)), and becoming converted to the "tidal theory" of planetary formation. That theory holds that planets form when another passing star rips away a sun's nebular material, and thus that planetary systems are vanishingly rare in the cosmos. Joshi quotes a 1935 Lovecraft letter to Emil Petaja that cites Eddington for a guess that "the cosmos may possess about *six* worlds with highly developed life at any one time."

THE DESTINATIONS · 151

his cosmic mill. In *Mountains of Madness* and "Whisperer in Darkness" he also scientizes the Gothic's haunted castle and monstrous persecution, translating them into effective modern terms for horror or myth. In short, he transforms outer space back into something like the Babylonian heavens: the realm of dangerous gods and spirits.

Jason Colavito specifically argues that Lovecraft's powerful fictionalization of the "ancient astronaut" motif, in "Call of Cthulhu" and *Mountains of Madness* especially, laid the groundwork for that theme's pseudoscientific explosion in Erich von Däniken's epochal bestseller *Chariots of the Gods* (1968). Von Däniken admittedly plagiarized the work of two modern French occultists, Louis Pauwels and Jacques Bergier, whose *The Morning of the Magicians* (1960) name-checked Lovecraft as "the greatest poet and champion of the theory of parallel universes" and detonated its own somewhat smaller nonsense tsunami at the beginning of the decade. Pauwels and Bergier published French translations of Lovecraft in the 1950s; Bergier even claimed to have corresponded with him in 1935.

Colavito's thesis positing HPL as the necessary and sufficient origin of the "ancient aliens" mytheme runs ahead of the evidence, as Bergier and Pauwels draw on many other sources in their gallimaufry, not least Charles Fort and Theosophy. Lovecraft certainly didn't originate the concept. Ancient Martian astronauts built the Pyramids, for example, in Garrett P. Serviss' *Edison's Conquest of Mars* (1898),[64] a rejoinder and unauthorized sequel to Wells' novel. In the 1920s, the Theosophical authors Charles Leadbeater and Alice Bailey both wrote extensively about the "Lords of the Flame" who descended to Earth from Venus and uplifted human (well, Lemurian) civilization 18 million years ago. I strongly suspect that von Däniken was also an avid reader of Paul Albert Müller's "Sun Koh" serial adventure stories (1933-1939), about the Nazi Doc Savage manqué (less Nazi in his postwar 1945-1953 appearances) who

---

64. Lovecraft admired Serviss as an astronomer, quoting his article on the nova near Algol at the end of "Beyond the Wall of Sleep," for instance. He also devoured Serviss' sci-fi adventure stories as a teenager.

descends from an Atlantean Maya kingdom and discovers alien tech-nologies in ancient ruins on Earth.[65]

> *"Thus long spaces of time wore on—ages longer than the brain of man could grasp, since the beings of Yaddith die only after prolonged cycles. After many hundred revolutions the Carter-facet seemed to gain on the Zkauba-facet, and would spend vast periods calculating the distance of Yaddith in space and time from the human earth that was to be. The figures were staggering—aeons of light-years beyond counting—but the immemorial lore of Yaddith fitted Carter to grasp such things."*

> — H.P. Lovecraft and E. Hoffmann Price,
> "Through the Gates of the Silver Key"

Lovecraft's alien invasions nearly always compromise human individu-ality, an interesting approach for an author who purported unconcern with individual human problems. Yekubians and Yithians and "star brothers" possess humans, the Mi-Go remove our brains and wash them, Cthulhu deforms our dreams and his Deep Ones taint our genetics. The Colour corrodes us into indistinguishable dust and madness. Only the crinoid El-der Things preserve our souls even while vivisecting us, and in fairness they created us in the first place. Lovecraft turns this pattern intriguingly on its head in "Through the Gates of the Silver Key," in which Randolph Carter invades the planet Yaddith and possesses its leading sorcerer, Zkauba.

Lovecraft invented Yaddith in the sonnet "Alienation" in *Fungi From Yuggoth*, as just another throwaway danger of the Outside: "He had seen Yaddith, yet retained his mind." But something about it must have stuck, and when HPL needed a world where Randolph Carter "retained his mind" inside an alien form, he picked Yaddith. He provides that "dim, fantastic world," billions of years in our past and millions of light-years

---

65. The *Science Fiction Encyclopedia* also suggests the 1950s UFO novels of Walter Ernsting (featuring an-cient alien visitations) as another likely influence on von Däniken. Ernsting, best known as the co-creator of Perry Rhodan, may have encountered Lovecraft's work in British sf compilations, and definitely read the Sun Koh adventures.

distant in an "unsuspected galaxy," with lush details suitable to a major Lovecraftian locus. It orbits "five multi-coloured suns," its metallic buildings rise alongside "cryptical floating cylinders," and like that other Carterian destination Kadath it sports "dizzy black crags."

The near-immortal folk of Yaddith resemble "curiously articulated" bipedal tapirs, with claws and "rugose, partly squamous" hide. But they can pass as human on Earth with a mask and mittens, and their libraries hold "the massed lore of ten thousand worlds living and dead." Yaddith even has its own Pnakotic manuscripts, the Tablets of Nhing. Libraries and immortality! What more does Randolph Carter or his creator need to signal that the Yaddithians, like the Elder Things, are "Men!" They even fight a never-ending battle against literal underground subversion, by the gigantic, viscous, tunneling bholes. (Lovecraft does at least describe the bholes as "bleached," which makes a change.) In this fairly shallow story, although Carter and Zkauba are literally twinned, Yaddith twins only with its future self, sunless and overrun with idiotic victorious bholes.[66] Yaddith is the imperiled Lovecraftian city on fast-forward, the Outside succumbing to itself.

"A sickened, sensitive shadow writhing in hands that are not hands, and whirled blindly past ghastly midnights of rotting creation, corpses of dead worlds with sores that were cities, charnel winds that brush the pallid stars and make them flicker low. Beyond the worlds vague ghosts of monstrous things; half-seen columns of unsanctified temples that rest on nameless rocks beneath space and reach up to dizzy vacua above the spheres of light and darkness."

— H.P. LOVECRAFT, "NYARLATHOTEP"

Yaddith, and Yuggoth, and all of Lovecraft's stars and planets, lie in deep interstellar space, in that "vast, unplumbed abyss of night wherein

---

66. Both Claes van der Hyl ("Diary of Alonzo Typer") and Robert Blake ("Haunter of the Dark") appeal to Yaddith for aid ("may the Lords of Yaddith succor me") or protection ("Yaddith grant [the lightning] will keep up!"), implying that at least some of Yaddith's wizards transcended its doom.

whirled suns and worlds of an even profounder blackness," as he says in "Haunter of the Dark." Lovecraft thrilled to the parallels between Outer Space and the Underground. Time after time Lovecraft interchanges the "abyss" or "gulf" of space with those of the underworld. As we've seen, all of Lovecraft's voids ultimately become the same void, be they dizzyingly below or infinitely above the Earth. Maurice Lévy calls this pattern the "reversed abysm" of the Lovecraftian cosmos. It makes a startling contrast with Lovecraft's "Copernican Revolution" of horror to note that for HPL the center of the Earth becomes literally the same as the center of the Universe.

In "Rats in the Walls," Delapore's endless mental progression downward ends in caverns "where Nyarlathotep the mad faceless god, howls blindly to the piping of two amorphous idiot flute-players." This of course prefigures Lovecraft's later descriptions of the daemon-sultan Azathoth, who bubbles chaotically "in inconceivable, unlighted chambers beyond time amidst the muffled, maddening beating of vile drums and the thin, monotonous whine of accursed flutes." Azathoth simultaneously exists "in the Gulf," outside the universe (often, "outside angled space"), and at the "centre of all infinity" or the "centre of ultimate Chaos." Given that Azathoth might be anywhere, then why not be at the center of the Earth as well? Or at least be there in the presence of his mighty messenger? And given that the Earth, already raddled with horrors and conquered by aliens, is as doomed as Yaddith, what's to separate it from the rest of the universe? We have traveled to Outer Space, and found it already here.

OKLAHOMA

"In 1925 I went into Oklahoma looking for snake lore, and I came out with a fear of snakes that will last me the rest of my life."

— H.P. LOVECRAFT AND ZEALIA BISHOP, "THE CURSE OF YIG"

If you asked the casual Lovecraft fan to rank the states of the Union in order of their Lovecraftian-ness, I suspect Oklahoma would land pretty far down the list. Landlocked, brash, commercial, and barely older than Lovecraft himself, it does not immediately recommend itself as a suitable horror setting for the Old Gentleman. Indeed, as he wrote in 1928: "I can imagine the desolation of a type of country which lacks the beauty & traditional associations of rural New England, as Oklahoma must." But thanks to a fortuitous application from a would-be writer of light romances, Lovecraft Country extends far into the west, to the red clay of the state where I in turn fortuitously encountered H.P. Lovecraft.

"Also, I worked up the geographic & other incidental colour—getting some data from the alleged authoress, who knows Oklahoma, but more from books."

— H.P. LOVECRAFT, LETTER TO AUGUST DERLETH (OCTOBER 6, 1929)

Zealia Brown Reed, aspiring author, probably obtained her referral to Lovecraft from his friend Samuel Loveman. In the spring of 1927 she hired him to revise and edit her nascent short stories, among them "When a Woman is Tempted" and "The Unchaining." After providing her with (apparently sensible) guidance on plot construction, points of view, and other fundamentals of her chosen craft, he then steered her away from "superficial, modern fiction" and toward horror writing. In 1930, she remarried, becoming Zealia Bishop, the name under which August Derleth published her collected collaborations with Lovecraft in 1953.

Those three collaborations include Lovecraft's two Oklahoma stories, "The Curse of Yig" and "The Mound," but Zealia herself was originally from North Carolina and lived in Cleveland when she first wrote to Lovecraft. The Oklahoma setting, plot germs, and "incidental colour" came via her half-sister Grace Compton, who she visited in February 1928. Grace and Zealia apparently swapped yarns with some old settlers, among them Grace's mother-in-law "Grandma" Sally Compton, who appears in both "The Curse of Yig" and "The Mound." Indeed, Lovecraft describes Grandma Compton in the latter tale as "a veritable mine of anecdote and folklore," implying that she was the original source of both story seeds.[67]

"They were very curious, these open-air ghost tales; and though they sounded flat and prosaic in the mouths of the white people, they had earmarks of linkage with some of the richest and obscurest phases of native mythology. All of them were woven around the vast, lonely, artificial-looking mounds in the western part of the state, and all of them involved apparitions of exceedingly strange aspect and equipment."

— H.P. Lovecraft and Zealia Bishop, "The Mound"

Bishop (or Lovecraft) lays the action of both stories near the small town of Binger, Oklahoma, in Caddo County in the west-central part of the state. According to Bishop's later memoir, Grace Compton lived on a "ranch in Oklahoma, a barren lonely place near the Texas border." This, sad to say, doesn't narrow it down much, and although barren enough, Caddo County lies a considerable distance from the Texas border. I note that the 1930 U.S. Census lists a "Grace L. Compton" living in Texas County, Oklahoma, in the barren lonely Oklahoma panhandle very close to the Texas border; Lovecraftian scholarship has not as yet unbent itself to trace the Comptons any further.

---

67. Dr. McNeill from "Curse of Yig" is named for the boys' Western adventure author Everett McNeil, a friend of Lovecraft's.

While I have no trouble believing in nests of Yig-protected rattlesnakes near Binger, I can state definitively that there are no mounds "a third of a mile west" of there, as the story would have it. Zealia supplied the following kernel of lore to Lovecraft: "There is an Indian mound near here, which is haunted by a headless ghost. Sometimes it is a woman." The actual mound in question is, appropriately enough, Ghost Mound, ten miles south of Hydro, Oklahoma, and 17 miles northwest of Binger.[68] Ghost Mound is actually taller than Lovecraft's mound, dominating the landscape even more than its fictional cousin does. Its ghostly legends describe mysterious white-clad figures, moving lights, and a human footprint in the rock-hard mud at the top of the mound left by a maiden who vanished (or died) while leaping off it. A different (possibly fictional) dead Native woman gave her name to Dead Woman Mound, five miles closer to Hydro, another possible source for the garbled story that reached Lovecraft from that barren ranch.

"Why would it never stop? Day and night, week on week, it was always going in exhaustless relays, as persistently as the red dusty winds that carried it."

— H.P. LOVECRAFT AND ZEALIA BISHOP, "THE CURSE OF YIG"

Lovecraft's frequent invocations of the wind and dust in "Curse of Yig" come perhaps from Zealia's local color, or from the 1925 frontier novel *The Wind*, by Dorothy Scarborough. Wind also blows into "The Mound," where "winds and forces" directly oppose the narrator as he tries to dig into the Binger mound, unleashing the "sinister up-pushing of a cold wind from below."

More likely, if Lovecraft heard of Oklahoma's famous wind, it simply joined the jet stream of his pre-existing nightmare symbolism. "The Hound" passes in "a wind, stronger than the night-wind," similar to the

68. I should point out that some local Binger partisans apparently root for Cougar Mound, eight miles west of Binger. Despite an entirely-too-plausible career path in which I involve myself in ferocious Lovecraftian Oklahoma mound-legend controversies, I'm satisfied with the consensus on Ghost Mound.

wind after the storm in "The Lurking Fear," the "vortex of withering, ice-cold wind" in "The Unnamable," and the "sudden, east-blowing wind" of "The Haunter of the Dark." Fetid winds likewise blow up during Curwen's sorceries in *Charles Dexter Ward*, and herald the return of Edward Derby in "The Thing on the Doorstep." Windstorms accompany the climaxes of "Juan Romero," "The Tree," and "The Moon-Bog."

A wind whistles from the abyss beneath "The Nameless City," "a howling tumult of ice-cold wind" emerges from the basement in "The Horror at Red Hook," and a "cavern wind" blows from the vaults "Under the Pyramids." A "demon mountain wind" that "held a particular strain of conscious malignity" blew out of the crinoid city *At the Mountains of Madness*, and the monstrous polyps control and even embody the winds blowing "out of the great huts under the ground, where terrible things have happened" in "The Shadow Out of Time." All of these match the "cold wind from below" the eponymous Mound.

> *"I had always felt, from well-defined undertones of legend and archaeology, that great Quetzalcoatl—benign snake-god of the Mexicans—had had an older and darker prototype; and during recent months I had well-nigh proved it in a series of researches stretching from Guatemala to the Oklahoma plains."*
>
> — H.P. LOVECRAFT AND ZEALIA BISHOP, "THE CURSE OF YIG"

Of course, another potential source of hideous tortures and strange mounds comes from south of Oklahoma, from Mesoamerica and specifically the Aztecs. Lovecraft seems to have granted "the ancient and noble Aztec" a certain honorary Classical status, based on their urban civilization and the sophistication of their mythology. (He owned at least two books dealing with pre-Columbian Mexico.) Juan Romero invokes the Aztec sun god Huitzilopochtli shortly before his titular transition, having previously hailed the sun "as if in the performance of some rite whose nature he did not himself comprehend." Romero's atavistic Aztec knowledge recalls the race-memory rituals from the later "Red Hook," a transition in itself from the earlier Lovecraftian motif of a population of isolated unnatural survivals.

This more usual Lovecraft antique cult shows up in "The Electric Executioner" (a rewrite of "The Automatic Executioner" by Adolphe de Castro) when Feldon rants, "God, if you knew the tribes I know! In the mountains—in the mountains—Anahuac—Tenochtitlan—the old ones." The narrator goes on to hysterically invoke Cthulhutl, Niguratl-Yig, and Yog-Sototl, inspiring Feldon to homicidal mania. De Castro's original story lacked not only these Mesoamerican Mythos names, but all the Aztec touches that Lovecraft added to the original story in a sort of desperate whimsy. His equation of the Mayan Kulkulkan and Aztec Quetzalcoatl with Yig in the Oklahoma stories seems more like an idea he took (fictively) seriously.[69]

> *"It was unmistakably a human shape, and I knew at once that I was seeing the daytime 'Indian ghost.' I did not wonder at the description, for surely the tall, lean, darkly robed being with the filleted black hair and seamed, coppery, expressionless, aquiline face looked more like an Indian than anything else in my previous experience. And yet my trained ethnologist's eye told me at once that this was no redskin of any sort hitherto known to history, but a creature of vast racial variation and of a wholly different culture-stream."*

— H.P. LOVECRAFT, "THE MOUND"

Native Americans appear in Lovecraft fairly often, even outside the Wichitas, Kickapoos, Pawnees, and Caddos in "The Mound" and "The Curse of Yig." Lovecraft mentions the Paiutes and Nez Perces in "Transition of Juan Romero" and "The Tree on the Hill," mostly as scene-setting elements. Named individual Natives surprisingly appear in a generally positive light, beginning with Juan Romero, who "gave not the least im-

---

69. Perhaps Lovecraft's interest in the Aztecs communicated itself to his protégé Robert Barlow. The latter became an anthropologist concentrating on Mesoamerican studies, teaching Nahuatl and Mayan at the Universidad Nacional and Mexico City College.

pression of Caucasian blood." "The Mound" adds the brave and informative Wichitas Grey Eagle and Charging Buffalo, heroes both, although Grey Eagle owes some of his longevity to his talisman of "Tulu metal." Similarly, the Wampanoag headman and "wonder-worker" Misquamacus both instructs the wizard Billington in sorcery and pens up the Thing that Billington summoned in the unpublished fragment "Of Evill Sorceries Done in New-England …" that Derleth turned into *The Lurker at the Threshold*. One imagines a similar track record for the "court astronomer of Pre-Inca Peru" in "Shadow Out of Time."

Even the unsavory mixed-breed John Eagle merely finds the titular "Diary of Alonzo Typer" rather than engaging in direct evil, unlike the "unhallowed rites and conclaves of the Indians" near Dunwich, or the degenerate "Esquimaux" cultists in "Call of Cthulhu." At least one of Joseph Curwen's "sullen pair of aged Narragansett servants" in *Charles Dexter Ward* comes from mixed stock. Like Misquamacus, "sartain half-breed red Indians" in "He" both teach the titular wizard Mythos lore and return (in tomahawk-wielding ghost-shoggoth form) to kill him. The "Peruvian of Indian blood" does nothing worse in "Out of the Aeons" than suffer a seizure in the Cabot Museum. In general Lovecraft agrees with his madman in "The Electric Executioner" that "the full-blood Indians—the real children of the feathered serpent—are sacred and inviolate except for proper sacrificial victims …" which is a much better deal than Lovecraft's white folks get.

American Indians also provide Lovecraft (and his characters) with evocative legends of, and plausible alternatives to, the Mythos. The Aleutians boast "prehistoric Indian specimens" of mummies in "Out of the Aeons," possible echoes of Ghatanothoan activity. Pennacook legend describes the Mi-Go in "Whisperer in Darkness" while the narrator of "The Shunned House" wishes for a Narragansett Indian legend about that unwholesome edifice. Meanwhile, anthropologists write off standing stones on Sentinel Hill as "the burial-places of the Pocumtucks" in "Dunwich Horror," and in Maine as Indian relics in "The Thing on the Doorstep." According to

"Colour Out of Space" and "Dreams in the Witch House" the locals know the stone altar in the Miskatonic River near Arkham is "older than the Indians," much like the white polypous thing in "Call of Cthulhu."

As Bret Kramer puts it, "More often for Lovecraft Natives were a marker to demonstrate the age or alien nature of a place or knowledge … Linking some place or knowledge to Native people is used to re-enforce their potency and imply a malign nature to the reader."[70] The Natives also wisely shun the Outside, as in "Tree on the Hill," "The Mound," and "Whisperer." It's in those latter tales that Lovecraft most clearly palms the card of Native precedence, instead presenting K'n-yani and Mi-Go as the true First Peoples. This relegates the Natives to "marker" status, but more positively allows HPL to transfer the Puritan horror of the frontier to his Outside entities.

"Oklahoma is a lot more than a mere pioneers' and promoters' frontier. There are old, old tribes with old, old memories there; and when the tom-toms beat ceaselessly over brooding plains in the autumn the spirits of men are brought dangerously close to primal, whispered things."

— H.P. LOVECRAFT AND ZEALIA BISHOP, "THE MOUND"

Lovecraft evokes that fear in *Supernatural Horror in Literature*, explicitly tying it to the country and to the Native Americans as symbols: "The vast and gloomy virgin forests in whose perpetual twilight all terrors might well lurk; the hordes of coppery Indians whose strange, saturnine visages and violent customs hinted strongly at traces of infernal origin …" In "The Mound," written eighteen months later, Lovecraft almost exactly recapitulates that fear. K'n-yan is a "vast and gloomy" land of "perpetual twilight" whose coppery folk bear "strange … visages" and practice extremely "violent customs" learned from deeper underground.

70. Angela Carter notes that the panoply of Native nomenclature in Lovecraft Country—Miskatonic, Pawtuxet, Manuxet—provides an uncanny survival of the extirpated Natives in "many settled regions abounding in graveyards." As she puts it: "The very absence of the Indians from their own forests embodies the estrangement of the alien country."

Besides the two Oklahoma stories, Lovecraft only sets one tale in the West, the early and repudiated "Transition of Juan Romero." It takes place in the Cactus Mountains of an unspecified region, which given the combination of silver mines and a mention of "Piutes" is most likely Nye County in southern Nevada, home of the Cactus Range. It, too, deals with a vast red-litten subterranean chasm, one that vanishes after a storm. Lovecraft knew little of the West besides the roughest of dime-novel notions, writing to Zealia in 1928 that he knew more of "Ctesiphon & the Parthian Empire, Samarcand & the Sogdianian plains beyond the Oxus, or Timbuctoo & the mysteries of the Saharan Hoggar region" than of Oklahoma.

I note that all the regions he mentioned were frontiers of the Classical world of antiquity: Ctesiphon and the Saharan Hoggar generally marking the eastern and southern frontiers of Rome, while Alexander's empire ended in "the Sogdianian plains beyond the Oxus." Oklahoma, too, serves as a frontier where both in the 1889 of "Yig" and in Lovecraft's present, civilization yields to wilderness. Lovecraft's Oklahoma tales also explicitly cross the frontier between Native and white, while "Juan Romero" does the same with the frontier between Mexican and Anglo.

Lovecraft thus extends Oklahoma into his own frontier, contrasting the recent settlement of the state with the "stupefying—almost horrible—ancientness of the West," limning his eternal frontier between the deep past and shallow present. His winds cross frontiers, blowing the literal atmosphere of one place to another, contaminating what should remain separate. In "The Mound," despite opening with the question, Lovecraft never explicitly develops the notion of the frontier as the "outside rim," rather treating the matter recursively. K'n-yan becomes (and very much transgresses) the border between humanity and Other, sitting atop its own too-porous boundaries with the pits of red-litten Yoth and black N'kai beneath it. He completed "The Mound" in January 1930, and the next month began "The Whisperer in Darkness." This true and magisterial examination of the Lovecraftian frontier returns to the east, and so do we.

VERMONT

"Something is alive that is dead elsewhere; something that we, or the blood that is in us, can recognize as more closely akin to ourselves than anything in the busy cosmopolis to the southward."

—H.P. LOVECRAFT, "VERMONT—A FIRST IMPRESSION" (1927)

With the exception of two brief mentions in "Sweet Ermengarde" and "The Shadow Over Innsmouth," both as character shorthand, Vermont for the Lovecraftian means ever and always "The Whisperer in Darkness." The Green Mountain State is the back of beyond, where the Mi-Go lurk, a haunted, desolate Transylvania just over the border from "the busy cosmopolis to the southward." And yet, and yet. By now, we have become used to Lovecraft's locations containing their own contradictions. Even those two passing mentions noted above cast Vermont in different lights: one as the home of gullible rubes, and the other as a font of hard-headed Yankees with no time for foolish stories about fish-men. In "Whisperer," Lovecraft likewise divides Vermonters into the skeptical "educated persons" and the rustic believers of "the more ignorant sort." And he never —never *quite*—lets us know which ones are correct.

"The whole matter began, so far as I am concerned, with the historic and unprecedented Vermont floods of November 3, 1927."

—H.P. LOVECRAFT, "THE WHISPERER IN DARKNESS"

"The Whisperer in Darkness" is a Fortean mystery, beginning with strange lights in the skies, bizarre footprints, and weird cryptid bodies found in the floods. Our hero Albert Wilmarth, the scientific-minded anthropologist, whipsaws between doubt, fear, and hope repeatedly over the course of the story. His interlocutor, Henry Akeley, is a local aristocrat "of character, education, and intelligence" but also "a recluse with very little worldly sophistication." Akeley begins as two people in one body, and continues horrifically down that path over the course of the novelette. What, exactly, happens, remains a question: Wilmarth reminds us that there is no proof of anything he says, and the story hints that Wilmarth might have dreamed the final shocking discovery—and possibly confabulated the horrific so-called truth about the Mi-Go, the Outer Ones, in a paranoid folie à deux.

This despite Lovecraft's insistence on the trappings of reason throughout: anthropological monographs, railroad timetables, photographic evidence, even a record cylinder. But all that evidence contradicts itself even before it disappears. Trying to assemble a coherent theory from the data nearly drives Wilmarth mad, even before he reaches Akeley's remote cabin. "Whisperer" is about rationality drowned by too much input, and it can be read as a kind of Heisenbergian updating of the old Newtonian horror universe. In this world, you can't even specifically locate the monsters—are they fungi? lobsters? alive? dead? sorcerers? scientists? ancient? modern? good? evil? Nyarlathotep? winged Indian demons? aliens?—much less find their wolvesbane or garlic and defeat them. Lovecraft takes the shadows and uncertainty and moves them from literary technique to scientific description—the Outer Ones are uncertain and indefinable, no matter how much you know about them. The seemingly clumsy morass of exposition is, again, part of the point. There's too much data, and it absolutely cannot be assembled into a coherent picture. If you doubt any of it, you must doubt all of it—and sure enough, it all vanishes, along with Akeley.

"My 'Whisperers in Darkness' will reflect a Vermont visit made in the same year [1928]. I am very fond of giving weird tales a minutely realistic setting as a sort of foil for the unreal extravagancies of the central theme."

—H.P. LOVECRAFT, LETTER TO J. VERNON SHEA (JUNE 19, 1931)

So let's go back to the "minutely realistic setting," and start again. Lovecraft first visited Vermont in August of 1927, a brief trip to see the poet Arthur Goodenough. The landscape—and especially rural Vermont's lack of connection to the commercial, immigrant-plagued world of Lovecraft's southern New England—charmed him into writing the panegyric "Vermont —A First Impression," much of which he recycled in a darker key for "Whisperer."

In June of 1928, he returned for a two-week stay with the editor Vrest Orton at a farmhouse near Brattleboro that (along with Goodenough's home) became the model for the Akeley place in "Whisperer." The "Pendrifter" column mentioned in the tale actually appeared in the Brattleboro *Reformer.* HPL borrowed the name Akeley from a local eccentric artist named Bert Akley, and other names (Wilmarth, Davenport, Noyes, Lee's Swamp) came from graveyards and local families. As he did in "Dunwich," Lovecraft repurposed local legendry, this time Abnaki tales of winged gods and monsters that HPL reassigned to the extinct Pennacook tribe in order to tweak them into the desired literary and cosmic form.

> *"The nearness and intimacy of the little domed hills have become almost breath-taking. Their steepness and abruptness hold nothing in common with the humdrum, standardized world we know, and we cannot help feeling that their outlines have some strange and almost-forgotten meaning, like vast hieroglyphs left by a rumored titan race . . ."*

> —H.P. LOVECRAFT, "VERMONT—A FIRST IMPRESSION" (1927)

Just so, he tweaked the wild landscape of Vermont into a place of horror and wonder. Lovecraft replicated the above description almost exactly in section VI of "Whisperer": the "little, domed hills" became "dwarfed," only one of the adjectives HPL applies to hills he thought (in a letter to Donald Wandrei) "worthy of Machen's Gwent country." "Whisperer" shews us "wild, domed hills," a "bald, lonely hill," "haunted hills," "lonely green hills," "grim, green sentinels," "shunned hills," both "wild hills" and "haunted hills" and "wild, haunted hills," "silent and problematical hills" and (tying for best adjective) "green and cryptical hills," and finally "half-unknown hills." Atop these hills, of course, are monoliths, and "caves of problematical depth," and an incised black stone also straight out of Machen.

Other changes Lovecraft rang on his "first impression" include a new line: "The dense, unvisited woods on those inaccessible slopes seemed to harbour alien and incredible things," and indeed they do: the Outer Ones. Further, the hills in "Whisperer" contrast not just with the "standardized" world but with the objective world, a sign that Vermont is a doorstep to Lovecraft's supersensible Outside. Their meaning is not "almost-forgotten" in the tale, but "aeon-forgotten," deepening the cosmic vistas of Lovecraftian deep time.

> *"There would be odd survivals of that continuous native life whose deep roots make it the one authentic outgrowth of the landscape—the continuous native life which keeps alive strange ancient memories, and fertilises the soil for shadowy, marvellous, and seldom-mentioned beliefs."*
>
> —H.P. LOVECRAFT, "THE WHISPERER IN DARKNESS"

Lovecraft transposes his own delight in the "deep roots" of Vermonters and their folkways into a Gothic terror, a terror of the terroir, if you will. As he wrote to August Derleth, he wrote "Whisperer" in order to "crystallise a powerful imaginative impression given to me by a certain landscape"—namely, those "green and cryptical hills." Note, in that context, that Lovecraft makes his weird fiction just as much an "authentic outgrowth of the landscape" as any of the "odd survivals" or "strange ancient memories" of the Vermont that he or Wilmarth explored in 1928. For Lovecraft, "continuous native life" is itself weird horror, and vice versa. Even more than the Marblehead-Kingsport duality we've noticed before, Vermont is perhaps Lovecraft's greatest triumph of the dualistic setting: delight and dread intermixed so finely as to be inseparable. With "Vermont—A First Impression" overlaid onto "Whisperer," the double nature of Lovecraft's settings leaps into stereoscopic clarity.

> *"I could tell that I was at the gateway of a region half-bewitched through the piling-up of unbroken time-accumulations; a region where old, strange things have had a chance to grow and linger because they have never been stirred up."*

> —H.P. LOVECRAFT, "THE WHISPERER IN DARKNESS"

In an October 1935 letter to Alvin Perry, Lovecraft mentions "the general impression of weirdness in Vermont's landscape," an impression doubtless intensified by the sheer emptiness of Vermont to the citified Lovecraft. For all his love of rambling nature walks, Lovecraft seldom praises the wilderness in the tones he uses for Randolph Carter's sunset city, or for his own beloved Providence. Although he delights in the isolated, forgotten towns and trackless forests of Vermont, he responds to them with a thrill of horror as well.

The "shunned hills" of this "wild, lonely region" certainly appear of a piece with other Lovecraftian wildernesses, such the "strangely domed hills" outside Dunwich or the abomination of desolation in "The Colour Out of Space." Akeley's Dark Mountain might well be Tempest Mountain in "The Lurking Fear," and the Mi-Go's haunts atop the crag echo the god-tainted summit of Kingsport Head in "The Strange High House in the Mist," or even beetling Mt. Hatheg-Kla in "The Other Gods." Throughout Lovecraft, mountains (of madness, or any other kind) are seldom benevolent, and never safe. However, they often hold great potential knowledge, such as the true form of the gods carved into Mt. Ngranek in *The Dream-Quest of Unknown Kadath.*

> *"The ways of the Vermonters became settled; and once their habitual paths and dwellings were established according to a certain fixed plan, they remembered less and less what fears and avoidances had determined that plan . . ."*

> —H.P. LOVECRAFT, "THE WHISPERER IN DARKNESS"

Lovecraft's Vermonters, both red and white, eventually learned to avoid those "silent and problematical hills." The Natives and the Winged Ones came to a modus vivendi; so, eventually, do the white colonists and the Mi-Go. The positive space of human settlement and the negative space of the Outer Ones define each other; the act of establishing a boundary also establishes an inextricable linkage. If Vermont is, in Lovecraft's "First Impression" words, "a surviving fragment of the old America," then America is defined by the Outer Ones: the "fears and avoidances" are inextricably part of the map and the territory.

Akeley and Wilmarth want to keep the boundary inviolate, keep the two aspects of Vermont separate, but fear that collapse and contamination are inevitable. Akeley and Wilmarth worry that "promoters and real estate men flooding Vermont with herds of summer people" from Lovecraft's swarming "cosmopolis to the south" will upset that balance, cross boundaries that should not be crossed. With the same italicized fear he expresses of being taken by the aliens, Akeley writes: *People must be kept away from these hills.*

> *"As we passed out of Brattleboro, my sense of constraint and foreboding increased, for a vague quality in the hill-crowded countryside with its towering, threatening, close-pressing green and granite slopes hinted at obscure secrets and immemorial survivals which might or might not be hostile to mankind."*

—H.P. LOVECRAFT, "THE WHISPERER IN DARKNESS"

What Akeley fears, and Wilmarth senses, is "the contagion of the morbid barrier-breaking"—that the boundary cannot hold, neither within themselves nor out in the woods. Vermont is already a fantastic, mythical realm, alive with monsters. Its woods are "a fantastic world of hushed unreality." In its hills, "Time had lost itself in the labyrinths behind." Wilmarth sees a "strangely calming element of cosmic beauty in the hypnotic landscape," and notes that "even the sunlight assumed a supernal glamour." He compares the vista of Vermont to the view in the background of a Renaissance painting; the unearthly impression intensifies in the total silence outside the Akeley farm. The boundaries become overlays. Just as Akeley doubles both Wilmarth and the Mi-Go, Dark Mountain (and the inside of Akeley's fine colonial house, choked in darkness and alien odors) doubles both Vermont and Yuggoth.

In that remote countryside, first and foremost, both Vermont (a "black, mysteriously forested slope") and Yuggoth (a lightless "world of fungoid gardens") are dark. Human eyes have just begun to chart their reaches; both have traces of extinct primordial races left in enigmatic profusion. Vermont features "archaic covered bridges linger[ing] fear-somely out of the past" while Yuggoth features "mysterious Cyclopean bridges—things built by some elder race." A "gurgling and insidious trickle of strange waters from numberless hidden fountains in the shad-owy woods" typifies Vermont's rivers, compared to the "black rivers of pitch" on Yuggoth. The Outer Ones were on Earth before mankind; it is humanity that trespasses on Yuggoth's mines, not the other way around. It is this realization that trickles away within Wilmarth, as he listens to the whisperer offering ineffable truths and impossible voyages outside time and space.

"The houses, each taken by itself, may be ugly enough; yet their arrangements in curving hill lanes and alleys, and the massed silhouette made by their blended roofs and chimneys against the sky, may possess a charm, poignancy, and absolute art value of the highest sort."

—H.P. LOVECRAFT, LETTER TO WOODBURN HARRIS (MARCH 1, 1929)

The individual houses of Brattleboro or Marblehead are homely, even ugly. The town, the collective, the civilization is beautiful. The Outer Ones are hideous; their offer of knowledge is transcendent. The Mi-Go are the first of Lovecraft's great races: monsters, yes, but also "men!" The scientific determination of the crinoids in *Mountains of Madness*, the genetic glory of the Deep Ones in "Shadow Over Innsmouth," the cool bibliomania of the Great Race in "Shadow Out of Time"—all begin with the Faustian seductions of the fungi from Yuggoth. Wilmarth's "zeal for the unknown" is Lovecraft's "adventurous expectancy." Wilmarth wishes so desperately "to be linked with the vast outside" that he disregards every hint of common sense. In his "ardour for strange delvings" (so like the Mi-Go with their appetite for curious mines) he wishes "to come close to the nighted and abysmal secrets of the infinite and the ultimate ..." And in Vermont, those nighted secrets wait for whoever dares to climb the hills.

THE BRITISH ISLES

"Gabinius had, the rumour ran, come upon a cliffside cavern where strange folk met together and made the Elder Sign in the dark; strange folk whom the Britons knew not save in fear, and who were the last to survive from a great land in the west that had sunk, leaving only the islands with the raths and circles and shrines of which Stonehenge was the greatest."

— H.P. LOVECRAFT, "THE DESCENDANT"

Lovecraft archly and eerily prefigures Howard's Hyboria in this passage, written perhaps in mid-1927. Two years before Kull and five years before Conan, he depicts the British Isles as remnants of a sunken continent. But with the exception of the revision tale "The Horror in the Museum" (written in October of 1932), this fragment marks the last time Lovecraft set a tale in England and ends a "British Cycle," if you will, running from "Facts Concerning the Late Arthur Jermyn and His Family" and "Celephaïs" through twin bromantic horror stories "Hypnos" and "The Hound" and climaxing in "The Rats in the Walls."

HPL at least briefly features England in three later stories. Kuranes, having tired of Celephaïs, comes on stage in *The Dream-Quest of Unknown Kadath* and reminisces about his English home, going so far as to re-create a petit England in the Dreamlands. Lovecraft identifies Sussex as the home of the Eltdown Shards (or at least their translator, the Reverend Arthur Brooke Winters-Hall) in his portion of "The Challenge From Beyond." And finally and curiously, Charles Dexter Ward doesn't pay nearly enough attention to London.

*"That he said nothing of antiquarian rambles in the glamorous old city
with its luring skyline of ancient domes and steeples and its tangles of
roads and alleys whose mystic convolutions and sudden vistas alternately
beckon and surprise, was taken by his parents as a good index of the degree
to which his new interests had engrossed his mind."*

— H.P. LOVECRAFT, *THE CASE OF CHARLES DEXTER WARD*

The man who is tired of London, to contradict Lovecraft's much-loved Dr.
Johnson, may just be busy researching the resurrection of his dead ancestor. To
an even greater extent than Boston, London generally represents the conventional, rational world in Lovecraft's tales: the "indifferent millions of London"
care nothing for Kuranes' agonies, the narrator flees to London for imagined
refuge from "The Hound," Delapore goes to London to obtain "eminent authorities" and "archaeologists and scientific men," and Ward's neglect of "antiquarian rambles" in London signposts his entry into an occult world.

That said, fictioneers had been casting London as an occult world for at least
four decades by the time Lovecraft got around to it, beginning with Robert
Louis Stevenson in *New Arabian Nights* (1882). That story collection kicked
off a trend, portraying London as a fantastic, or at least Hermetic, metropolis,
full of weird adventures just around the corner from its staid Victorian landmarks: a "Baghdad-on-the-Thames," in the later words of Lin Carter (with a
little help from Henry Mancini). Carter's tag specifically referred to Arthur
Machen's *The Three Impostors* (1895), another linked story cycle of mysterious
secrets in London. Machen later wrote, in his 1923 memoir *Things Near and
Far:* "All the wonders lie within a stone's throw of King's Cross Station."

That was just before Lovecraft assures us, in the story "He," that London is
"a sentient perpetuation" of "Old London" and that this is a good thing, which
seems palpably unlikely given the regular run of Lovecraft's sentient perpetu-
ations. The British Museum holds the *Necronomicon* (per the "Dunwich Horror") and it holds Ward's attention, but it never receives Lovecraftian focus.
Set in Southwark, "The Horror in the Museum" evokes London's famous

wax museum, Madame Tussaud's, but it might have been set anywhere. It's in "Hypnos" where Lovecraft most fully contrasts secret London and public London, staging the meeting of the narrator and his muse that most quotidian of locations, a railway station. (Recall the role of railroads as mundane extrusions in "Shadow Over Innsmouth" and "Whisperer in Darkness," for example.) The two then pursue magical pathworking and artistic exaltation in "hoary Kent," followed by drug binges amongst the bohemian set in the heart of London. The story finally ends with mundane London victorious and the complete effacement of the narrator's magical master.

Lovecraft didn't know London well enough to make "Hypnos" the equal of Stevenson or Machen, a fault he attempted to rectify in the spring of 1927 with a major research deep dive. This "very minute study of London from books, maps, & pictures" was preparation for writing a series of tales set in London, which eventually yielded only "The Descendant." Aside from that fragment's superb opening line, "In London there is a man who screams when the church bells ring," and the *Fungi From Yuggoth* poem "St. Toad's," inspired by a London dream during that research binge, there's not much left of Lovecraft's London.

> *"England! Old England! in my love for thee*
> *No dream is mine, but blessed memory;*
> *Such haunting images and hidden fires*
> *Course with the bounding blood of British sires:*
> *From British bodies, minds, and souls I come,*
> *And from them draw the vision of their home."*

— H.P. LOVECRAFT, "AN AMERICAN TO MOTHER ENGLAND" (1916)

His fogginess on London notwithstanding, Lovecraft firmly emphasizes his own English ancestry throughout his letters and his poetry, and every so often in his fiction. But as we've seen throughout this Tour, the more HPL fervently adores a thing, the darker and more fuscous he paints it. For Lovecraft, the matter of England becomes the matter of blood:

"Arthur Jermyn," "Celephaïs," "Rats in the Walls," and "The Descendant" all deal with ancestry, and specifically with deep English ancestry. Lord Northam in "The Descendant" and (arguably) Delapore in "Rats in the Walls" trace their lineage into the North of England, and Delapore follows his deeper yet, as we'll do ourselves on this Stop.

In "Celephaïs," Kuranes' final ride literally traces his lifeline backward, from London through the Surrey Downs "toward the region where Kuranes and his ancestors were born" and back through "thirteen generations" past knights on horseback through villages "Chaucer or men before him might have seen" to end up in his ancestral Trevor Towers manor somewhere in Somerset or Devonshire.[71] This, not coincidentally, is where Lovecraft believed his own ancestral roots lay; he tugs on them again when the narrator of "The Mound" harkens back to his forefathers, those "settled, homekeeping gentlemen of Somerset and Devon."

In the character Arthur Jermyn, Lovecraft paints his double: "a poet and a dreamer" of dubious yet aristocratic blood. Lovecraft's mother described her son as "hideous," and Arthur Jermyn's features inspire repulsion. Kenneth W. Faig draws parallels between the institutionalizations of Sir Wade and Sir Robert Jermyn and the confinement in Butler Hospital of Lovecraft's father Winfield. Like Winfield Lovecraft, Sir Alfred Jermyn suffers his breakdown in Chicago; Lovecraft like Arthur Jermyn returns to his beloved family home after his father's attack. We can't narrow the location of Jermyn House down more specifically than "the moor," almost a synecdoche for Gothic England.

"... [A]ncient faiths and ancient rites stirred stealthily, and the pale moon of Britain looked sometimes on strange deeds in the Roman ruins of Caerleon and Hexham, and by the towers along Hadrian's crumbling wall."

— H.P. LOVECRAFT, *THE CASE OF CHARLES DEXTER WARD*

71. In *The Dream-Quest of Unknown Kadath*, Kuranes' dream version of his home is "a little Cornish fishing village" stocked with "such people as had the most English faces." This combination, plus the cliff his body falls over in "Celephaïs," argues for either Cornwall or more likely Devon (the next county eastward) as his ancestral county.

England's original Goths, of course, were the Saxons, who toppled Roman civilization in England and then fell to the Normans, leaving those ur-Gothic ruins ("the debased Romanesque of the bungling Saxons") behind. For all their atmospheric qualities, Lovecraft mostly skips over the centuries between his beloved Rome and his properly feudal England. The main exception to Lovecraft's Saxon darkness comes in *Charles Dexter Ward*, with the brief appearance of the mysterious magus from jar "No. 118." He writes in the "Saxon miniscules of the 8th or 9th century A.D." and wields enough rude power to terrify Curwen and demolish Orne and Hutchinson.

But that's all. Even the architecture of Northam Keep skips directly from "the masonry of Hadrian's Wall" to the medieval fortifications of Edward III's reign, just as the Northam blood remains a Roman lineage "which Pict and Saxon, Dane and Norman, were powerless to obliterate." In his 1927 letter to Clark Ashton Smith on the topic of St. Toad's, Lovecraft mentions a dream of its "pre-Norman crypt," a possible echo of the cultic peak of Exham Priory "about 1000 A.D." But like Exham itself, Lovecraft goes deeper, into the Roman past of Britain.

> *"Anchester had been the camp of the third Augustan legion, as many remains attest, and it was said that the temple of Cybele was splendid and thronged with worshippers who performed nameless ceremonies at the bidding of a Phrygian priest."*
>
> — H.P. LOVECRAFT, "THE RATS IN THE WALLS"

Lovecraft, like Alexander Pope and Oliver Goldsmith, strongly identified his own beloved eighteenth century with the "Augustan Age," and England with Rome. His degenerate cults and monsters threaten "the severe and harmonious classicism of the age of the Caesars" in 30 A.D. and 1730 A.D. alike. Thus, for Lovecraft, Roman Britain doubles down on civilization.

His Roman Britain hosts the "Third Augustan Legion," which in our history remained in North Africa for its entire existence. J.-M. Rajala plausibly suggests Lovecraft simply incremented up one from the historical Second Augustan Legion, based in Caerleon in Wales, possibly in order to leave that part of Roman Britain to Arthur Machen. David Haden further postulates that the "African" Third Legion proved more congenial to Lovecraft as a transmitter of degenerate cults than the wholesome "British" Second Legion in Caerleon.

Lovecraft's Third Legion is stationed at Lindum (modern Lincoln) in "The Descendant," and in the fictitious "Anchester" in "Rats in the Walls." There turns out to be an Ancaster in Lincolnshire, on a Roman town site even, which you'd think would settle the matter. But Lovecraft deploys his legion even farther north. Northam Keep and its Roman foundation lie "on the Yorkshire coast," hard by Hadrian's Wall, for example. Jedediah Orne's mention in *Charles Dexter Ward* of "Sylvanus Cocidius" appearing "in ye Vault under ye Roman Wall" also points north: Hadrian's Wall features numerous images and dedications to Cocidius, a British forest god, the equivalent of the Roman Sylvanus. And finally, Hexham itself lies only a few miles south of the Wall.

"And this week workmen have blown up Exham Priory, and are busy obliterating the traces of its foundations."

— H.P. LOVECRAFT, "THE RATS IN THE WALLS"

Both S.T. Joshi and David Haden consider Hexham Priory the model in name for Lovecraft's Exham Priory. Haden notes the story's mention (twice!) of the aurora, further implying a northern location. Haden goes further still and identifies Anchester (three miles east of Exham) with the city of Corbridge, the Roman Corstopitum, three miles east of Hexham. And indeed, in 1909, archaeologists discovered idols and inscriptions of Cybele and Atys (who figure in "Rats in the Walls") in Corbridge. Further, Haden has uncovered the story of Dilston Castle, abandoned near Hexham by the evocatively named *Rat*cliffe family after the last Earl's execution—under an aurora borealis.

The home of St. John and the narrator in "The Hound" provides Love-craft with something of a rehearsal for Exham Priory. The Decadent grave-robbing lads dwell in "great stone house," an "ancient manor-house on a bleak and unfrequented moor" complete with a corpse-stuffed "se-cret room, far, far underground." Haden suggests more models: the "stone mangers" in Aryton Castle (near Corbridge) paralleling the "stone pens" in Exham Priory, and the position of Dilston Castle on a "steep bank" reminiscent of Exham Priory's "steep precipice."

But why would Lovecraft stumble upon all these details in the Hexham chapter of *Highways and Byways of Northumberland* (1921)? Because his own paternal grandmother Helen Allgood descended from the Allgoods of Nunwick, "near Hexham" as he wrote to Frank Belknap Long in 1927, emphasizing "I knew all that before!" Lovecraft's father—the madman, whose blood Lovecraft worried might have polluted him—thus descends from Jermyn House *and* from Exham Priory!

"For all his love of Ireland, America had not left him untouched, and he hated the beautiful wasted space."

— H.P. LOVECRAFT, "THE MOON-BOG"

Let's leave Exham behind, for the time being, and visit the other isle in question: Ireland. Lovecraft sets only "The Moon-Bog" in Ireland, specifi-cally in Kilderry. This is not the Kilderry in County Kerry in the far west of Ireland, but a fictitious one in County Meath northwest of Dublin. Denys Barry's last name (from the Welsh-Norman de Barry family) would indi-cate County Kerry, but the story explicitly calls out not just County Meath but nearby Ballylough in Ulster.[72] Besides a reference to Greek temples from the Irish legendary *Book of Invasions*, Lovecraft does very little with the country, preferring to concentrate on the classical haunts thereunder. The titular bog might be anywhere.

---

72. Or he might have just made up the name: the story's Ballylough is south of Kilderry, and large enough to have the area's railway station. The actual Ballylough is north of County Meath, and barely registers on maps. There is a larger (pop. <2,000 in 1920) town of Ballyloughcoe in County Westmeath, which Lovecraft might have borrowed. However, he wrote "The Moon-Bog" in less than a day, with evidently minimal research.

Ireland also appears in "The Call of Cthulhu," depicted as a primitive island "full of wild rumour and legendry" roiled by the rise of Cthulhu, just like Haiti and the Philippines and Brooklyn. "The Whisperer in Darkness" also primitivizes Ireland, citing "wild Wales and Ireland" with "their strange, small, and terrible races of troglodytes and burrowers." Finally, HPL compares the Old Ones' city in Antarctica to the Giants' Causeway north of County Antrim in Ulster: again, Ireland the primeval.

As against that, Lovecraft's Irish characters are, with stunning originality, for the most part cops. But not primitive ones, to be sure. The policeman in "Haunter of the Dark" is a "great wholesome Irishman" and Malone in "The Horror at Red Hook" is "a Dublin University man born in a Georgian villa near Phoenix Park." (Along with his poetic past, that Georgian villa tips us off as to Malone's real worth.) Even the Irish immigrant mob in Providence in "Haunter of the Dark" has the bravery and public spirit to drive the Starry Wisdom cult out of town in 1869.

"We did not pause long, but shiveringly began to clear a passage down the steps. It was then that Sir William, examining the hewn walls, made the odd observation that the passage, according to the direction of the strokes, must have been chiselled from beneath."

— H.P. LOVECRAFT, "THE RATS IN THE WALLS"

Lovecraft's Ireland, therefore, is primitive, fallen from its Greek past, but its sons are stalwart and true. England represents civilization, built on its Roman past, but beset by (and productive of) degenerates. In both "The Moon-Bog" and the later "Rats in the Walls" an American returns to his ancestral home and restores it, uncovering something ancient and uncanny beneath the surface. But Denys Barry is a colonizer in Ireland, with no true roots: Artemis draws him up out of her bog-temple and into the sky. Delapore, however, belongs to the land of England, drawn back by blood and pulled down by atavism: Cybele buries him and his sanity deep in the earth, driving him down beneath Britain, to Nyarlathotep.

LENG

"Mythologists have placed Leng in Central Asia; but the racial memory of man—or of his predecessors—is long, and it may well be that certain tales have come down from lands and mountains and temples of horror earlier than Asia and earlier than any human world we know. ... Leng, wherever in space or time it might brood, was not a region I would care to be in or near."

— H.P. LOVECRAFT, *AT THE MOUNTAINS OF MADNESS*

We first hear of Leng in "Celephaïs," and hear more of it in "The Hound." We actually penetrate that brooding plateau in *The Dream-Quest of Unknown Kadath,* and in the poem "The Elder Pharos" in the *Fungi From Yuggoth* cycle. From a certain speculative viewpoint, almost all the action of *At the Mountains of Madness* occurs in Leng, and it's by this point that even the uncanniest of geographers becomes a trifle nervous. Lovecraft weaves a few new threads into our disturbing Leng rug in an extended citation in "Through the Gates of the Silver Key."

Leng also surfaces fleetingly in "Whisperer in Darkness," but what doesn't? "Out of the Aeons" briefly name-checks our dread country, as does its fellow Hazel Heald revision tale "The Horror in the Museum." Both provide Leng as a somewhat contradictory provenance for incidental malignities, introducing fragments of detail that resolutely refuse to cohere. As we search for Leng, we encounter such fragments repeatedly, the earliest perhaps being an early hint in "Beyond the Wall of Sleep." In that 1919 tale, a star-entity informs the narrator that: "We shall meet again— perhaps in the shining mists of Orion's Sword, perhaps on a bleak plateau in prehistoric Asia." Leng might also be one of the "farther uplands of Thibet" mentioned in "The Last Test" as a source of the "black fever."

"... once barely escaping from the high-priest not to be described, which wears a yellow silken mask over its face and dwells all alone in a prehistoric stone monastery on the cold desert plateau of Leng."

– H.P. LOVECRAFT, "CELEPHAÏS"

So where is Leng? Clearly it's in the Dreamlands, a land of "horrible stone villages" ruled by the High Priest in the Yellow Mask. Lovecraft derived this image not from Robert W. Chambers' King in Yellow (which he wouldn't encounter until 1927) but from the Veiled Prophet, the sorcerer Mokanna in Thomas Moore's 1817 epic poem "Lalla-Rookh."[73] "Celephaïs" also first identifies Leng as a "cold desert plateau," one of the few signifiers to stick to Leng throughout its transmogrifications.

In *Dream-Quest*, Lovecraft provides the greatest tranche of information on Leng. He all but reveals the High Priest in the Yellow Mask as a moonbeast, in cahoots with Nyarlathotep's servant the "slant-eyed merchant." That worthy's nationality remains discreetly hidden, although he boasts of trade with Leng and "looked queerly intelligent when the cold waste was spoken of." This provides Carter, and us, a connection between Leng and Kadath in the Cold Waste to which we shall return. The merchant further resembles the "squat, slant-eyed" slaves in the city of Inganok, who "drifted somehow across or around the impassible peaks from valleys beyond Leng."

However, the men of Leng themselves have wide mouths, dwarfish tails, and hooves; they wear turbans to disguise their horns. They kidnap Carter and shanghai him on a black galley they sail between Dylath-Leen and the Moon. (A Freudian critic, should any of that antique breed survive, could surely make hay out of Lovecraft's fear-fantasy of being kidnapped by nofooling satyrs.) The men of Leng, it turns out, serve the moon-beasts. As a final filip, we hear that purple spiders infest the valleys of Leng.

---

73. Lovecraft read Moore; his narrator quotes Moore's 1840 poem "Alciphron" while digging in "The Nameless City."

Although Lovecraft mentions "evil fires ... seen at night from afar" beforehand, in "The Elder Pharos" we suddenly hear that the monastery of the Veiled Priest is also a mighty lighthouse emitting a blue beacon beam. That poem also describes the alien Thing that "wears a silken mask / of yellow" and as much as states that this "last Elder One" speaks to Nyarlathotep ("Chaos with the beat of drums") so it's definitely the Dreamland Leng so lit. In *Dream-Quest,* a possibly related "pallid beacon" shines from a window of the gods' castle atop Kadath, in the "carven mountains" north of both Inganok and Leng. In the poem, the Elder Pharos attracted seekers "in man's first youth"; Will Murray suggests that it's a navigational beacon for galleys from the Moon. Finding Leng isn't so easy, it seems, as we'll shortly discover.

> *"... we recognised it as the thing hinted of in the forbidden* Necronomicon *of the mad Arab Abdul Alhazred; the ghastly soul-symbol of the corpse-eating cult of inaccessible Leng, in Central Asia. All too well did we trace the sinister lineaments described by the old Arab daemonologist; lineaments, he wrote, drawn from the souls of those who vexed and gnawed at the dead."*
>
> — H.P. LOVECRAFT, "THE HOUND"

Where is Leng? Lovecraft explicitly places it "in Central Asia." Even a few Dream details mesh with that location, beginning with the "high impassible mountains" that cut Leng off from Inganok. The men of Leng once dwelt in Sarkomand, which "lies in the valley below Leng" guarded by statues of titanic winged lions. A ship for "Lelag-Leng" gets as close as one can to Sarkomand by sea nowadays, apparently.

Lovecraft derived the name "Sarkomand" fairly clearly from the Central Asian city of Samarkand, best known to him from James Elroy Flecker's 1913 poem "The Golden Journey to Samarkand." Samarkand, while not the "primordial" city of Lovecraft's depiction, does pre-date the Persian Empire, and lies in the valley below the Pamir plateau in what would have been Russian Turkestan to Lovecraft.[74] Tamerlane made Samarkand his capital, flying his lion-and-sun standard above the city; lions likewise decorate the Sher-Dor Madrassa in the city's Registan, or main square.

The Leng of "The Hound" points east of Samarkand toward China, its "soul-symbol" being "exquisitely carved in antique Oriental fashion from a small piece of green jade." Further, the "corpse-eating cult" of Leng echoes a practice ascribed to the Bonpa practitioners of Tibet by the anarchist and occultist Alexandra David-Néel: "A morsel of … transformed flesh, when eaten, will produce a special kind of ecstasy and bestow knowledge and supernormal powers upon the person partaking of it." The flesh comes, at least in her version, from the tongue of a corpse bitten off during the *Ro-langs* ritual. Given that David-Néel described this necrophagy in 1929 (and Lovecraft entered it into his Commonplace Book in 1933) we remain at a loss for the actual source where in 1922 Lovecraft encountered exotic Tibetan magic, if indeed he did. (In 1927, he namechecks "Bonpa priests" in "The Last Test.") His edition (the 9th) of the *Britannica* does use the inviting phrase "professional corpse butchers" when describing the Tibetan funerary custom of exposing the dead to be devoured by "beasts and birds of prey."

It's also barely possible that Lovecraft stumbled onto a mention somewhere of the actual Tibetan kingdom of Ling, also called Tsang-Ling in some sources. Ling's main claim to fame comes from being the home country of Tibet's epic hero, King Gesar. However, Lovecraft shows no sign of familiarity with Tibetan epics, and his *Britannica* doesn't mention Ling or King Gesar in its survey of Tibetan geography.[75] Likewise, no map in that edition depicts the mining village of Leng-hu (Lenghu today) in Tsinghai province. Tsinghai was part of Tibet before the Chinese con-

---

74. It's unlikely Lovecraft ever heard of the small city of Lenger in modern-day southern Kazakhstan. Its name apparently comes from a Turkic word meaning "station" or "rest-house."

75. In the history section, it does mention the unrelated, but assonant, Liang dynasty; the 11th edition (1910) also mentions "Kesar" and uses the word *ling* to mean a book of the epic.

quest in 1724, but Leng-hu itself only dates from the discovery of oil in the territory after Lovecraft wrote.

> *"Thanks for the sinister glimpse of Bho-Blôk, the Daemon Lama of Night & Abhorred Leng. Rrrrgh ... but all the hidden, festering evil of pathless Thibet leers from those balefully arching brows!"*

— H.P. LOVECRAFT, LETTER TO ROBERT BLOCH (LATE JUNE, 1933)

The brief references to Leng in "Through the Gates of the Silver Key" and "Out of the Aeons" likewise seem to place that dire tableland in Asia, though not as specifically as "The Hound" does. In the first of those, Lovecraft mentions a yogi who visited "Yian-Ho, the hidden legacy of sinister, aeon-old Leng," implying (though certainly not mandating) a physical country somewhere in Asia. Yian-Ho, which we shall visit again in a bit, becomes the heir or successor to Leng, much as Irem of the Pillars does to the Nameless City: Lovecraft evoking his ongoing twinning pattern while tying this new city into his older mythology. Even more clearly, "Out of the Aeons" places cults of the Pacific god Ghatanothoa "in ill-fated Atlantis, and on the abhorred plateau of Leng." Paralleling the physical (albeit vanished) Atlantis with Leng again implies an Earthly geographical location, somewhat distant from the Pacific.

In April 1933, between finishing "Gates" and writing "Aeons," Lovecraft began corresponding with Robert Bloch, a young writer fascinated by HPL's burgeoning mythos, and especially, it seems, by Leng. In May, he defines Leng to Bloch in a letter as "a cold & horrible plateau inhabited by a nameless race of priests who dwell inside windowless stone towers & traffic with Outside powers." Lovecraft further added that humans visiting Leng never return. Bloch sketched a self-portrait as the "Lama of Leng," and Lovecraft dubbed him "Bho-Blôk," inditing later letters to Bloch "At the Pharos in Leng" and at the "Citadel of Leng." He famously gave Bloch permission to kill him in a story, including a document to that effect witnessed by the "Tcho-Tcho Lama of Leng." In 1933, the Dalai and Panchen Lamas still governed Tibet, of course. Lovecraft's epistolary lama, along with David-Néel's necrophagous legends, leads Robert M. Price to essentially identify Leng with Tibet, in much the same way that Kingsport "is" Marblehead or Arkham "is" Salem.[76]

> *"All this while the land was getting higher, and finally they came to a windswept table-land which seemed the very roof of a blasted and tenantless world. There, all alone in the hush and the dusk and the cold, rose the uncouth stones of a squat windowless building, around which a circle of crude monoliths stood. In all this arrangement there was nothing human, and Carter surmised from old tales that he was indeed come to that most dreadful and legendary of all places ..."*
>
> — H.P. LOVECRAFT, *THE DREAM-QUEST OF UNKNOWN KADATH*

But the boundary of Leng is hardly clear-cut. The Dreamlands and Central Asia overlap throughout the legend-pattern: for example, the "sinister lineaments" in "The Hound" depict canine corpse-eaters, evoking the ghouls of the Dreamlands. The fires and stone huts could come from nightmares or travelers' tales alike. The music of Dreamland Leng includes "a shrill droning of pipes and a nauseous rattle of crotala," which Lovecraft marks as "Asiatic" music throughout his stories, for example in "Red Hook" and the "yellow, squint-eyed" future New York of "He."

The notion of a "cold desert plateau" full of weird noises likewise evokes the "singing sands" of the Takla Makan wasteland in Xinjiang, crossed by Marco Polo and other medieval wonder-mongers. Travelers in that cold desert plateau heard and saw eerily familiar voices and shapes, ascribed to demons by the locals. In 1245, Joannes de Pian described those locals as deformed, beardless cannibals; Marco Polo seems to refer to Tibet when he describes "extraordinary marvels and sorceries" of "diabolic art" practiced nearby. Perhaps significantly, Lovecraft's letter to Bloch of mid-

---

76. Lovecraft's December 1927 letter to Frank Belknap Long in which he humorously boasts of slaying "the yellow-veiled priest at Lhasa" also clearly demonstrates at least his willingness to conflate Tibet and Leng.

April 1935 comes from the "Desert beyond Leng," dated at the "Hour of the Shapes in the Sands."

Lovecraft's Yian-Ho derives from the city of Yian created by Robert W. Chambers in the story "Maker of Moons" (1896). In Chambers' telling, the city of Yian exists both in the real Chinese interior and in dreams, and it too exudes alien music: "the air is filled with the music of silver bells." (In Chambers' later novel *Slayer of Souls* (1920), Yian eventually falls to a black-magical cult of conspiratorial Kurds á la "Red Hook.") If Yian-Ho descends from Leng, then perhaps its ancestral plateau likewise exists across dimensions, linked by alien music and predatory masked lamas.

> *"Certainly, we were in one of the strangest, weirdest, and most terrible of all the corners of earth's globe. Of all existing lands it was infinitely the most ancient; and the conviction grew upon us that this hideous upland must indeed be the fabled nightmare plateau of Leng which even the mad author of the* Necronomicon *was reluctant to discuss."*

> — H.P. LOVECRAFT, *AT THE MOUNTAINS OF MADNESS*

Where is Leng? Even Asia and Dreamland don't cover enough ground—in 1931, Lovecraft moves Leng to Antarctica. As HPL supposedly "demythologizes" his legendry in *At the Mountains of Madness*, Leng shifts from a cultist country on the "roof of the world" to a racial memory of an alien colony on a "hideous upland" at the bottom of the globe. The city of the crinoids, after all, also sits on a plateau or "table-land," and it, too, spawns horrors that survive death. Leng isn't alone: in that novel Lovecraft also transports "Ib in the land of Mnar" from the putative Dreamlands to the waking, if still "whispered" and "pre-human," Earth.

Of course, the putative "demythologizing" doesn't take even in this novel. If anything, as we've seen, Lovecraft *remythologizes* Antarctica itself: "Like [a] land of mystery in a dream or gateway to forbidden world of untrodden wonder." Antarctica and Dreamland aren't that far apart, for all the geological data dumping. Dyer believes that "the whole white world would dissolve into a gold, silver, and scarlet land of Dunsanian dreams." The crinoid city looms "loomed like a dream-phantasy," while the titular mountains "loomed dream-like." The seven explicit descriptions or comparisons in the novel of the city and plateau to dreams don't include the two separate mentions of Alhazred's insistence that shoggoths exist only in dreams, or the seven other uses of "nightmare" as an adjective for the city or its architecture, four of them the bald "nightmare city."

As a cherry on our Dreamland-Antarctica sundae, recall Danforth ranting of the "elder pharos" as he looks back at the titular Mountains, themselves "beyond doubt the unknown archetype of that dreaded Kadath in the Cold Waste beyond abhorrent Leng, whereof unholy primal legends hint evasively." In the Dreamlands, Leng lurks beyond the impassable mountains, while in Antarctica, the mountains lie on the other side of Leng. Is this Lovecraft's mistake, or a hint that Antarctica-Leng mirrors Dream-Leng?

> *"Something about the scene reminded me of the strange and disturbing Asian paintings of Nicholas Roerich, and of the still stranger and more disturbing descriptions of the evilly fabled plateau of Leng which occur in the dreaded* Necronomicon *of the mad Arab Abdul Alhazred."*
>
> — H.P. LOVECRAFT, *AT THE MOUNTAINS OF MADNESS*

Lovecraft also blends Antarctica with Asia, not least in the novel's repeated evocations of Nicholas Roerich. Roerich, a Theosophical mystic and painter, also explored Central Asia (including Tibet) between 1925 and 1929 searching for the hidden mystical city of Shambhala, a Buddhist legend and possible model for Chambers' Yian.[77] It's not just Roerich; Dyer's chain of free association links the two locations as well: "of the daemoniac plateau of Leng, of the Mi-Go, or Abominable Snow-Men of

---

77. Lovecraft also glancingly inserts "Shamballah" into his mythos, with mentions in "The Diary of Alonzo Typer" and "The Tree on the Hill." Lovecraft's Shamballah, built by Lemurians 50 million years ago, remains "inviolate still behind its walls of psychic force in the eastern desert." It also (as a proper Lovecraftian cavern-city ought) emits tenuous mists connected with "madness and delirium."

the Himalayas." The "Elder Pharos" comes at it the other way, referring to the "last Elder One," who might be a crinoid Old One or something else. For what it's worth, "Out of the Aeons" also mentions the "Elder Ones" of Yuggoth.

A similar confusion reigns in "The Horror in the Museum," which refers to "the Dhol chants attributed to malign and non-human Leng." "Dhol" probably comes from Machen's Dôls, one of a series of mysterious terms in "The White People" that could colorably refer to the supposedly Asiatic "Picts" of pre-Celtic Britain. Lovecraft here identifies Leng not as Asiatic but "non-human," although "chants" implies humanoid throats, not crinoid-creature vacuoles. That phase-state between non-human and humanoid recalls the Theosophical notion that life began in Tibet, supposedly the first land to rise from the ocean. In a 1931 letter to Robert E. Howard, Lovecraft endorses a sober version of this theory: "That the human race started on some plateau in central Asia is almost certain." And what do we find but a reference to "man's first youth" in "The Elder Pharos," and of course the shattering bas-relief revelation in *Mountains* that the crinoid beings created mankind as a joke in Antarctica.

"On the walls of the corridors were painted frightful scenes older than history, and in a style unknown to the archaeologists of earth. After countless aeons their pigments were brilliant still, for the cold and dryness of hideous Leng keep alive many primal things."

— H.P. LOVECRAFT, *THE DREAM-QUEST OF UNKNOWN KADATH*

Those pre-human histories incised on the Cyclopean walls of Antarctic Leng have their own precursor: the "archaic frescoes" painted on the stone corridors of the citadel of Dreamlands Leng. Both bas-relief and fresco chronicle cycles of inhuman history and alien warfare, and those cycles echo and rhyme each other. Both depict their natives battling domestic foes: shoggoths and purple spiders, respectively. Both describe wars with alien invaders: the men of Leng against the moon-beasts, and the crinoid creatures vs. the Cthulhu-spawn and Mi-Go. The mention of "the gifts of the Men of Leng" in the Mi-Go ritual in "Whisperer in Darkness" opens up an intriguing potential identification (at least on an iconic level) of the moon-beasts with the fungi from Yuggoth: they have pinkish cilia, buzzing or fluting, rudimentary flight, human trafficking, and Nyarlathotepworship in common.

Let's try the tapestry of Leng on our own looms, then. Lovecraft first plants his "bleak plateau" unnamed in Central Asia in "Beyond the Wall of Sleep" (1919), and weaves it into the Dreamlands of "Celephaïs" (1920) before pulling it back to almost-Tibet in "The Hound" (1922). The *Dream-Quest* (1926) and "The Elder Pharos" (1929) provide high Dreamlands color and the longest explicit treatment of the Leng legend. In "Whisperer" (1930) Lovecraft seems to twist all his Leng threads together: the "Men of Leng" come from Dreamland, but its place next to Yian in the faux Akeley's rant aligns it with Central Asia. Finally, a mention of Leng's "pits of primal life" prefigures its possible transference to elder Antarctica, where Leng theoretically manifests in *Mountains of Madness* (1931), but retains strong features both of Tibet and Dream. We've noticed that Leng in "Horror in the Museum" (1932) points both to Antarctica and Central Asia, but (perhaps under Bloch's enthusiastic influence) Lovecraft closes the loop with Leng fully returned to quasi-Tibet in "Through the Gates of the Silver Key," "Out of the Aeons" (both 1933), and his letters to Bloch.

"Certainly, men reached Leng from very different oceans."

— H.P. LOVECRAFT, *THE DREAM-QUEST OF UNKNOWN KADATH*

With that quote, Randolph Carter summarizes our geographical roundelay as well as anyone can. But where, in the final analysis, is Leng? One answer obtrudes itself, through every story and every fragment. Leng is Lovecraft's actual, literal nightmare country. Neither we nor Lovecraft can get away from it, no matter how much he shifts it around the globe and we attempt to "demythologize" it. Look at the signifiers: Leng is, first and foremost, cold. Lovecraft famously hated the cold, yearning for Florida through his Providence winters. Further anathema to the antiquarian soul, Leng has no architecture, just white domes and primitive stone towers. Antarctic Leng features the crinoid city, of course, but its architecture degenerates visibly across the eons—and Lovecraft hates and fears decay far more than he does mere savagery.

Lovecraft finds and creates in Leng a hateful symbol of his feared racial future, as well, when decay (architectural and otherwise) of white-English "mankind" leads to its overthrow. Leng's rulers are never Lovecraft's "men" but always his phobic "aliens": Asiatics, or moon-beasts, or Mi-Go, or revolted slave-shoggoths. Randolph Carter, Lovecraft's alter ego, reports that Lovecraft's first nightmares, the night-gaunts, flock atop the peaks above Leng. His hateful shantak-birds hunt below them; Leng lies beneath two layers of winged terror. Need a final proof? Leng has no cats. As Randolph Carter's narrator reports: "They told him how sorry they were that no cats would stay in the land of Inganok, and how they thought the hidden nearness of Leng was to blame for it."

DEEP TIME

*"Looking back to our sensations, and recalling our dazedness at viewing
this monstrous survival from aeons we had thought pre-human, I can
only wonder that we preserved the semblance of equilibrium which we
did. Of course we knew that something—chronology, scientific theory, or
our own consciousness—was woefully awry ..."*

— H.P. LOVECRAFT, *AT THE MOUNTAINS OF MADNESS*

Although H.G. Wells beat H.P. Lovecraft to the subject of dizzying
cosmic eons in *The Time Machine* (1895) and Olaf Stapledon exceeded his
reach in *Last and First Men* (1930), both those science-fictioneers looked
to the future. It was Lovecraft who first fictionally looked back in awe and
terror at the illimitable, unknowable prehistory and paleontology of the
planet, who first explored the horror of Deep Time and the undead past.

HPL begins to touch on the notion of the astronomical past influencing
the present in "Polaris," where his viewpoint character switches from a modern dream to the death of the city Olathoë 26,000 years ago, one entire preces-
sion of the zodiac behind him. In "The Temple," he enters legendary time, as
his U-boat commander encounters the "terrible antiquity" of Atlantis. The real
advent of Deep Time into the Lovecraftian cosmos comes with his first pre-
human archaeological horror story, "The Nameless City." Finally, "The Call of
Cthulhu" invokes an almost unutterable horror of Deep Time as the keystone
of Lovecraft's mythology, after which point he seldom leaves it unmentioned.

"The Last Test" and "The Mound" tentatively approach the concept as a
kindred horror to biology and decadence, respectively, but it only becomes
Lovecraft's central horrific effect and main theme with the last of his great

chronicles: *At the Mountains of Madness* and "The Shadow Out of Time." In both those stories, the dizzying, vertiginous pressure of geological eras, of time itself, serves as the core horror. For Lovecraft, Deep Time becomes the ultimate abyss, containing annihilating monsters and annihilating truths.

> *"The science of geology … is indeed something in which I might become interested under the proper set of chance conditions; insomuch as it is directly concern'd with that main stream of cosmick pageantry which begins in blank aether and ends in the perfection of … Georgian architecture."*

— H.P. LOVECRAFT, LETTER TO JAMES F. MORTON (OCTOBER 31, 1930)

Although Thomas Carlyle coined the phrase in 1832, and John McPhee first used it about geological time in 1981, the concept of Deep Time springs from Lovecraft's beloved Augustan Age. In *Theory of the Earth* (1785), the geologist James Hutton proposed a slow, endless cycle of rocky strata forming in the molten core of the earth, thrusting up through its crust, and eroding away again. In 1788, Hutton showed the mathematician John Playfair a prize example of upthrust unconformity at Siccar Point, and Playfair prefigured Lovecraft when he wrote: "the mind seemed to grow giddy by looking so far into the abyss of time."

As Charles Lyell and others demonstrated the slow changes in the Earth recorded in sedimentary layers, scientists extended their guesses at the age of the planet from 75,000 years (Buffon, 1779, based on its cooling rate) to 20 million (Lord Kelvin, 1862, based on the thermodynamic age of the Sun) to 100 million (Joly, 1897, based on the rate of salt deposition in the oceans). In 1911, Arthur Holmes introduced the theory of dating rocks by the rate of radioactive decay, which pushed the Earth's age into the billions of years. Radiometric dating slowly penetrated geology, finally becoming accepted wisdom in a report of the U.S. National Academy of Sciences in 1931—mere months after Lovecraft finished *At the Mountains of Madness*.

Lovecraft retained his schoolboy interest in geology his whole life, and geologists appear in his work more often than any other type of scientist.

His geologists sometimes serve as protagonists, as witnesses to the horror of Deep Time, most notably William Dyer in *Mountains of Madness* and George Campbell in "The Challenge From Beyond." Dyer also guest-stars in the other great Deep Time story, "The Shadow Out of Time." The mining engineers "with some knowledge of geology" Robert B.F. Mackenzie in "Shadow Out of Time" and the unnamed narrator of "Transition of Juan Romero" probably count here as well.

Other nameless geologists simply exist to be baffled and mystified by the Outside: by the scroll cover in "The Green Meadow," the statue of Cthulhu in "Call of Cthulhu," the noises in the Dunwich hills in "The Dunwich Horror," and the amulet of Tulu-metal in "The Mound." Finally, "three professors," three unwise men, shatter the meteoric inclusion with "a geologist's hammer" and symbolically release "The Colour Out of Space."

> *"All at once I came upon a place where the bed-rock rose stark through the sand and formed a low cliff; and here I saw with joy what seemed to promise further traces of the antediluvian people. Hewn rudely on the face of the cliff were the unmistakable facades of several small, squat rock houses or temples; whose interiors might preserve many secrets of ages too remote for calculation, though sandstorms had long since effaced any carvings which may have been outside."*

> — H.P. LOVECRAFT, "THE NAMELESS CITY"

The archaeological horror of "The Nameless City" rapidly becomes paleontological horror, as the excavator discovers signs of prehistoric reptile life beneath the ruins. This rehearsal for *At the Mountains of Madness* has a quasi-academic narrator (more occultist than scientist), a lost city in a desert, evidence of vast geological change, images on the walls depicting inhuman (and prehuman) history, and finally fluid, unnatural survivors at the bottom of a pit. Lovecraft describes the city not just as "primeval" and "antediluvian," but "Paleozoic and abysmal," literally linking Deep Time and the gulfs of space or Tartarus. Lovecraft also introduces the

Theosophical notion of sunken continents in this story, setting the city's founding 10 million years ago (Mya), "before Africa rose from the waves."

Finally, "The Nameless City" provides the paradigmatic Lovecraftian quote on Deep Time:

> *"That is not dead which can eternal lie,*
> *And with strange aeons even death may die."*

Needless to say, Lovecraft uses the term "aeons" poetically here, not scientifically. Geologically, an eon marks the time between major changes to the Earth's biosphere, on a scale of hundreds of millions to billions of years: only four eons have begun since the planet formed. Eras of dozens to hundreds of million years in duration make up each eon; our Phanerozoic Eon comprises three eras: Paleozoic, Mesozoic, and Cenozoic. Eras are subdivided into periods, such as the familiar Triassic, Jurassic, and Cretaceous Periods of the Mesozoic Era, each between 50 and 80 million years long. Periods divide into epochs, which further split into ages. Lovecraft uses all these terms interchangeably.

> *"Old Castro remembered bits of hideous legend that paled the speculations*
> *of theosophists and made man and the world seem recent and transient*
> *indeed. There had been aeons when other Things ruled on the earth …*
> *They all died vast epochs of time before men came, but there were arts*
> *which could revive Them when the stars had come round again to the right*
> *positions in the cycle of eternity."*

> — H.P. LOVECRAFT, "THE CALL OF CTHULHU"

In "The Call of Cthulhu" Lovecraft speaks of "measureless aeons" and "vast epochs," aiming for a Gothic-geological sturm und drang. Cthulhu, he says, came to Earth "vigintillions of years" ago, which manages to dwarf even the age of the universe: a billion billion consecutive universes would only last a few octillionths of a vigintillion years. An American vigintillion, 10^{63} that is: Lovecraft would have meant a British ("long-scale") vigintillion, 10^{120} or not quite a vigintillion vigintillions. Numeric accuracy aside, the concept of entire spans of existence wiped out by the endless pressure of Time—and of a Thing that can survive even that—orchestrates the scope and power of this first of his masterpieces.

He attempts something similar in the background of "The Last Test" the next year (1927) when he has Clarendon expatiate on "whole forgotten cycles of evolution with beings and races and wisdom and diseases—all lived through and gone before the first amoeba ever stirred in the tropic seas geology tells us about." But a virus isn't Cthulhu, and Adolphe de Castro's romances are no match for Old Castro's theology, so he moves on. In "The Mound" (1930), the K'n-yani appear as the result of "one or two million years" of evolution and eugenics, future humans derived from a past (alien-tainted?) offshoot. Bulwer-Lytton did much the same (complete with descent from frog-creatures) for his hollow-earth Vril-ya species in *The Coming Race* (1871).

Most interestingly, in "The Mound" Lovecraft uses the multiple-recension technique he began in "Picture in the House" to layer eras on top of themselves for a "folded" narrative impression of Deep Time improving on Bulwer-Lytton's deliberately tangled temporal mystifaction. The narrator's (contemporary) reading of Zamacona's (near-medieval) version of the decadent K'n-yani (legendary) myths of their (paleontological) origin marvelously garbles even Lovecraft's cosmology, casting "Tulu" as a benevolent father-god who brought all humans to Earth in equality "as soon as its crust was fit to live on." Lovecraft even plays with re-de-mythologization of his Dreamlands, referring to a K'n-yani legend that "between glacial ages" they built a surface civilization "at the South Pole near the mountain Kadath."

"For this latter we headed; and when at last we were able actually to touch its weathered Cyclopean blocks, we felt that we had established an unprecedented and almost blasphemous link with forgotten aeons normally closed to our species."

— H.P. LOVECRAFT, *AT THE MOUNTAINS OF MADNESS*

And then the year after that, he does it right. The Old Ones at the South Pole are no longer ancient "future humans" straight out of Bulwer-Lytton, but proper Lovecraftian Things built on truly alien lines. *At the Mountains of Madness* presents the "cycles of life" from "The Last Test" and the primordial ghost-city from "The Nameless City" in the cold, pitiless light of modern science, only later drifting into mysticism as the geologists' minds collapse under the pressure of Deep Time. Lake's original speculations ("will mean to biology what Einstein has meant to … physics") turn out to be both more and less radical than the truth: that alien life created earthly life, and remains here today. The Old One city deforms time, allowing "rudimentary fishes, molluscs and corals" to survive 300 million years out of time from the Silurian into the Oligocene. Better still, even the Old Ones themselves suffer from Deep Time, resurrected after the fall of their civilization and hunted by the shoggoths they thought defeated epochs ago.

At some point before February 1931, when he started the novel, Lovecraft must have found an article or museum pamphlet that provided him some rough estimates and dates for "historical geology," as the field was called then. Having sorted through both his available *Britannica* editions, all the known geological texts in his library, and those mentioned in his 1936 "Suggestions for a Reading Guide," I can only say it wasn't any of those works. All these sources—Lovecraft mentions specifically Geikie's *Geology Primer* (1874), Longwell's *Foundations of Geology* (1930), Norton's *Elements of Geology* (1929), and Miller's *Introduction to Geology* (1928)—share the general 19th-century reluctance to do more than estimate the age of the earth and share the relative thickness of the geological deposits associated with each era.

Lovecraft's geochronological dates, as given in his fiction, fall somewhere between the sedimentary deposit dates of geologists like Charles Schuchert, who in 1914 tentatively dated the beginning of the Triassic to 13 Mya, and the earliest radiometric dates of Joseph Barrell, who in 1917 dated the same event to 190 Mya. Lovecraft does at least strike a blow for Wegener's then-controversial theory of continental drift, confirming it (extremely propter hoc) by the bas-relief maps on the walls of Kadath. Lovecraft also uses slightly idiosyncratic terminology, implying that the

"Archaean Age" immediately predates the Cambrian and repeatedly referring to "the Comanchian" era or period. More usually the Comanchean, this now-deprecated Age (not an era) comprises the latter half (c. 125 Mya to 100 Mya) of the Early Cretaceous. Lovecraft, meanwhile, somewhere derived dates (I deduce from the context) between 60 and 30 Mya for "Comanchian times." Did his mineralogist friend James F. Morton send him a theoretical sketched précis of some sort, now lost?

> *"Primal myth and modern delusion joined in their assumption that mankind is only one—perhaps the least—of the highly evolved and dominant races of this planet's long and largely unknown career. Things of inconceivable shape, they implied, had reared towers to the sky and delved into every secret of Nature before the first amphibian forbear of man had crawled out of the hot sea three hundred million years ago. Some had come down from the stars; a few were as old as the cosmos itself; others had arisen swiftly from terrene germs as far behind the first germs of our life-cycle as those germs are behind ourselves. Spans of thousands of millions of years, and linkages with other galaxies and universes, were freely spoken of. Indeed, there was no such thing as time in its humanly accepted sense."*

> — H.P. LOVECRAFT, "THE SHADOW OUT OF TIME"

Various hints of Deep Time recur in "The Horror in the Museum," tying Rhan-Tegoth to ancient Lomar, which must thus predate his freezing three million years ago. "Out of the Aeons" (1933) mentions that "spawn of Yuggoth had perished aeons before," possibly a reference to the Mi-Go, which species he dates to the Jurassic in *Mountains of Madness*. In "Whisperer in Darkness" he says that the fungi found ruins of "an elder race extinct and forgotten" on Yuggoth when they colonized it, Deep Time in Deep Space, but this is only one of the promising leads that "Out of the Aeons" squanders.

In November 1934, Lovecraft returned to the Triassic age in force, recapitulating his first scratchings at the rim of Deep Time with a massively expanded version of "Polaris." In "The Shadow Out of Time" we have the narrator pulled back and forth between a city in the primordial past and a modern dreaming existence—and as we've mentioned before, Lovecraft's first version of this story was set in ancient Lomar, not alien Pnakotus. In this story even more than *Mountains*, the "stupefying gulfs of time" are themselves the horror, the Great Race merely being the mechanisms by which Peaslee finds himself fallen into that void.

Lovecraft restrains his geological info-dumping this time around, settling for a decorous setting "somewhat less than 150,000,000 years ago, when the Paleozoic age was giving place to the Mesozoic"—the early Triassic, in other words. The Great Race last at least another hundred million years, sending themselves forward to escape the spectral polyps' escape 50 Mya. From Lovecraft's description of the Yithians as a "relatively late race," we can slot their arrival on the table after the Elder Things. Meanwhile, the Great Race fights off "octopoid and reptilian invaders," allowing us to date them before the onset of the Cthulhu-spawn of R'lyeh and the reptile-folk of Valusia.

HPL's segment of "The Challenge From Beyond" (written six months after he finished "Shadow Out of Time") simply recapitulates the psionic kidnapping from "Shadow" again, switching (or adding) space and time. Lovecraft dates the Yekubian cube significantly later than the "pre-Carboniferous Eltdown Shards" that describe it, likely an artifact of haste, not a sign of deliberate time-slippage. Finally, "The Haunter of the Dark" provides a suitably primordial provenance for the Shining Trapezohedron by name-checking the crinoid Elder Things, the serpent-men of Valusia, and "aeons later" the first humans. However, the horror no longer comes from those aeons, but from transcending them while joined within the soul of Nyarlathotep.

> *"It is told that in the immemorial years when the world was young, before ever the men of Sarnath came to the land of Mnar, another city stood beside the lake; the grey stone city of Ib, which was old as the lake itself, and peopled with beings not pleasing to behold."*

> — H.P. LOVECRAFT, "THE DOOM THAT CAME TO SARNATH"

When Thomas Carlyle coined the term "deep time" in "Boswell's 'Life of Johnson'" (1832) he implied (and then re-stated throughout his other works, most notably *Sartor Resartus* (1833-34)) a conception similar to the "face of the deep" that pre-dated Creation: a spiritual ocean of time, reflecting the divine. The anthropologist Mircea Eliade conveys something of the same meaning when using the term *illud tempus* (Latin, literally "that time") to refer to the "mythic time" before (historical) time begins.

Lovecraft, of course, reconciles mythic time with geological time in a common Deep Time: contemplating "strange aeons" whether stratigraphic or mythopoetic leads to awe and, inevitably, terror. In "The Nameless City" he ties his Dreamland cities of Sarnath and Ib to (historical) Chaldaea and to a time "before men existed." In "Call of Cthulhu" he puts it perfectly and succinctly: "In the elder time chosen men had talked with the entombed Old Ones in dreams, but then something had happened." In *Mountains of Madness* and "Shadow Out of Time," he reverses the process, mythologizing the scientific horror of Deep Time behind Alhazred's ravings and recasting the *Necronomicon* as a Triassic dream-journal.

> *"Theosophists have guessed at the awesome grandeur of the cosmic cycle wherein our world and human race form transient incidents. They have hinted at strange survivals in terms which would freeze the blood if not masked by a bland optimism."*
>
> — H.P. LOVECRAFT, "THE CALL OF CTHULHU"

Lovecraft encountered a different attempt to reconcile mysticism and scientific time, the doctrine of Theosophy, some time before writing "The Call of Cthulhu." Promulgated beginning in 1875 by Helena Petrovna Blavatsky (HPB, a fine parallel to our own HPL), Theosophy combined primarily Hindu myth with the new Victorian scientific doctrines of geological deep time and evolution. Blavatsky contrasted those supposedly revolutionary ideas with the ancient acceptance in supposedly "primitive" India of cosmic time-scales and cycles of creation and extinction.

In his *Aryabhatiya* (c. 510 A.D.) the Indian astronomer Aryabhata provides the dates that Blavatsky used for the Yuga cycle, the mahayuga ("great yuga"). Each mahayuga lasts 4.32 million years, divided between Satya, Treta, Dvapara, and finally Kali Yugas. The current mahayuga began 3.89 Mya; the current Kali Yuga began in 3102 B.C. and will last 426,880 more years before the cycle restarts with the next Satya Yuga. Each maha-yuga equals one thousandth of a day (1.44 minutes) of Brahma; a Brah-ma-day, or *kalpa*, lasts 1,000 mahayugas or 4.32 billion years; a day and a night of Brahma lasts 8.64 billion years. (Randolph Carter rides these cycles of "unreckoned kalpas" during his fall from the shantak's back in *Dream-Quest*.) According to Aryabhata, 50 years have elapsed of the current Brahma, making the universe approximately 155.5 trillion years old, or ten thousand times older than current cosmological thinking puts it.

Lovecraft imbibed Theosophy passively at first, via other occult fiction, then mainlined it starting in 1926 or so when he discovered its specific resonances with his own invented mythologies. In his excitement, he name-drops the Theosophist W. Scott-Elliot's *Atlantis and the Lost Lemuria* (a 1925 fixup of two earlier works) in "The Call of Cthulhu." Scott-Elliot describes Blavatsky's series of alien "root races" that emerge, spawn sub-races, war, and die, a cyclic sequence in which the next root race emerges from the previous one at a numerologically significant eon. Lovecraft's collaborator and correspondent E. Hoffmann Price, who at various times called himself a Theosophist, provided him with "more of the stuff," some of which apparently spawned their sub-races into his fiction.

Blavatsky's First Root Race, the Polarians, are a race of pure mentation, just like Lovecraft's Yithians. The Second Root Race, the Hyperboreans, aren't Lovecraft and Smith's furry Voormis or arch prehumans, but ec-toplasmic "sweat-born" creatures not unlike shoggoths or the "formless spawn" of Tsathoggua. The Third, Lemurian, Root Race has no skeleton; later occultists associate these "egg-born" with crystals and mining. Those parallels to the Mi-Go only go so far, as the Lemurians resemble three-eyed goliaths, not winged lobsters. Lovecraft's giant, coppery K'n-yani settled Atlantis and Lemuria, making them a closer parallel. According to Scott-Elliot, the gaseous "fire-born" Lords of Venus incarnate into the rubbery Lemurians and enlighten them, a possible model (suggests Robert M. Price) for Lovecraft's Yithians possessing the invertebrate cone-creatures of the Ordovician Earth.

> *"It was really the first draught of reliable surface information they had had since the refugees straggled back from Atlantis and Lemuria aeons before ..."*

> — H.P. LOVECRAFT AND ZEALIA BISHOP, "THE MOUND"

Blavatsky didn't invent Lemuria. That particular lost continent began as a scientific hypothesis by desperate Darwinians. To explain the spread of lemur fossils between Madagascar and India, in 1864 the zoologist Philip Sclater postulated a land bridge between them that he named for those darling proto-primates. Beginning in 1868 Lovecraft's ultra-Darwinian idol Ernst Haeckel, on a waste-not want-not principle, proposed that Lemuria also held the missing fossils of early humanity. Thus, in "The Haunter of the Dark" Lovecraft places the Shining Trapezohedron "in Lemuria [beheld by] the first human beings."

For good measure he also puts Madame Blavatsky's spurious *Book of Dzyan* into the Starry Wisdom library in that same story, and into the hands of Alonzo Typer in "Diary of Alonzo Typer." Even that sad tale sniffs a bit of Theosophical Deep Time, as here we learn that Dzyan's first six chapters "antedate the Earth" and hear "of the city Shamballah, built by the Lemurians fifty million years ago ..." HPB jumped onto that "scientific" lost continent with both feet, embracing Lemuria in her "Mahatma letters" in 1882. In 1904, Scott-Elliot expanded "Lost Lemuria" into the Pacific, where a different charlatan, James Churchward, renamed it Mu in *The Lost Continent of Mu* (1926). Lovecraft then moved Ghatanothoa among other horrors onto it, in slapdash fashion, differentiating it by implication from the previous sunken Pacific continent that hosted R'lyeh.

> *"It cannot be described, this awesome chain of events that depopulated the whole Earth; the range is too tremendous for any to picture or encompass. Of the people of Earth's fortunate ages, billions of years before, only a few prophets and madmen could have conceived that which was to come—could have grasped visions of the still, dead lands, and long-empty sea-beds."*

— H.P. LOVECRAFT AND ROBERT H. BARLOW, "TILL A' THE SEAS"

It only remains for us to look into the future with Lovecraft as Deep Time continues until humanity, the earth, and the universe all die out. "Till A' the Seas" (1935) remains the only work of Lovecraft's to look that far ahead in detail: among other nice touches, the 16th-century Rio de Janeiro becomes "Yuanario, their immemorially ancient capital." The horror of human extinction becomes simple destiny here, more bathetic than horrifying. Lovecraft projects cosmic indifferentism more memorably in "Shadow Out of Time," as the Great Race migrates into the "hardy cole-opterans" who rule Earth fifty million years from now, and then into the "bulbous vegetable entities of Mercury" as the Sun shrinks. Some cursed races will cling "to the cold planet and [burrow] to its horror-filled core," but at least we'll be dead.

For Lovecraft, the horror isn't survival to the end, or even human futility in such survival, as it was for Wells. For Lovecraft, the horror lies in repeating prehistory, as the narrator of "Polaris" must, as the resurrected Elder Things must, as Randolph Carter must in endless cycles whether launched from Kadath or Yaddith, as Nathaniel Peaslee must in his dreams, and as we all must when Cthulhu awakens and the "stars come right again." The past isn't dead, as Faulkner assures us. It isn't even past. For Lovecraft, this simultaneity opens the great abysm of Deep Time, and then traps us all in the vault.

DEEP TIME COMPARATIVE TABLE

THEOSOPHICAL TIME	LOVECRAFTIAN TIME	GEOLOGICAL TIME
	"Archaean Age" Elder Things arrive [1000 Mya] Cone-shaped beings [1000 Mya] Spectral polyps dominate Solar System [600 Mya]	Pre-Cambrian *2040-1500 Mya* Archaean Eon 4000 Mya Proterozoic Eon 2500 Mya
First (Polarian) Root Race	Cambrian [500 Mya]	Cambrian Period *550-540 Mya* 541 Mya
	Ordovician [300 Mya] Great Race arrive from Yith?	Ordovician Period *480 Mya* 485 Mya
	Arrival of Cthulhu? Sinking of R'lyeh? Eltdown Shards ["pre-Carboniferous"]	Silurian Period *390-380 Mya* 444 Mya Devonian Period *350 Mya* 419 Mya
Second (Hyperborean) Root Race	Valusia [>100 Mya]	Carboniferous Period *300 Mya* 359 Mya
	Shoggoth revolt [150 Mya] Yekubian cube hits [150 Mya]	Permian Period *240-215 Mya* 299 Mya
Third (Lemurian) Root Race {34.5 Mya}	Peaslee in Pnakotus [<150 Mya]	Triassic Period *200-190 Mya* 252 Mya
	Mi-Go arrive	Jurassic Period *175-155 Mya* 201 Mya
Lords of Flame arrive from Venus {18.5 Mya} Fourth sub-race emerges, beginning of sexual reproduction {16.5 Mya} Lemuria sinks {9.7 Mya}	"Comanchian Era" [60-30 Mya] Elder Thing city at Kadath [50 Mya] Lemurians build Shamballah [50 Mya] Polyps escape; Great Race flees into future [50 Mya]	Lower (Early) Cretaceous Epoch *140-120 Mya* 145 Mya Upper (Later) Cretaceous Epoch *110-95 Mya* 100 Mya

Mya = millions of years ago; Kya = thousands of years ago

DEEP TIME COMPARATIVE TABLE

THEOSOPHICAL TIME	LOVECRAFTIAN TIME	GEOLOGICAL TIME
	Elder Thing 'corpses' [40 Mya]	Eocene Epoch *60–55 Mya* 66 Mya (Paleocene Period)
Eocene begins {9 Mya} Fourth (Atlantean) Root Race {4.5 Mya}	Upper cavern above Elder Thing city closes	Oligocene Epoch *35 Mya* 34 Mya
	Nameless City built [10 Mya]	Miocene Epoch *19 Mya* 23 Mya
		Pliocene Epoch *7 Mya* 5.33 Mya
Fifth (Aryan) Root Race {1 Mya} Atlantis sinks {850 Kya}	Lomar founded? Rhan-Tegoth frozen [3 Mya] K'n-yan settled [2 Mya] Antarctic ice sheet buries Elder Thing city [500 Kya] Mu sinks [170 Kya] Lomar falls to Inutos [26 Kya] Doom of Sarnath [10 Kya]	Pleistocene Epoch 2.58 Mya

Mya = millions of years ago; Kya = thousands of years ago

This table compares the various eras of Deep Time: Theosophical, Lovecraftian, and modern geological. Conveniently, both Theosophy and Lovecraft tie their mythologies to geological periods, and for much the same reason: verisimilitude in the hoax.

Theosophical dates and periodicities {in curly brackets} derive from Arthur E. Powell, *The Solar System* (1930) and W. Scott Elliot, *The Story of Atlantis and the Lost Lemuria* (1925). Lovecraftian dates [in square brackets] are those appearing in the text of his stories, not those extrapolated and ret-conned by later scholars and authors. I have gingerly interpolated four Lovecraftian events with question marks—those he ties to no date or geological period—as noted in the main text.

The table provides two sets of geological dates for the beginning of the various periods and epochs: those contemporary with Lovecraft (from Joseph Barrell, "Rhythms and the Measurements of Geologic Time" (1917) and Schuchert and Dunbar's *Textbook of Geology* (1933)) in *italics* (Barrell provides the lower values) and the current geochronology, as given in Wikipedia.

THE SOUTH

"The South is in some respects my favourite part of America; its climate, atmosphere, blood, traditions, and social-political views all being closer to my own liking than those of any other region."

— H.P. LOVECRAFT, "TRAVELS IN THE PROVINCES OF AMERICA" (1929)

Like many northerners, H.P. Lovecraft loved his city but hated the cold. This ambivalence may not lurk behind his "shadow cities"—duality resides too close to every other aspect of Lovecraft's life and art—but it turned his head south more often than the routine portrait of HPL as reclusive regionalist normally admits. Although he never wrote a great story, or any story, truly utilizing a Southern setting in the way he did New England, perhaps we can see a new side of Lovecraft Country in this southern light.

Lovecraft sets three stories, in some large part, in the South. "The Statement of Randolph Carter" occurs in Florida (where Daniel Upton's father retires in "Thing on the Doorstep"). "Medusa's Coil" unfolds in Cape Girardeau, Missouri, southern in geography, culture, and allegiance during the Civil War. The de Russy family in that story originates in Louisiana, where Inspector Legrasse confronts the Cthulhu cult in a bravura sequence of "The Call of Cthulhu." In that swamp combat south of New Orleans, Lovecraft manages to turn pulp stereotype into something approaching the complexity and landscape sense of his New England tales.

The frame story of "Through the Gates of the Silver Key" transpires in the New Orleans home of Etienne-Laurent de Marigny (who also gets

name- and city-checked in "Out of the Aeons") although past a certain
louche decorating scheme it has little of the Crescent City about it. The
Delapores of "Rats in the Walls" hail from Virginia, as does the ethnolo-
gist narrator of "The Mound."[78] The Old Dominion can also boast the
"vast limestone cavern systems" explored by Nathaniel Peaslee during his
Yithian possession in "Shadow Out of Time." We pass two more incidental indicators on our Southern itinerary: the Davis family leaves Arkansas
for Oklahoma in "Curse of Yig," and "Through the Gates of the Silver
Key" also identifies Harley Warren's home state as South Carolina. With
HPL's brief mention of El Paso in "The Electric Executioner" his only nod
to his compadre Robert E. Howard's Texas, he completely passes by five of
the eleven states of the Confederacy.

> *"But I did not hesitate long, for as a Virginian I felt the blood of ancestral
> fighters and gentlemen-adventurers pounding a protest against retreat
> from any peril known or unknown."*
>
> — H.P. LOVECRAFT AND ZEALIA BISHOP, "THE MOUND"

Teasing what is specifically Southern out of Lovecraft's fiction sets us
quite the challenge. His love of traditional ways, near-obsessions with
ancestry and being a gentleman, and generally reactionary approach to
the modern seem to put him on the solidly Southron side of Yankee-
dom to the modern reader. Even in his own time, he felt an instinctive
kinship with the South, hailing the "Great Lost Cause" of rebellion and
famously hanging a picture of Jefferson Davis on his wall during his
early amateur journalism years.[79] It may be more productive to examine
what Lovecraft thought of the South, what he thought was worth noting or treating as "Southern."

---

78. Kenton J. Stanfield, the crystal prospector hero of "In the Walls of Eryx," likewise comes from Richmond, Virginia—although that's probably a little gentle (and ironic) fun poked at Edgar Rice Burroughs'
Virginian swashbuckler John Carter of Barsoom.

79. He remained Yankee and writerly enough to mock the South for its moralism in "The Unnamable,"
in which that region (with the Pacific coast) panics and bans one of Carter's more gruesome tales.

Of course, where those qualities were qualities he already admired, he deploys his characteristic doubling technique, seemingly involuntarily. The narrator of "The Mound" harkens to his Virginia ancestors and plunges forward—only to discover and experience utter horror at the revelation he uncovers underground. This, in miniature, recapitulates the tale of the Delapores, likewise "proud and honourable, if somewhat reserved" Virginia gentlemen since the days of James I. In "Rats in the Walls," the last Delapore moves to Bolton, in the "greyness of Massachusetts," as a child, and buries himself in uncongenial "stolid Yankee" business matters. Only after his son dies does he follow the atavistic call of his ancestors and rebuild his estate, only to uncover an abyss of cannibal disaster and disgrace. Courage and family feeling, two of Lovecraft's high virtues, lead to destruction.

Passing over the (coincidental?) detail of a Virginia gentleman who owns a cat named "Nigger-Man"[80]—one who turns on him when Delapore's bestial nature emerges—still more goes south with the story, and the names, in "Rats in the Walls." Lovecraft names the Delapore plantation in Virginia "Carfax," an obvious tribute to the home of the vampire in Bram Stoker's *Dracula.* And then he burns it down, as if to highlight its unworthy succession to the true home of the de la Poer family, just as Bram Stoker (with his sprawling plot and conventional, sexually charged monster) proved unworthy of his literary ancestor Edgar Allan Poe. Lovecraft barely conceals Poe's name in "de la Poer," and indeed Poe's Providence inamorata Sarah Helen *Power* Whitman (inaccurately) traced both her heritage and Poe's to a common ancestor, the Norman bishop Roger Le Poer, Lord Chancellor to Henry I. Lovecraft knew all this, just as he knew his "god of fiction" likewise considered himself a Southern gentleman, despite a career spent in the North.

---

80. The cat's name is the same as that of Lovecraft's childhood cat, who ran away following the family's move out of 454 Angell Street, when HPL was fourteen.

"But Charleston is still Charleston, and the culture we know and respect is not dead there. Dilution there may be, but in the main there is more alive than in any other place in America. The original families still hold sway ... and still uphold the basic truths and values of a civilisation which is genuine because it represents a settled adjustment between people and landscape, old enough to have created the overtones needful to a sense of interest and significance."

— H.P. LOVECRAFT, "AN ACCOUNT OF CHARLESTON" (1930)

When Lovecraft visited Richmond, Virginia in May of 1929 he made pilgrimage to the "Poe Shrine" near the poet's childhood home. He was so taken with this first real encounter with Southern-ness that he even forgave Richmond's shabby, pedestrian architecture, terming the city "subtly delightful" in a paroxysm of politesse. He revisited the Poe Shrine and associated Poe sites upon his returns to Richmond in 1930 and 1931. The latter visit capped his first trip to Florida, where he enjoyed the heat and the many antiquarian sights of St. Augustine, the oldest European city in America. In May 1932, he took a longer trip deeper into the South, visiting Chattanooga and Memphis, Tennessee, and Vicksburg and Natchez, Mississippi. The relative commercial failure of Natchez prevented the rebuilding of its antique architecture, leading Lovecraft to rank this sleepy river port with "Quebec, Salem, Marblehead, & Newburyport."

He reached the climax—both geographical and architectural—of this trip in New Orleans, which rocketed to the heights of his appreciation. He particularly delighted in the number and variety of courtyards to discover, spending over two weeks in the city. On the way back north in late June, he approvingly toured Mobile, Alabama, another un-modernized town, and stopped again for Poe genuflection in Richmond. In April 1934, Lovecraft returned to Florida for the first of two extended stays with his young protégé Robert Barlow, rustication and conversation replacing tourism in the state's empty center.

But as much as he enjoyed New Orleans, and as long as he loafed in Florida, Lovecraft's truest Southern love was the city of Charleston, South Carolina. At that time an almost entirely 18th-century city architecturally, but prosperous enough to seem like a (much) warmer Providence, Charleston seduced Lovecraft at first sight. On April 29, 1930, the day after his arrival, he wrote to Derleth: "I'd move here in a second if my sentimental attachment to New England were less strong." He produced a massive travelogue of the city, declaring it "probably the most civilised spot in the United States."

> *"There was something provocatively fascinating in the tree-girt, decrepit pile before me, for it spoke of the graces and spaciousness of a bygone era and a far more southerly environment. It was a typical wooden plantation house of the classic, early nineteenth-century pattern, with two and a half stories and a great Ionic portico whose pillars reached up as far as the attic and supported a triangular pediment. Its state of decay was extreme and obvious; one of the vast columns having rotted and fallen to the ground, while the upper piazza or balcony had sagged dangerously low."*

> — H.P. LOVECRAFT AND ZEALIA BISHOP, "MEDUSA'S COIL"

But Lovecraft never wrote a tale set in Charleston, or St. Augustine, or Natchez. He even gives New Orleans short fictive shrift: "Through the Gates of the Silver Key" could be set in the Bronx for all it would matter to the story. When Charles Dexter Ward goes "south to talk with a strange old mulatto who dwelt in a swamp," it's almost a perfect parody of Lovecraft's southern exposure.[81] Lovecraft sets his true southern stories not in cities, but in swamps and ruins.

The haunted, ruined de Russy house in "Medusa's Coil," for example, is a nearly perfect Lovecraftian metaphor, or it would have been if the

---

81. Joshi and Klinger both speculate that Ward's consultant was one of the Cthulhu cultists from "Call of Cthulhu," but this looks more like one of Lovecraft's standard occult-tourism checkoffs.

rest of the story hadn't come so badly unglued. To Lovecraft, the South provides a touchstone for his other fiction, as it provides the purest ore of his archetypes: haunted ruins, broken lineages, desolate countryside, racial "contamination," plausible rituals and cults.[82] His abject rurals, as he assures us in their first appearance in "Beyond the Wall of Sleep," "correspond exactly to the decadent element of 'white trash' in the South." (In "Shadow Over Innsmouth," such normal human degeneracy proves to be a head-fake at the real horror of alien taint.) "The Statement of Randolph Carter" even has an underground abyss, as does the border-state border-case "The Mound."

Lovecraft was an urban Yankee, after all, and it is the opposite of those qualities that he hailed in time-frozen Natchez and New Orleans, and that he at the same time feared about the South. The rural, empty South becomes the shadow country of Lovecraft's northern Boston and Providence and Arkham, an "Upstate" for the whole country. His temptation by the heat of Florida, and moreso by the stasis of Charleston, merely completes the Jungian cycle of contradictions.

"He altogether abandoned the slave trade, alleging that its profits were constantly decreasing."

— H.P. LOVECRAFT, *THE CASE OF CHARLES DEXTER WARD*

Of course Charleston originally built its prosperity on the back of the slave trade, both directly as a slave market, and indirectly as an exporter of slave-produced commodities such as indigo, rice, and cotton. Lovecraft blithely disregarded (at best) this history in his rhapsodies, brushing past the "Slave Mart" and expressing relief at the failure of Denmark Vesey's "insurrection of the numerous blacks." But for whatever reason—with one huge exception, which we'll get to—Lovecraft's depiction of slavery in his fiction turns on its institutional horrors.

---

82. Lovecraft's treatment of Voodoo deserves a whole essay of its own, maybe in the next volume of our Tour.

His metaphorical uses of slavery—to morphine (in "Dagon") and religion (in "The Picture in the House")—emphasize its crippling dehumanization. Although he doesn't explicitly describe the prisoners beneath Exham Priory in "Rats in the Walls" as slaves, he wrings every ounce of horror from the spectacle of human beings used as livestock. Here as elsewhere, he indicts degeneracy, not race per se, the cult's enforced inbreeding and devolution degrading white Briton stock. Lovecraft furthermore depicts the active slave traders in his stories—Joseph Curwen in *Charles Dexter Ward,* and the Men of Leng in *Dream-Quest of Unknown Kadath*—as unequivocally evil, equating their slaving to human sacrifice and cannibalism. Even the Men of Leng find themselves enslaved in Inganok, food for the moon-beasts.

Lovecraft's interweaves his most detailed—and most literally horrible—slave narrative with the "captivity narrative" of Pánfilo de Zamacona, prisoner of K'n-yan under "The Mound." (A mound in the border-Southern state of Oklahoma, to boot.) The Old Ones of K'n-yan keep two classes of slaves. The lowest class, to which Zamacona (rightfully) fears consignment, is the "reanimated corpses," or y'm-bhi.[83] While Lovecraft signals disgust at this concept, it falls closer to the traditional horror end of the spectrum. He puts more creative, individual bite into the other class, the gyaa-yothn: "half-human" slaves engineered from "[nonhuman] ancient conquered enemies, from outer-world stragglers ... and from the naturally inferior members of the ruling race of Tsath."

Lovecraft doesn't hide from the implications here. Yes, his gyaa-yothn have black fur, "anthropoid blood," and flat noses and bulging lips ... but they evoke pity along with disgust. And their (idealized, brachycephalic Nordic-Amerind) masters, by contrast, evoke horror and even contempt. HPL paints the Old Ones as degenerate, sadistic materialists, whose practice of racial eugenics emerges organically as part and parcel of their de-

---

83. Lovecraft clearly derives "y'm-bhi" from the Caribbean living-dead enslaved "zombie," a word and concept sensationally re-introduced to pulp audiences earlier that year by William Seabrook's breathless travelogue of Haiti, *The Magic Island.*

based culture—in a story written in December 1929, perhaps six months after his first extended stay in the South.

> *"Formless protoplasm able to mock and reflect all forms and organs and processes—viscous agglutinations of bubbling cells—rubbery fifteen-foot spheroids infinitely plastic and ductile—slaves of suggestion, builders of cities—more and more sullen, more and more intelligent, more and more amphibious, more and more imitative—Great God! What madness made even those blasphemous Old Ones willing to use and to carve such things?"*

— H.P. LOVECRAFT, *AT THE MOUNTAINS OF MADNESS*

Then, a little more than a year later, he takes it all back. Like the K'n-yani Old Ones, the crinoid Old Ones in Antarctica genetically engineered a slave race, the shoggoths. But Lovecraft depicts these slavers as noble, comparing them to his beloved Romans, and in a famous peroration Professor Dyer assures the reader that vegetable-radiate aliens they might be, but "they were men!" By contrast, the shoggoths are nothing but a hideous mass: a "nightmare plastic column of foetid *black* iridescence," and sadly (as China Miéville points out in his introduction to the novel) Lovecraft's color choice seems deliberate here. Like the city fathers of Charleston, the Old Ones of Kadath faced a slave insurrection, the shoggoth rebellion in the Permian period finally put down with "weapons of molecular disturbance."

The Old Ones' civilization exhausts itself in decadence at the end, and their proud citadel becomes the property of the shoggoths at last. Dyer describes the new shoggoth bas-relief carvings as evincing a "profound and calamitous degradation of skill" reminiscent of "ungainly Palmyrene [Syrian] sculptures fashioned in the Roman manner." Even a geologist can recognize the shoggoths as (non-European) inferiors aping a superior (European) tradition. And what, coincidentally, does Lovecraft single out for mention three separate times in his extended Charleston travelogue? His observation that, during the Victorian era in Charleston, "[a]rchitectural details became heavy and almost crude as negro craftsmen replaced skill'd white carvers."

In January 1930, Lovecraft finishes "The Mound," a tale of thorough-going vileness centered on eugenic slavery. In April 1930, Lovecraft discovers a southern twin city of Providence: Charleston, a slave-built city seemingly untouched by hateful modernity or equality. In February 1931, freezing in a New England winter, he remembers the warmth of Charleston, and writes of another perfect city built by slaves, now fallen under a blanket of ice. A city, need I point out, that he places in Antarctica—as far South as it can possibly lie.

THE SWAMP

"My dreams occasionally approach'd the phantastical in character, tho'
falling somewhat short of coherence. One scene is especially stamp'd upon
my recollection—that of a dank, fœtid, reed-choak'd marsh under a grey
autumn sky, with a rugged cliff of lichen-crusted stone rising to the north."

— H.P. LOVECRAFT, LETTER TO DONALD WANDREI (NOVEMBER 24, 1927)

There is probably an excellent monograph, or series of monographs, one
could write on the topic of Lovecraft's specific dream images as expressed
in his fiction. If some discrete object-sensation-image appears multiple
times in his works, even if never quite in central fashion, it almost always appeared at some point earlier in his dreams. That certainly seems
to be the case with the dream-swamp he describes in the letter to Wandrei above: a Lovecraftian locus immediately recognizable as such, even
though its actual use as a main setting remained rare.

Only "The Statement of Randolph Carter" and "The Moon-Bog" set
their climactic action in the swamp, to which we can add major scenes in
"The Call of Cthulhu," "The Quest of Iranon," and "The Shadow Over
Innsmouth." Lovecraft briefly mentions the marshy nature of the Jurassic
in "The Shadow Out of Time," the "unhealthy shimmer" of the salt marsh
in the pre-colonial Manhattan of "He," and the similarly time-lost mud
flat in "Dagon." He further stages the action next to, but not in, swamps
or marshes in "The Whisperer in Darkness," "Medusa's Coil," "Polaris,"
"Two Black Bottles," and "The Tomb." The swamp provides major imagery to prose poems like "What the Moon Brings" and the fragment "The
Thing in the Moonlight," and to some of HPL's actual poems such as "On

Receiving a Picture of the Marshes at Ipswich" (1917), "Despair" (1919), "The Nightmare Lake" (1919), and "The Outpost" (1930).

> *"I saw the stretching marshy shore,*
> *And the foul things those marshes bore:*
> *Lizards and snakes convuls'd and dying;*
> *Ravens and vampires putrefying;*
> *All these, and hov'ring o'er the dead,*
> *Necrophagi that on them fed."*

— H.P. LOVECRAFT, "THE NIGHTMARE LAKE" (1919)

The swamp in the American imagination began as the Biblical "desert" in the sense of a land without human presence, as the punishment of a land removed from God: "But the miry places thereof and the marshes thereof shall not be healed; they shall be given to salt" (Ezekiel 47:11). The swamp is the haunt of monsters, as in *Beowulf,* or in the historical American experience the hiding place of escaped slaves, pirates, and Indians. Not just its dark hiding places, but its existence athwart social (and state) boundaries, make the swamp a threat to order.

American Gothic and Romantic writers additionally cast the swamp as a melancholy and fatal landscape.[84] Standout examples include Thomas Moore's "The Lake of the Dismal Swamp" (written in 1803 during a sojourn in Virginia), Longfellow's *Evangeline* (1847), and Poe's "Ulalume" (1847). Poe's "dank tarn" in "The Fall of the House of Usher" (1839) further limns the swamp as a source and home of infectious miasma and madness, the irrational made natural, the exalted unconscious. In *The Confidence-Man* (1857), Melville conventionally parallels the swamps around Cairo with disease and with lies—but in that proto-Lovecraftian text, infection is the only way to know reality, and disease is the only truth.

By Melville's 1850s, the Romantic tendency to glorify the tragic— and a new desire for a disappearing rural world among increasingly ur-

---

84. The verb "to swamp" takes on the meaning "to overwhelm" or "to drown" shortly after 1800.

ban readers—begins to turn the swamp around. Harriet Beecher Stowe uses the Biblical desert instead as the traditional dwelling of prophets in exile, in her novel of slave rebellion *Dred, A Tale of the Dismal Swamp* (1856). Henry Thoreau meanwhile re-imagines the swamp in "Walking, or the Wild" (1862) as a place of refreshment and reinvigoration, a reservoir of natural force. Walt Whitman celebrates the swamp's natural riot of life in "O Magnet-South" (1860), which contains amidst his earthy joy a Lovecraftian tone: "O the strange fascination of these half-known half-impassable swamps, infested by reptiles, resounding with the bellow of the alligator, the sad noises of the night-owl and the wild-cat."

> *"You say to me that there is nothing in the swamp or near it which could form the setting of that frightful episode. I reply that I know nothing beyond what I saw."*
>
> — H.P. LOVECRAFT, "THE STATEMENT OF RANDOLPH CARTER"

This is the conventional picture of the swamp that Lovecraft's stand-in Randolph Carter enters along the Gainesville Pike in 1919 with his abusive mentor Harley Warren, fretting at "the gross luxuriance of the unhealthy vegetation."[85] In the dream that inspired this story, Lovecraft and his friend Samuel Loveman merely violate a grave in "a very strange and very ancient cemetery" of the New England sort. Lovecraft added the swamp—specifically named Big Cypress Swamp in the tale—and moved the location south, presumably to Florida where the most prominent real-world examples of a Gainesville and a Big Cypress Swamp occur, though not remotely near each other.[86]

---

85. Early Lovecraft has strong feelings about trees that might have fed on human corpses: this story, "The Tree," "The Lurking Fear," and "The Unnamable" all share this motif.

86. There are also a Gainesville and a Big Cypress Swamp in Georgia, although the Big Cypress Swamp in Georgia lies closer to Gainesville, Florida than it does to the northern-Georgia Gainesville. Virginia also boasts a Gainesville Pike (in northern Virginia) and many big cypress swamps (in southern and eastern Virginia) though none so specifically named. But it's most likely that Lovecraft hastily picked a town name in Florida without looking at the map: in his first draft, he misspelled it "Gainsville."

Throughout the short story, Carter refers to "miasmas" and "vapors" and implies his memory remains uncertain, as if the experience were a dream. This is straight Usher stuff, in which the swamp or tarn where earth becomes water and air similarly interpenetrates dream and reality, madness and truth. "Polaris," written eighteen months or so before "Statement," likewise interweaves dream and waking, past and present, myth and reality. Its narrator lives in the house "south of the sinister swamp" but he can see the "red-leaved trees of the swamp" nearby. A little over a year after "Statement" Lovecraft returned glancingly to the swamp, at the climax of "Quest of Iranon." Iranon's (possibly fantastic) search for the city Aira, in a (probably) Dreamland tale, ends in a "marshy quicksand" of unknowable truth.

> *"The bog was the cause of all these troubles, as Barry told me the night I came to the castle. I had reached Kilderry in the summer sunset, as the gold of the sky lighted the green of the hills and groves and the blue of the bog, where on a far islet a strange olden ruin glistened spectrally."*
>
> — H.P. LOVECRAFT, "THE MOON-BOG"

Lovecraft's other early swamp story, 1921's "The Moon-Bog," similarly involves dreams, death, and madness, and gaps in a narrator's memory. All classic Lovecraftian elements, all part of our emerging swamp complex. It even begins with a proper Lovecraftian phobia: "And now I shudder when I hear the frogs piping in swamps, or see the moon in lonely places." But in this story, the primordial evil doesn't emerge from the bog, but from Denys Barry's plan to drain the bog. Barry sins against Nature and Nature's (Greek) gods, and they reach down from the moon and repay his hubris.[87]

Unusually, Lovecraft also casts it as an aesthetic crime to drain the bog, "to strip ... its moss and green heather, and kill the tiny shell-paved streamlets

---

87. This would be an excellent place to note the parallels and differences between "The Moon-Bog" and John Buchan's weird tale "The Grove of Ashtaroth" (1910), except I have no evidence that Lovecraft ever read that Buchan story, much less before 1921. He seems to have read most of his Buchan during a spate of classics consumption while revising *Supernatural Horror in Literature* in 1933.

and quiet blue pools fringed with rushes." Draining the bog is like knocking down a Georgian building, destroying something beautiful out of nothing but capitalist greed or materialist blindness. Thus even Lovecraft isn't wholly immune to Thoreau's sense of the swamp as a place of respite, reconstruction, even healing. The bog certainly holds a sort of resurrection, halfway between Henry Thoreau and Harley Warren perhaps. But it's still "brooding" and conceals "sunless secrets [with] terrible sights lying black under the unmeasured depth of age-old peat." The sin, ultimately, lies in attempting to discover the truth, to piece together the past on solid ground.

> *"It was a quest of the grotesque and the terrible—a search for Dark Swamp, in northwestern Rhode-Island, of which [C.M.] Eddy had heard sinister whispers among the rusticks. They whisper that it is very remote and very strange, and that no one has ever been completely thro' it because of the treacherous and unfathomable potholes, and the antient trees whose thick boles grow so closely together that passage is difficult and darkness omnipresent even at noon, and other things .... It is a very peculiar place, and no house was ever built within two miles of it."*

> — H.P. LOVECRAFT, LETTER TO FRANK
> BELKNAP LONG (NOVEMBER 8, 1923)

No discussion of the Lovecraftian swamp should omit the comic interlude of the search for Dark Swamp on November 4, 1923. Lovecraft's friend and sometime collaborator C.M. Eddy had heard "sinister whispers" of a fabled "Dark Swamp" in the area of Chepachet, in northwestern Rhode Island. According to "the rusticks," an anomalous flight of rabbits out of the territory was because of something in the Swamp: "One very antient man with a flint-lock said that IT had mov'd ..." So Lovecraft and Eddy set out to discover it (and even IT), in search of quasi-Thoreauvian inspiration perhaps.

In Chepachet they asked around the bar, and the drinkers sent them to the town clerk. That worthy said the Swamp had "a queer reputation" but that he had never seen it, and maybe they should ask one Sprague, who had guided a Brown University botanical expedition thither in 1911. Sprague explained that he hadn't been the guide, that was a fellow named Fred Barnes, who in turn had better things to do and sent them on to James Reynolds via another tavern. Mr. Reynolds in turn informed them that the Swamp was on the property of the farmer Ernest Law. Farmer Law received their compliments and pointed out the Swamp, "a very odd place" between two hills, two miles away "by a winding road." Having walked seventeen miles and killed the whole day with zero Swamp to speak of, Lovecraft and Eddy turned around and headed homeward ... and never returned.[88]

> "At the end of the passable road they alighted, and for miles splashed on in silence through the terrible cypress woods where day never came. Ugly roots and malignant hanging nooses of Spanish moss beset them, and now and then a pile of dank stones or fragment of a rotting wall intensified by its hint of morbid habitation a depression which every malformed tree and every fungous islet combined to create."

> — H.P. Lovecraft, "The Call of Cthulhu"

We shall never know what great tale of the swamp we missed thanks to the dilatory yokels of Chepachet, but Lovecraft returned to the "terrible cypress woods" with a vengeance in 1926 in "The Call of Cthulhu." Perhaps his return to Providence that year reminded him of his previous adventure, or perhaps with his actual feet back on firmer social soil he felt freer to fictively venture again into the mire. Here he provides us with actual swamp-dwellers, his "abject rurals" exported from Upstate. As in those earlier tales, he separates the innocent and terrified "primitive but good-natured" swamp squatters from the degenerate Cthulhu cultists. The cultists inhabit an area of swamp that even the squatters fear to enter, an ur-swamp, a "black morass."

The police push through the ur-swamp and reach "a natural glade of the swamp ... a grassy island of perhaps an acre's extent, clear of trees and tolerably dry." In the midst of chaos, an order. But this order proves worse than

---

88. To the Swamp, that is. They returned home just fine.

even "the blackest of the African voodoo circles," as it orbits the inhuman titan-god Cthulhu. Islands in the swamp may just be narrative necessities (characters have to be able to stand and move for action to happen, after all) but they do recur a lot. Not just in "Call" but in "The Moon-Bog," "Shadow Over Innsmouth," and "Two Black Bottles" (and Lovecraft's poem "The Outpost") this pattern recurs: a fane of the Outside, acting as a crystallizing catalyst of the Unnatural in the midst of fluid Nature.

> *"If this were so, I would have to make my retreat across country away from any road; but how could I do that in view of the marshy and creek-riddled nature of all the surrounding region? For a moment my brain reeled—both from sheer hopelessness and from a rapid increase in the omnipresent fishy odour."*

> — H.P. LOVECRAFT, "THE SHADOW OVER INNSMOUTH"

In "Whisperer in Darkness" the alien-colonized Dark Mountain "rises out of Lee's Swamp," perhaps pointing to a kindred archetype: the dead city in a swamp.[89] In "Quest of Iranon" we hear of "the marsh where Sarnath once stood," for example.

The fragment "The Thing in the Moonlight" begins in a swamp near a ruined city, and "He" describes the salt marsh on which Greenwich and New York City itself would eventually rise. If the squatters represent a dead society in a swamp, their terror (like Lovecraft's own fears) points to their hideous double, the shadow of this half-hidden archetype, specifically R'lyeh. Cthulhu's island combines swamp and city, at least in its adjectives. This "strange, dank" island of "mingled mud, ooze, and weedy Cyclopean masonry," features "oozy blocks" "dripping with green ooze." A "polarising miasma" distorts its sun, and "[o]ne could not be sure that the sea and ground were horizontal."

Innsmouth incarnates the dead city in a swamp even more fully than R'lyeh, if only because Lovecraft lingers long over the tale of its murder by … the

---

89. Honesty compels me to mention that the main Mi-Go colony at Round Hill is "east of here," apparently on the other side of Dark Mountain from Lee's Swamp ("the west slope").

Marshes. He situates the town, essentially, on an island in the swamp: "wide salt marshes, desolate and unpeopled" surround the town on the landward side. The only way out is the Rowley railway, abandoned now but still a "solid line of ballasted, weed-grown earth [that] stretched off to the northwest" to Rowley and civilization. The way out of the swamp of chaos and madness is the straight line of reason ... unless you carry the swamp out with you.

> *"I have drunk of the fog-foetid fountains*
> *That ooze down to the marsh and the main;*
> *And in hot cursed tarns I have seen things I care not to gaze on again."*

— H.P. LOVECRAFT, "NEMESIS" (1917)

The last line of this passage from "Nemesis" reveals again our swamp image, the "hot cursed tarn" that holds the horrible truth. But look at the two lines above it in an Innsmouthian light: the "fog-foetid fountains" themselves show the spoor of the swamp, as they "ooze down to the marsh" and the sea. And Lovecraft tells us he has drunk of that swamp water, made it his own hideous Hippocrene. He has been contaminated by that drink, and by what he has seen in those tarns.

To smell something involves actually inhaling particles of the thing smelled. The foulness comes inside your body, an inhalation leading to, becoming, an involuntary drink. This foetor proclaims and comprises almost all of Lovecraft's horrors; "as a foulness shall ye know Them," as he writes. Swamps smell bad, almost archetypically so, the source of their miasmas and vapors being "loathsomely redolent" rotting matter. Not that Lovecraft is any great fan of the swamp's outrageous and simultaneous fecundity, either: remember the Cthulhu cult's "animal fury and orgiastic license." Life and death mingle in decay, water and land blend, a plastic biology and geography that rhyme with the non-Euclidean geometry of the Outside. The swamp becomes a fractal synecdoche for the Lovecraftian world, a realm of chaos and miasma, blasted by God and shunned by man, dark and full of holes and monsters.

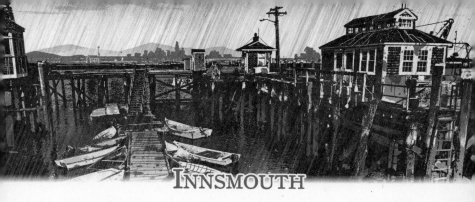

INNSMOUTH

"Then we reached the crest and beheld the outspread valley beyond, where the Manuxet joins the sea just north of the long line of cliffs that culminate in Kingsport Head and veer off toward Cape Ann. On the far, misty horizon I could just make out the dizzy profile of the Head, topped by the queer ancient house of which so many legends are told; but for the moment all my attention was captured by the nearer panorama just below me. I had, I realised, come face to face with rumour-shadowed Innsmouth."

— H.P. LOVECRAFT, "THE SHADOW OVER INNSMOUTH"

Once more Lovecraft looks down from a height at a city of dream, but this time he does so not with with wonder but with pity and horror. This time he looks, and we look, at Innsmouth. The decrepit fishing port on the coast of Miskatonic country first appears in 1929 in two of the *Fungi From Yuggoth* sonnets, "The Port" and "The Bells."[90] Robert Olmstead's[91] terrifying and terrified narrative "The Shadow Over Innsmouth" evokes and limns the titular town more fully than any other of Lovecraft's created conurbations, so much so that one can draw a street map of the city based on the story. Asenath Waite, the villain/ess of "The Thing on the Doorstep" hails from Innsmouth, and Walter Gilman almost finds his feet set on the road to Innsmouth in "The Dreams in the Witch House." It's not immediately

---

90. Robert Marten also suggests that Sonnet IX, "The Courtyard," takes place in Innsmouth, doubtless because of its placement immediately after "The Port" and its reference to "rotting, fish-eyed houses." That poem's corpses without "either hands or head" also evoke the fate of the idol of Dagon in 1 Samuel 5:4: "the head of Dagon and both his hands were cut off." However, Lovecraft based the "black courtyard" of the title on Union Place in Brooklyn, and almost titled the sonnet "Union Place."

91. The name of the narrator of "The Shadow Over Innsmouth" appears in Lovecraft's notes, though not in the actual text of the story.

relevant to our Tour, but Innsmouth has spawned more post-Lovecraft "Cthulhu Mythos" stories than Kingsport, Dunwich, or even Arkham.[92] In the memetic sense—as in all other senses—Innsmouth is "sticky."

> *"'Innsmouth' reflects a sort of exaggeration of ancient Newburyport, Mass., whose increasing quiescence & depopulation are getting to be almost spectral."*
>
> — H.P. LOVECRAFT, LETTER TO ROBERT BLOCH (MAY 9, 1933)

Lovecraft liked the name of the town well enough to recycle it from his 1920 Dreamland tale "Celephaïs," where "Innsmouth" refers to the seaside town in Devon or Cornwall over whose cliffs the Earth-bound body of Kuranes topples. One can imagine a parallel with Exeter and Plymouth, two cities in Devon that also provided their names to Massachusetts port cities. Robert Marten speculates that Lovecraft may have initially simply made a "whimsical reversal" of Exmouth (the port of Exeter in England) to "Innsmouth" for the 1920 story.

Marten also speculates that Lovecraft picked the name from his own early work because the story centers on an inn, Gilman House, as does one of its models, Algernon Blackwood's "Ancient Sorceries" (1908). Lovecraft admired this tale of a traveler who encounters a town full of bestial cultists (of cats, not fish) and mentions its "ancient inn yard" in 1928 when summarizing it in his Commonplace Book. Marten's theory ignores the original coinage, and assumes that Lovecraft was plotting his late-1931 story two years earlier while naming decrepit seaports in *Fungi From Yuggoth*. In my own mind, Marten is on safer ground with the reversed-Exmouth theory.[93]

---

92. See, for example, the stories in the latter half of *The Innsmouth Cycle* (Chaosium, 1998) and (just for a start) the anthologies *Shadows Over Innsmouth* (Fedogan & Bremer, 1994), *Weird Shadows Over Innsmouth* (Fedogan & Bremer, 2005), *Tales Out of Innsmouth* (Chaosium, 2006), *Innsmouth Nightmares* (PS Publishing, 2013), *Weirder Shadows Over Innsmouth* (Fedogan & Bremer, 2013), and *Innsmouth Tales* (Self-published, 2000/2015).

93. The Deep One city off the coast of Innsmouth, Y'ha-nthlei, derives from Dunsany's "god of little dreams" Yoharneth-Lahai, who appeared in his own sketch in *Gods of Pegāna* (1905). It would be neat if "the land of Honalee" where "Puff, the Magic Dragon" lived came from Lovecraft or Dunsany, but I have no evidence that the lyricist Leonard Lipton ever read either author. Peter Yarrow's parents originally settled in Providence, Rhode Island, though.

Marten is downright bulletproof when he insists that Lovecraft based the town of Innsmouth on Newburyport, Massachusetts. Andrew Rothovius argued unconvincingly for Ipswich, while Colin Wilson even more arbitrarily cites Cohasset, a rundown fishing port in Rhode Island. Will Murray writes that since Newburyport appears in the story, Innsmouth must "be" somewhere else, and suggested Gloucester as Lovecraft's real model. As far as that goes, Innsmouth must indeed be located on the Massachusetts coast "between Newburyport and Arkham," as HPL wrote to Clark Ashton Smith in November 1931, but there's no reason to erase, or particularly consider, Gloucester either.

Murray claims Gloucester's American Legion Hall as a close match for the Esoteric Order of Dagon Hall in Innsmouth, and notes the existence of the cupola'd (actually, dormered) Sargent-Murray-*Gilman*-Hough House in Gloucester.[94] As against that, Marten deploys nine street names in Newburyport identical to Innsmouth avenues (versus Murray's seven in Gloucester), Newburyport's semicircular "town square" unique in New England except for Innsmouth, and the roaring Merrimack River that inspired the otherwise-anomalous falls of Innsmouth's Manuxet. One might also usefully note the *sixteen* separate identifications of Newburyport as the model for Innsmouth in Lovecraft's letters.

> "[S]he assured me that the rumours of devil-worship were partly justified by a peculiar secret cult which had gained force there and engulfed all the orthodox churches. It was called, she said, 'The Esoteric Order of Dagon,' and was undoubtedly a debased, quasi-pagan thing imported from the East a century before, at a time when the Innsmouth fisheries seemed to be going barren."

> — H.P. LOVECRAFT, "THE SHADOW OVER INNSMOUTH"

Lovecraft also took at least some inspiration for Innsmouth from the setting of the horror-paranoia novel *The Place Called Dagon* (1927)

---

94. I'm sure this has occurred to others, but I think the Dexter-Jackson House in Newburyport with its solitary, somewhat ludicrous cupola must have inspired the "cupalo" on top of Zadok Allen's childhood house.

by Herbert Gorman. That novel, which Lovecraft read in early 1928, transpires between two towns in central Massachusetts: Marlborough, founded by refugee witch-cultists from the Salem trials, and Leeminster, founded by refugee orgiasts from Thomas Morton's Merrymount settlement.[95] Morton's brand of Maypole-dancing, rum-running, free-love religion took over the original (1625) settlement of Mount Wollaston in 1626 and he renamed it Merrymount or Mount Ma-re. When Puritan forces from Plymouth Colony under Miles Standish sacked Merrymount in 1629, they renamed it "Mount Dagon," and exiled Morton to the Isles of Shoals off Portsmouth, New Hampshire.[96] The Puritans starved Mount Dagon out the following winter, and burnt it in 1631. Merrymount is now a neighborhood in Quincy, Massachusetts.

Lovecraft absolutely knew the Merrymount story, from his own wide reading in colonial history as much as from Gorman's novel and the Nathaniel Hawthorne tale "The May-Pole of Merry Mount" (1832). He mentions it in a letter to Wilfred Blanch Talman in March 1931, somehow resisting the Dagon reference. Dagon, who HPL had invoked in his first published story, bubbled once more to the surface of Lovecraft's thinking somewhen in the fall of 1931. Morton's colonists, like Marsh's townsfolk, bred with "the Other," and were accused (by William Bradford and others) of reviving pagan rites. Lovecraft's version of history repeating itself thus casts the FBI as Puritan authorities and J. Edgar Hoover as a modern-day Miles Standish, destroying a new Mount Dagon in an overwhelming military raid.

---

95. Gorman's Leeminster takes its name from the central Massachusetts town of Leominster, about 25 miles east of Athol, near where Lovecraft fictively placed Dunwich. *The Place Called Dagon* reads very much like a less-cosmic, talkier version of "The Dunwich Horror," and I suspect it influenced that story even more than it did "Innsmouth."

96. Just up the coast from Newburyport, Lovecraft visited Portsmouth on the same October 1931 trip that sparked "Shadow Over Innsmouth." David Haden suggests the Isles helped inspire Devil Reef. The Isles have more than their share of dramatic legend and history, including anomalously ample fish catches, mysterious bars of silver, and notorious murders.

"Sails out of Innsmouth! echoing old renown
Of long-dead times. But now a too-swift night
Is closing in, and I have reached the height
Whence I so often scan the distant town.
The spires and roofs are there—but look! The gloom
Sinks on dark lanes, as lightless as the tomb!"

— H.P. LOVECRAFT, *FUNGI FROM YUGGOTH* VIII, "THE PORT" (1929)

Before Lovecraft consecrates Innsmouth to Dagon, he marries it to the sea in two sonnets. In Sonnet VIII, "The Port," the narrator walks north from Arkham to "the crest" of hills overlooking Innsmouth and sees a sail that strikes him as "evil with some portent beyond speech." However, when he reaches the height at nightfall, he sees Innsmouth spread out without any lights. Lovecraft's Commonplace Book for 1928 records the image of a ship leaving a dead port city, unlit at night. He still wrestled with the motif as late as 1934: "town fails to light up at night" appears in his Commonplace Book for that year. In the story, Innsmouth of course has a fearsome shadow over it, and no lights except the implacable moon.

In Sonnet XIX, "The Bells," the sound of midnight bells haunts the narrator, who explores his "dreams and memories" for the answer. He remembers "quiet Innsmouth, where the white gulls tarried / Around an ancient spire" but when he seeks it in dream, he reaches "submerged towers" where "sunless tides" ring the bells "on the dead sea floor." This poem recalls a legend, told of innumerable coastal towns in Britain including the original Dunwich in Suffolk and Forrabury in Cornwall near the "original" Innsmouth: A shipwreck, or a flood, carries the church bells out to sea, where they ring to herald storms. Poe's poem "The City in the Sea" (1831) provides another touchstone for Lovecraft's sonnet, although it focuses on the emotional impact of a dead city that even stills the sea around it. When the city finally sinks, Poe writes, "Hell, rising from a thousand thrones / Shall do it reverence."

"She was one of the Innsmouth Waites, and dark legends have clustered for generations about crumbling, half-deserted Innsmouth and its people."

— H.P. LOVECRAFT, "THE THING ON THE DOORSTEP"

And well might Hell honor Innsmouth. Even the citizens of witch-haunted Arkham detest Innsmouth, and not in a regional rivalry sort of way. Arkham's Methodist pastors urge their communicants to avoid Innsmouth's churches. In both "The Thing on the Doorstep" and "Dreams in the Witch House," Innsmouth acts as a looming locus of evil. In the first story, Innsmouth acts as the dangerous Outside reflection of seemingly orderly Arkham, full of witches and sorcery and blackmailing servants. In the second, Innsmouth becomes a weirdly resonant echo of a triple-sunned Outside which also provides enigmatic alien metalwork. Innsmouth serves as Arkham's dark twin in "Doorstep," and as the figurative "human twin" to hyperspatial true horror in "Witch House."[97]

In all three stories, the central figures escape from Innsmouth. Robert Olmstead in "Shadow" escapes along the rusted Rowley railway spur, along a straight (or at least engineered) line northwest to modernity and civilization. In "Doorstep," Asenath (or Ephraim) Waite escapes from the death-house city of Innsmouth by covert infiltration, embodying Lovecraft's fears of sex, identity loss, and foreign blood in one package. Her husband Edward Derby then escapes (temporarily) from Asenath's symbolic Innsmouth by smashing her skull with a candlestick, a somewhat under-analyzed response to Lovecraftian horror. Gilman's escape from the pull of Innsmouth (or the "infinite north" along its azimuth) is the most interesting of the batch. He cannot escape it alone, so he balances vectors,

---

97. Robert Waugh points out that Innsmouth also twins Kingsport: both ancient, undermined with warrens and tunnels, architecturally pure but secretly decadent, outside time, symbolically devoted (as Robert M. Price theorizes) to "St. Toad." Kingsport's god looks down from the heights, Innsmouth's lurks below the depths; Kingsport is the whitening, Innsmouth the sepulcher. Lovecraft's work repays nearly endless examination from different perspectives through this lens; even in this book, I barely scrape the surface of the possibilities. If you doubt the depth of Lovecraft's art and skill after reading Waugh's essay "Landscapes, Selves, and Others in Lovecraft" then there is simply no reasoning with you.

THE DESTINATIONS · 227

using the pull toward the stars (to the point between Hydra and Argo Navis) to countermand the pull to the sea. Equilibrium and math become the opposite of madness and impulse.

> *"But the real thing behind the way folks feel is simply race prejudice—and I don't say I'm blaming those that hold it. I hate those Innsmouth folks myself, and I wouldn't care to go to their town. I s'pose you know—though I can see you're a Westerner by your talk—what a lot our New England ships used to have to do with queer ports in Africa, Asia, the South Seas, and everywhere else, and what queer kinds of people they sometimes brought back with 'em."*

— H.P. LOVECRAFT, "THE SHADOW OVER INNSMOUTH"

Once we start pulling up the cellar doors of Innsmouth looking for sub-textual fish-frogs, pretty soon we hit Lovecraft's bass line of degeneration and decay linked to racial mixing. A quarter of Rhode Islanders were for-eign-born in 1930, something Lovecraft very definitely noticed. His own beloved Providence hosted vibrant communities of Italians, Irish, Poles, and Portuguese, among others. He responded to them fictively in varying fashions: killing them in "The Terrible Old Man," patronizing them in "Dreams in the Witch House," and even valorizing them in "Haunter of the Dark." In "Shadow Over Innsmouth" he takes a sort of middle path: the Deep Ones and Dagon cultists "scattered" the would-be Polish and Portuguese immigrants to Innsmouth "in a peculiarly drastic fashion."

Lovecraft very possibly painted the "Kanaky" Deep One influx into Innsmouth as his response to another immigrant group: the relatively large population of Cape Verdeans in Providence.[98] Whaling ships from New Bedford, and merchant ships in general from Providence, heavily recruited crews from Brava and the other Cape Verde Islands off west Africa, considering the islanders near-perfect sailors: disciplined, honest, able, and cheap. By 1930, Cape Verdean shiphands had bought or salvaged

---

98. I haven't been able to track down the blog post where I originally ran across this theory. It may have been one by the excellent Lovecraftian writer and editor Paula R. Stiles.

their own ships, and owned virtually every sailing ship in New Bedford. Descendants of whaling crewmen became independent fishermen and pursued their own shore trades, most notably in two cities: New Bedford and Providence.

Portugal long encouraged intermarriage between Europeans and natives in its colonies, including Cape Verde, and the resulting blend confounded the U.S. Census then and now. Cape Verdean immigration to the U.S. reached 1,500 per year by 1923; one might estimate Cape Verdean numbers in the Providence area of between three and five thousand (about 2% of the population) in 1930.[99] Lovecraft very likely noticed this distinctive, clearly mixed-race group: the Louisiana Cthulhu cult in "Call of Cthulhu" is "largely West Indians or Brava Portuguese from the Cape Verde Islands." Joseph Curwen's servant Gomes is also Cape Verdean, infiltrating sacred Providence itself at the side of an Anglo necromancer.

> "Innsmouth? ... Used to be almost a city—quite a port before the War of
> 1812—but all gone to pieces in the last hundred years or so. No railroad
> now—B. & M. never went through, and the branch line from Rowley
> was given up years ago. More empty houses than there are people, I
> guess, and no business to speak of .... Once they had quite a few mills,
> but nothing's left now except one gold refinery running on the leanest
> kind of part time."

> — H.P. LOVECRAFT, "THE SHADOW OVER INNSMOUTH"

The only thing more common than racial subtexts in Lovecraft is pointing out racial subtexts in Lovecraft. Far less often do critics seek an economic subtext in HPL, despite the presence of an economics professor as the protagonist of "The Shadow Out of Time." Lovecraft, of course, keenly felt his own fall into ever-less-genteel poverty, and responded strongly when he saw his own plight mirrored in his surround-

---

99. Those who see the (black, enslaved) shoggoths as signifiers of Lovecraft's fear of racial uprising may note at this juncture that the Deep Ones plan to raise a shoggoth in the abyss off Innsmouth.

ings. Lovecraft visited Newburyport in April 1923[100] and August 1927, and even on those visits noticed the town's "sand-choked harbour" and "utter, hushed stagnation," and the unpaved streets of its "marvellous slum labyrinths." Visiting again in October 1931, he again saw rows of shuttered 18th-century houses, sunken and ruined warehouses, and rotting docks—and almost immediately started writing "The Shadow Over Innsmouth."

The difference was that in October 1931 he feared the same thing happening to Providence. The unemployment rate in December 1931 was 15.3% nationally, but unemployment in highly industrialized Rhode Island regularly tracked higher, possibly reaching 25% when Lovecraft was writing this story.[101] Providence specifically suffered from the crash in the market for jewelry, one of the city's major manufactures; unemployment in Providence rose to 32% over the 1931-1932 period. The Great Depression had transformed Lovecraft from a reactionary Yankee aristocrat into a technocratic dirigiste enthusiastic for "a kind of fascistic socialism." This change shows in this story, from Olmstead's thin travel budget to the economic panic and gold-lust driving the embrace of Dagon, the explicit identification of the cult leaders with the town's leading capitalists, and possibly even to the un-Lovecraftian ending in which Olmstead decides to surrender to his blood and join the Deep Ones forever. Whatever else is wrong with Innsmouth, unlike Providence it could still manufacture jewelry.

"Everything cleaned up in the mornin'—but they was traces.... *Obed he kinder takes charge an' says things is goin' to be changed ... others'll worship with us at meetin'-time, an' sarten haouses hez got to entertain* guests ... they *wanted to mix like they done with the Kanakys ...."*

— H.P. LOVECRAFT, "THE SHADOW OVER INNSMOUTH"

100. On this visit, he met Miss Helen Tilton, the superintendent of the library reading room. She became Olmstead's informant Anna Tilton of the Newburyport Historical Society in "Shadow."

101. During the period 1930-1933, of all the states of the union, Rhode Island had the third-highest unemployment rate on average. Only Michigan and Nevada suffered more.

In the course of arguing (entirely successfully) that "Shadow Over Innsmouth" narrates a rite of passage, Robert M. Price points out that Innsmouth is itself "an interstitial space of liminality," as he puts it. A liminal space exists between two other spaces: a doorway exists between inside and outside, for example. And we all know what Lovecraft thinks of Doorways between Inside and Outside. Innsmouth is such a doorway, the threshold of the "gate o' hell" off Devil Reef, through which the Deep One taint enters America. Geographically and symbolically, Innsmouth lies between Newburyport (economic ruin caused by capitalism) and Arkham (moral ruin caused by witchcraft), and reflects both.[102] It's also a seaport on the coast, literally lying between land and water. To underline that, it's surrounded by a salt marsh—also a condition between solid earth and liquid sea—and ruled by Marshes.

The Marshes, of course, are themselves interstitial beings, existing and interfacing between humanity and alien Deep Ones. The Innsmouth folk are triply liminal: amphibian (breathing water and air), hybrid (human and Deep One), fish-frogs ("half ichthyic and half batrachian"). Innsmouth is crumbling but not a ruin, described not just in "Shadow" but "Doorstep" and "Witch House" as "half-deserted." Innsmouth is transformative, changing Olmsteads into Marshes and humans into Deep Ones; it is alchemical, changing a "funny-shaped lead thingumajig" into gold. Innsmouth lies outside of the natural time-sequence; it has no clocks, "only black gaping holes where clock-dials should have been" and a bell that tolls "hoarse strokes" right out of the sonnet.

Last but not least, Innsmouth embodies and enmeshes that most hideously transitive of senses: the sense of smell. As we noted in our Stop in the Swamp, to smell an odor is to be contaminated by it, and Innsmouth has "stench-cursed streets." Lovecraft continuously fortifies its fishy "odour" (a word he uses 11 times in the tale), its "smell" (7 times), and its "malodorous" (2 times), "foul" (once) "stench" (3 times). He even smudges

---

102. James Kneale makes the fascinating point that Innsmouth also lies almost equidistant between Jerusalem and Ponape, the home of the Cthulhu cult in the tale.

the boundary between scent and hearing, as Innsmouth's hybrids "flopped noisomely past" the cowering Olmstead.

But Olmstead only cowers there in the grassy ravine because Innsmouth drew him to its squamous bosom first. All Lovecraft's cities are twin cities, and Innsmouth (which has its own twin city offshore in Y'hanthlei) combines repulsion and attraction. The mystery of a hidden city and a beautiful tiara compel Olmstead to discover repellent inhabitants and decaying buildings. Innsmouth boasts "fine but ruinous old churches," while Devil Reef combines "beckoning superadded to grim repulsion." Olmstead's blood attracts, his nose revolts. In Innsmouth, the Jungian mysterium coniunctionis becomes a coming-of-age fertility rite, a literal mystery of interpenetration between hinterland Ohio and the archetypally feminine sea.[103]

> "[C]ould not an hallucination have been repeated under the quasi-hypnotic spell of that ancient, haunted, and shadowed town? Such places have strange properties ...."

— H.P. LOVECRAFT, "THE SHADOW OVER INNSMOUTH"

Lovecraft emphasizes the thin-ness of boundaries constantly in his work, as we noted in our Dreamland Stop early in our Tour. Dreams, infiltration, contamination, madness, uncanny survival, unnatural hybridity; all these core Lovecraftian concepts fructify in Innsmouth and in its core story. Moreover, all of these erode or even erase boundaries. Lovecraft fears the act of penetrating boundaries—of oozing through them, or teleporting across them, or revealing them to be mere arbitrary lines by a trick of mathematics or perspective. To Lovecraft, the liminal space always conceals (or rather reveals) the terrifying place. No map can contain or define it, and no Rowley railway spur can lead one out of it.

This, then, is what a rationalist atheist considers blasphemous. It's not just Lovecraft's bigotry that depends on black-and-white categories, but

---

103. I have almost as little regard for Jungian interpretations of literature as I do for Freudian ones, but I have to admit that "Shadow" is one story where a Jungian reading seems almost too obvious.

his epistemology, even his ontology. The rational mind depends on categories and lines and cause-to-effect relationships to function: to allow
overlaps and blurs and synchronicities is to open the way to mysticism and
chaos, to "an actual contagious madness," in Olmstead's words. Lovecraft
turned those subversive hybridities into art, horrific suspicion becoming
inspiration and vice versa. He fictively swam out to the brooding reef of
his subconscious, looked down into the economic abyss, saw a city with no
lights, and heard the bells of Innsmouth.

Apocalypse

"The increasing thunder must have affected my dreams, for in the brief time I slept there came to me apocalyptic visions."

— H.P. Lovecraft, "The Lurking Fear"

Of Lovecraft's first two mature tales, "The Tomb" deals with transcending death; in classic Lovecraftian fashion, evading death becomes more horrible than simply dying. "Dagon," meanwhile, grapples with (as its narrator shrinks from) death on a larger scale: that of civilizations, of our species, and perhaps even our planet. A horror author as ambivalent toward personal death as Lovecraft was[104] gravitates toward those two edge cases: Undeath and Apocalypse. Perhaps in some later Tour we'll look into the unquiet grave with Jervas Dudley and Harley Warren—for now, let's get ringside seats to the end of everything.

"Then rose spires and monoliths that were weedy but not remembered; terrible spires and monoliths of lands that men never knew were lands. There was not any pounding now, but only the unearthly roaring and hissing of waters tumbling into the rift."

— H.P. Lovecraft and Winifred V. Jackson, "The Crawling Chaos"

Lovecraft vouchsafes us explicit visions of his early Apocalypse in four stories and one poem, written between November 1920 and August 1925. The first of them, the prose poem "Nyarlathotep," began as a dream; another dream in 1927 became the fragment "The Thing in the Moonlight."

---

104. Note, as just one of many examples, that the offer of paradise in "Ex Oblivione" is literally oblivion and nothingness.

The moon appears in all his apocalyptic visions, from the "greenish moon" in "Nyarlathotep" and the "ghastly moon" of "The Crawling Chaos" to the explicit lunar revelation of "What the Moon Brings" and the "glare of the moon" in his 1925 poem "The Cats." In "He" the "impious pyramids flung to the moon" echo the full moon that ushers in the personal apocalypse of the titular wizard.

Other common elements weave in and out of the six revelations: a rusting railway in "Nyarlathotep" and "The Thing in the Moonlight"; stone pyramids in "The Cats" and "He"; flowers in "Crawling Chaos" and "What the Moon Brings," and flowering fungi in "The Cats"; crumbling steeples in "The Cats" and a broken tower in "Nyarlathotep." Devil-lights burn in "He" and death-lights glow in "The Cats;" marshes glitter in "What the Moon Brings," "The Thing in the Moonlight," and "He," albeit in the past. Receding oceans reveal weedy spires in "Crawling Chaos" and "What the Moon Brings," Asiatics revel in "The Cats" and "He" and skulk in "Nyarlathotep," and cacophony echoes through "Crawling Chaos" and "He" along with the endless nightmare shrieks of "Nyarlathotep." From the chill winds from Outside at the beginning of "Nyarlathotep" to the metaphorical black "ocean of bitumen" that rises on the drums and horns of "He," Lovecraft's Apocalypse encompasses his entire mythos.

> *"I dream of a day when they may rise above the billows to drag down in their reeking talons the remnants of puny, war-exhausted mankind—of a day when the land shall sink, and the dark ocean floor shall ascend amidst universal pandemonium."*

— H.P. LOVECRAFT, "DAGON"

It is almost Lovecraftian convention to note that "Dagon" prefigures "The Call of Cthulhu," and indeed the eschatology of the entire Cthulhu Mythos, in the above sentence. This first hint of Apocalypse receives a perhaps-surprising echo in "Arthur Jermyn" when Lovecraft opens his narrative of the facts concerning him with this: "Science, already oppressive with its shocking revelations, will perhaps be the ultimate exterminator of our human species—if separate species we be—for its reserve of unguessed horrors could never be borne by mortal brains if loosed upon the world." Dagon's tectonic cataclysm from below combines with a hideous revelation from within, revealed not by divine prophecy but by cold science.

The world is itself an apocalypse waiting, and we must inevitably awaken and be destroyed. What we consider the commanding heights of reason will topple us into the abyss of madness, a psychological coloration of Dagon's geological doom. The originator of Deep Time, James Hutton, postulated a world of mountains and continents endlessly upthrust by volcanism and ground down by erosion, providing an Enlightenment gloss on the prophecy in Isaiah 40:4: "Every valley shall be exalted, and every mountain and hill shall be made low: and the crooked shall be made straight, and the rough places plain."

> *"That cult would never die till the stars came right again, and the secret priests would take great Cthulhu from His tomb to revive His subjects and resume His rule of earth. The time would be easy to know, for then mankind would have become as the Great Old Ones; free and wild and beyond good and evil, with laws and morals thrown aside and all men shouting and killing and revelling in joy. Then the liberated Old Ones would teach them new ways to shout and kill and revel and enjoy themselves, and all the earth would flame with a holocaust of ecstasy and freedom."*

— H.P. LOVECRAFT, "THE CALL OF CTHULHU"

The atheist Lovecraft presents his clearest and most famous Apocalypse in explicitly theological terms in "The Call of Cthulhu." The cult leader Old Castro describes a period of tribulation, during which Cthulhu sleeps and His priests must work in secret, followed by signs and wonders ("the stars come right") and then by His glorious resurrection and rule on Earth forever. If this sounds familiar, Lovecraft doubtless meant it to: "The Call of Cthulhu" borrows some of its structure from Christian belief, like "The Dunwich Horror" does more thoroughly two years later. "The Dunwich Horror" is Lovecraft's Gospel, as Donald R. Burleson among others has pointed out, and "Call of Cthulhu" is (in part) his Book of Revelation.

Lovecraft scholar (and Biblical scholar) Robert M. Price notes the specific parallels between Thurston's tale and apocalyptic scripture. The story begins with Professor Angell collecting newspaper clippings of dire current events pointing to a greater cosmic truth, a mirroring of millenarian preachers and publications in the 1920s as now. Angell's clippings could be summarized by Luke in his Gospel (Luke 21:25): "And there shall be signs in the sun, and in the moon, and in the stars; and upon the earth distress of nations, with perplexity; the sea and the waves roaring." Old Castro predicts a massive breakdown in conventional morality heralding the End Times, just as the Apostle Paul does in his letters to Timothy (2 Timothy 3:1-2): "This know also, that in the last days perilous times shall come. For men shall be lovers of their own selves, covetous, boasters, proud, blasphemers, disobedient to parents, unthankful, unholy."[105]

But Cthulhu will rise again, as will His followers; Paul promises much the same (1 Thessalonians 4:16): "For the Lord himself shall descend from heaven with a shout, with the voice of the archangel, and with the trump of God: and the dead in Christ shall rise first." And finally, the true believers celebrate in the new Earth ruled by Cthulhu after a cleansing fire; compare 2 Peter 3:10-13: "But the day of the Lord will come … the earth

---

105. Most apocalyptic literature focuses on wars, earthquakes, and the like as signposting the End Times. Old Castro's belief that libertinism and anarchy usher in the Old Ones may be Lovecraft's devoted (though hardly devout) reading of Cotton Mather shining through. Mather, a New England apocalypticist every bit HPL's equal, blamed the 1692 resurgence of Satan in Salem on the weakening moral (and political) hold of Puritanism on the people of Massachusetts. I owe this insight to Edward Ingebretsen, S.J.

also and the works that are therein shall be burned up. ... Nevertheless we, according to his promise, look for new heavens and a new earth, wherein dwelleth righteousness."

> *"Here likewise a rambling letter to the editor of a paper in South America, where a fanatic deduces a dire future from visions he has seen. A despatch from California describes a theosophist colony as donning white robes en masse for some 'glorious fulfilment' which never arrives ..."*

— H.P. LOVECRAFT, "THE CALL OF CTHULHU"

Lovecraft even provides metatextual false prophets (who of course prophesy truly if ignorantly) and apocalyptic literature within his own apocalyptic prophecy. Cthulhu's dreams awaken a thousand John the Baptists, Henry Wilcox among them, who serve as heralds of his rise. The St. John the Divine of the god of R'lyeh only emerges gradually in the story as this revelation's narrator, Francis Wayland Thurston. Cthulhu is of course his own Beast of Revelation or Midgard Serpent, come from the sea to overthrow the heavens. Lovecraft read Yeats, calling him "the greatest living poet" in 1932; he must have been familiar with Yeats' "The Second Coming" (1919), which likewise conflates Beast and Messiah heralded by times of chaos and alienation.

Lovecraft plays the same pattern over in stories of personal apocalypse, such as "The Horror at Red Hook." Robert Suydam begins as the John the Baptist figure, or perhaps the Christ figure (his personality shifts during the story) whose death heralds the return of the beast-messiah Lilith. Thomas Malone becomes the witness, the John the Divine who discovers a cavalcade of wonders, beholds the returned god, and sees his world destroyed. HPL had run a classical, Epicurean riff on the apocalypse motif in "Poetry and the Gods," a mid-1920 collaboration with Anna Helen Crofts. In that tale, the slumbering Greek gods promise in dreams the creation of a new poet, who shall properly herald their coming ... and, it is implied, awaken them with his song.

"And shadowed on a screen, I saw hooded forms amidst ruins, and yellow evil faces peering from behind fallen monuments. And I saw the world battling against blackness; against the waves of destruction from ultimate space; whirling, churning; struggling around the dimming, cooling sun."

— H.P. LOVECRAFT, "NYARLATHOTEP"

That herald appeared, if at first only to H.P. Lovecraft, in a dream some time in late 1920. But Nyarlathotep appeared not as a demigod or magus, or a prophet or cult leader, but as an electrical showman projecting a cinema film. The apocalypse he ushers in, despite its biblical clothing and rhythms, represents Lovecraft's scientific fears for "a season of social and political upheaval": machine mass-culture (note the mass hypnosis in the story) and degeneration, accelerated by "swarthy" non-Western newcomers.

The "yellow evil faces" in the ruins represent the "Yellow Peril" of Asiatic influx we discussed back when we made our Stop at the Pacific Ocean, which reappears in "He" and "The Shadow Out of Time." These fears perfectly track those of the eugenics movement in Britain and America: that white cultures weakened by urban disease and rural poverty degenerate and decay physically and morally, to be swept aside by more numerous and vigorous nonwhite populations. Eugenicists (and Lovecraft) condemned both Dunwichian inbreeding and Innsmouthian miscegenation ("outbreeding"), which they believed poisoned and weakened the native stock.

"The ever-present heat, as Earth drew nearer to the sun, withered and killed with pitiless rays. It had not come at once; long aeons had gone before any could feel the change. And all through those first ages man's adaptable form had followed the slow mutation and modelled itself to fit the more and more torrid air. ... Man, softened and exhausted, could cope no longer with the ruthlessly mounting heat. It seared him as he was, and evolution was too slow to mould new resistances in him."

— H.P. LOVECRAFT AND ROBERT H. BARLOW, "TILL A' THE SEAS"

Eugenics was part and parcel of the scientific consensus in Lovecraft's time, embraced by figures both progressive and patriarchal, as well as by leading biologists including Lovecraft's ultra-Darwinist hero Ernst Haeckel. Other elements of the "Nyarlathotep" future similarly reflect scientific fact circa 1920, such as the "dimming, cooling sun."[106] In 1862, Lord Kelvin proposed a chemical-mathematical model for the Sun's activity, arguing that constant consumption of its fuel would lead to its inevitable cooling and shrinking several million years in the future.

Kelvin's theory survived in its essentials until 1939, when Hans Bethe demonstrated the mechanics of solar hydrogen fusion. Likewise, contemporary astronomers believed in Norman Lockyer's 1890 theory of stellar evolution, in which stars evolved from hot nebular gas to diffuse giants to cool, compact stars. It wasn't until 1955 that Hoyle and Schwarzschild slotted red giants into the main sequence of stellar evolution and changed our Sun's future from dimming dwarf to red giant.[107] Thus, Lovecraft and Barlow's non-supernatural apocalypse "Till A' the Seas" depends on some gravitational surge, or a passing planet or star, to pull the Earth closer to the Sun. But even in this straight sf story, "degeneracy both physical and cultural," "degradation and debauchery," "madness and frenzy" usher in the final end.

"Man rules now where They ruled once; They shall soon rule where man rules now. After summer is winter, and after winter summer. They wait patient and potent, for here shall They reign again."

— *Necronomicon*, quoted in H.P. Lovecraft, "The Dunwich Horror"

Historians' work reflected eugenics-style biology as well, notably the grand-scale histories of Oswald Spengler. In *The Decline of the West* (1918-1922), Spengler considered civilizations as biological organisms, growing in spring, flourishing in summer, and dying in winter to be replaced by

---

106. It's not entirely impossible that Lovecraft here intentionally conflates the scientific "dimming, cooling sun" of the future with the contemporary anthropological notion that the solar wheel symbol (e.g., the swastika) represents the "Aryan race." I haven't seen any conclusive evidence to this effect in his letters or other writings, however.

107. Clark Ashton Smith paints a dim, blood-colored, tired sun into his far-future tales of Zothique, but the swollen giant red sun waits until Jack Vance's Dying Earth stories.

new shoots seeded by their destroyers. Lovecraft read Spengler in spring 1927, but was citing his theory in essays and letters as early as 1921. Spenglerian cyclical apocalypses made their way into Lovecraft's fiction by that year, when he wrote "The Nameless City." The City's reptile civilization burrows underground to escape the desert but still succumbs to "a slow decadence of the ancient stock," to be replaced by the human (but pre-Adamic, and equally doomed) civilization of Irem of the Pillars.

Ten years later, in *At the Mountains of Madness,* Lovecraft gives Spengler a full workout with the vastness of geology and paleontology thrown in for good measure. The crinoid Old Ones' bas-reliefs record the rise and fall of several civilizations, and (over millions of years) the inevitable decadence of their own. The cone creatures in "The Shadow Out of Time" suffer apocalypse twice: once when the Yithians replace them, and again when the possessors abandon their hosts to the polypous Elder Things. The capricious Great Race apparently escapes ultimate doom by endlessly fleeing it, possibly into a reborn universe of the sort Randolph Carter traverses in "Through the Gates of the Silver Key." The Yithians' "fascistic socialism" also escapes inevitable decadence by eugenically culling only the best minds of the species for immortality, and (Lovecraft hints) by constant warfare.

> *"I shall go to those poles when the earth is cleared off, if I can't break through with the Dho-Hna formula when I commit it. They from the air told me at Sabbat that it will be years before I can clear off the earth, and I guess grandfather will be dead then ... I wonder how I shall look when the earth is cleared and there are no earth beings on it. He that came with the Aklo Sabaoth said I may be transfigured, there being much of outside to work on."*

— H.P. LOVECRAFT, "THE DUNWICH HORROR"

Our Apocalypse may come, then, as the result of another species staving off its own end times. We pose no challenge to the Yithians, who simply leapfrog us for our superior coleopteran successors. But our ignorant swipes at other beings invite retaliation. "A good army of men" could thwart the Mi-Go, but "if that happened, more would come from outside." The Mi-Go drove the crinoids into the Antarctic, and chased the K'n-yani underground, so humanity stands little chance against them.

We have torpedoed a Deep One city in revulsion and horror—but "the reel horror" of the fish devils is not their past conspiracies but "what they're a-goin' to do!" Not content to degrade and contaminate our human blood, they're "a-bringin' things up aout o' whar they come from." More specifically, they're breeding a shoggoth in the trench off Devil Reef, one of the monstrous slave-weapons that nearly ended the crinoid Old Ones and all life on Earth in the Permian period. One wonders if the Deep Ones know exactly what they're doing themselves, or if like us, they have sown their own doom with their experiments.

Of course, we don't all just sit idly by and wait for science or degeneracy to end us. Joseph Curwen and his circle invite Yog-Sothoth into communion, threatening "all civilization, all natural law, perhaps even the … solar system and the universe."[108] Their delvings threaten "the cosmos" with "a horror beyond all human conception or calculation," such as the monstrous mathematics ("angles of the planes") that Wilbur Whateley seeks to master before clearing off the Earth. Between the Deep Ones and the followers of Yog-Sothoth, we approach the mythic hints in Lovecraft's early apocalypse "The Crawling Chaos": "I could not but feel that some noxious marine mind had declared a war of extermination upon all the solid ground, perhaps abetted by the angry sky."

> *"Soon from the sea a noxious birth began;*
> *Forgotten lands with weedy spires of gold;*
> *The ground was cleft, and mad auroras rolled*
> *Down on the quaking citadels of man.*
> *Then, crushing what he chanced to mould in play,*
> *The idiot Chaos blew Earth's dust away."*

— H.P. LOVECRAFT, *FUNGI FROM YUGGOTH* XXI, "NYARLATHOTEP" (1930)

---

108. Joseph Curwen ("J. C.") is another blasphemous Christ figure, or perhaps an Antichrist. Resurrected on Good Friday of 1927, he provides a parodic eternal life to his chosen.

At some point over the holiday break between December 27, 1929 and January 2, 1930, Lovecraft unveiled his final apocalypse, in a sonnet that recapitulated his first revelation a decade previously. Like the prose poem, the sonnet "Nyarlathotep" opens with the initial vision of the herald "out of Egypt," now an explicit wonder-worker and prophet. The prose poem's "waves of destruction from ultimate space" become "mad auroras" rolling down on our civilization. The sonnet draws on Lovecraft's other revelations: Nyarlathotep's red robes recall the "red and orange" robes of the Asiatics in "He," and the "weedy spires" and cleft ground both appear in "The Crawling Chaos," as does the ultimate destruction of the planet.

This unified Apocalypse echoes forward through Lovecraft's later writings like the cacophonous drums and clattering crotala of Leng. Nyarlathotep's revelation informs "Whisperer in Darkness" as cosmicism, "Dreams in the Witch House" as degeneration, and "Shadow Out of Time" as nihilism. The "mad auroras" above the Mountains of Madness threaten Kadath in the cold waste and those who would seek it out, in seaplanes or in dreams. Innsmouth decays on the edge of "forgotten lands with weedy spires of gold" and the idiot Chaos thwarts Randolph Carter's final quest to return from Yaddith. In "Haunter of the Dark," Nyarlathotep again comes out of Egypt, and his annihilatory parousia consumes Robert Blake.

Every discovery, every history, every story becomes a tale of Apocalypse. The narrators go mad from revelation, disintegrating their own reality as completely as Azathoth can. They "could not tell what they had heard." When madness describes (or de-scribes) the world, the world becomes Apocalypse, aflame with ecstasy and freedom or drowning under a black ocean. It cannot be parsed or understood. It becomes a blank tome, a dead, featureless whiteness like that of the Antarctic plateau. All that remains is war within, and with, our own minds. We can but echo the parodic doxology uttered by Danforth in his final manic glossolalia, the only cry of faith possible in the face of nothingness: "the original, the eternal, the undying." Selah.

PROVIDENCE

"But I want the familiar Old Providence of my childhood as a perpetual base for these necromancies & excursions—& in a good part of these necromancies & excursions I want certain transmuted features of Old Providence to form parts of the alien voids I visit or conjure up. I am as geographic-minded as a cat—places are everything to me."

— H.P. LOVECRAFT, LETTER TO CLARK
ASHTON SMITH (NOVEMBER 7, 1930)

If Lovecraft was, as his friend the poet Winfield Townley Scott said, his own greatest creation, so too his greatest fictional setting was his own beloved hometown: Providence, Rhode Island. Through his eyes, love and fear mixed to create the very ideal type of the Lovecraftian city, a mise en scène that grew from the simple sketched backdrop of "From Beyond" to the cosmic cockpit of "The Haunter of the Dark." In between those two tales he fused Providence antiquarianism with science fiction in "The Shunned House" and Providence history with pure horror in *The Case of Charles Dexter Ward*.

Three more Lovecraft fictions feature Rhode Island's queen of cities. The critical opening act of "The Call of Cthulhu" intermingles Providence's art world and chaotic dockyards with its Georgian academic calm to unsettling effect. Boston mystic (and Lovecraft alter ego) Randolph Carter only touches Providence at an angle, in his dreams in *The Dream-Quest of Unknown Kadath* and after his disappearance in "Through the Gates of the Silver Key." Providence makes up part of Carter's "sunset city" for which he defies Nyarlathotep; the "Providence mystic" Ward Phillips argues against probating Carter's estate. In both cases, Providence helps keep Randolph Carter alive, as Lovecraft certainly felt the city did in his own case.

> *"I am Providence, and Providence is myself—together indissolubly as one, we stand thro' the ages; a fixt monument set aeternally in the shadow of Durfee's ice-clad peak!"*[109]

> — H.P. LOVECRAFT, LETTER TO JAMES F. MORTON (MAY 16, 1926)

If Winfield Lovecraft hadn't contracted syphilis, H.P. Lovecraft would not have been Providence at all, because he would have grown up in Auburndale, Massachusetts. Although born in his mother's family mansion at 454 Angell Street in Providence, the infant HPL removed with his parents to Auburndale, home base for his father's sales route. Here Lovecraft's first memories formed, including his first architectural vista, looking down from the Auburndale railway bridge at age two-and-a-half. But his father's first serious collapse forced the sale of the family plot in Auburndale and the return of young Howard and his mother to Providence in 1893. He never truly left it behind again.

Even the two years he spent in exile in New York City could not erase his powerful imprinting on the scenery, the architecture, the skies and seas, of Providence. He absorbed the peculiar blend of commercialism and gentility, of Yankee conservatism and Rhode Island freethinking, which characterized his city. It was only six months into his remove to New York that he wrote the poem "Providence," which concludes: "For thou art of the soul of me / And always at my side!" In March of 1926, preparing to come home, he wrote to his aunt Lillian Clark, "Providence is part of me—I *am* Providence," although like Randolph Carter he generously credits other parts of New England active in his "inner life and imagination." He loved Marblehead, Quebec, and (eventually) Charleston to transports of ecstasy, but only Providence could be his true home. Barton Levi St. Armand sums it up:

109. This humorous hyperbole refers to Durfee Hill, 22 miles northwest of Providence, which towers 804 feet above sea level.

"Lovecraft would never have been Lovecraft without Providence—its history, its atmosphere, its legends, its peculiar and individual character."

"The nurse used to stop and sit on the benches of Prospect Terrace to chat with policemen; and one of the child's first memories was of the great westward sea of hazy roofs and domes and steeples and far hills which he saw one winter afternoon from that great railed embankment, all violet and mystic against a fevered, apocalyptic sunset of reds and golds and purples and curious greens."

— H.P. LOVECRAFT, *THE CASE OF CHARLES DEXTER WARD*

Lovecraft's vision of Providence came over a lifetime, and simultaneously broke over him in the golden hour. Excerpts from his letters demonstrate the power that specific juxtapositions of urban imagery unleashed in Lovecraft: "rare combinations of slope, curved street-line, roofs & gables & chimneys ... in the magic of late afternoon assume a mystic majesty and exotic significance" (to Donald Wandrei, 1927); "a strange sense of adventurous expectancy connected with landscape and architecture and sky-effects" (to August Derleth, 1930); and "half-known architectural or landscape vistas, especially in connexion with a sunset" (to Clark Ashton Smith, 1930). Matt Cardin identifies this as the Romantic sensation of *sehnsucht,* the bittersweet "infinite longing" for an impossible or forgotten past. Sunsets inevitably conjure the past, but also a kind of free-floating future, the end of things.

In his landmark essay "Sunset Terrace Imagery in Lovecraft," Peter Cannon leaves the psychologizing to others and sets about tracing the specific motif throughout Lovecraft's work. As we've seen earlier in this Tour, Lovecraft recycled his ecstatic first sight of Marblehead into all of Kingsport, unveiled from atop a hill, "outspread frostily in the gloaming." Lovecraft's first faery view of New York City came (as the narrator says in "He") "in the sunset from a bridge ... its incredible peaks and pyramids rising ... from pools of violet mist to play with the flaming clouds ..." In the *Dream-Quest,* Randolph Carter beholds his "sunset city" from "on the high terrace above it," and in "Silver Key" he looks down the hill outside Arkham at the "outspread countryside golden and glorified in the slanting floods of magic poured out by a western sun" and sees the impossible past of Kingsport's Congregational church steeple.

One can multiply instances effortlessly, from Charles Dexter Ward's joyous return to Providence "before and below him in the sunset" through "Expectancy" and "Continuity" (and several other sonnets) in *Fungi From Yuggoth* through Robert Blake's evening reveries gazing westward at "mystical sunsets" behind the Starry Wisdom steeple atop the "unknown, ethereal world" of Federal Hill. As that example (and the earlier example of Kingsport) shows, even in the grip of infinity and sehnsucht, Lovecraft builds (or finds) horror. In "Dreams in the Witch House" Walter Gilman gazes down from a balustraded terrace at a frighteningly alien world under the endless noon of three suns. In "The Shadow Over Innsmouth" Olmstead looks down at the half-ruined city in the morning (not the sunset) just as the narrator of "The Port" stares at it unlit by night. But even in Innsmouth, at sunset Olmstead feels "an air of mystic loveliness and peace."

> *"My pets are not pretty, for they come out of places where aesthetic standards are—very different."*

> — H.P. LOVECRAFT, "FROM BEYOND"

In "From Beyond," Crawford Tillinghast seeks infinity not in a Providence sunset, but in an "accursed electrical machine" that opens onto, or into, Hyperspace. He lives in an "ancient, lonely house set back from Benevolent Street" on the east side of Providence. Our narrator carries a revolver after having been mugged in East Providence, but the criminal hazards of that low-rent district pale before the nigh-existential dangers of the ultra-violet. Even though Lovecraft doesn't bother to really draw Providence out in the tale—a near impossibility anyhow since the action occurs almost entirely in one attic room—he clearly contrasts it with the unspeakable vistas unleashed by Tillinghast's device.

Lovecraft's protagonists often reflect himself, especially in the Providence stories. In this case, however, not the cipher of a narrator but the villain Crawford Tillinghast seems like the dark mirror of Lovecraft. Tillinghast is Lovecraft turning away from the city into the attic, where HPL spent much of his boyhood escaping into the infinite past. He pursues "science and philosophy" as Lovecraft had dreamed of doing, replacing HPL's failure ("despair") with "terrors unutterable and unimaginable." Likewise, Hyperspace becomes a dark mirror to Providence, full of half-seen dangers but infinitely compelling. However, its "aesthetic standards are—very different." The opposite of the perfectly, even celestially, beautiful city is the "hideous world" of abhorrent (electri)-city that is Hyperspace.

> *"The general fact is, that the house was never regarded by the solid part of the community as in any real sense 'haunted.' There were no widespread tales of rattling chains, cold currents of air, extinguished lights, or faces at the window. Extremists sometimes said the house was 'unlucky,' but that is as far as even they went."*

> — H.P. LOVECRAFT, "THE SHUNNED HOUSE"

With "The Shunned House" in 1924, Lovecraft moves his horrors into the real city of Providence, and into a real and identifiable house in that city. Now generally called the Stephen Harris House, Lovecraft knew the house at 135 Benefit Street as the Babbitt house, because his aunt Lillian Clark lived there as a caretaker for the Babbitt family in 1919-1920. He played up the house's eerie decrepitude during that period in his 1920 poem "The House." Stumbling upon a similarly ivy-choked house in Elizabeth, New Jersey, HPL rushed back to Flatbush and wrote this story, contrasting the almost anodyne "unlucky" reputation of the "shunned house" in his fictive modern day with a hideous truth literally buried beneath it.

In this tale, present-day Providence—armed with absolutely contemporary weapons such as Crookes tubes and flamethrowers—confronts a Gothic shadow from its past. Lovecraft makes much of the irony that Poe walked past the house without seeing the true horror within. In a 1936 poem, "In a Sequester'd Providence Churchyard Where Once Poe Walk'd," he plays with a different irony, of common passersby walking through St. John's Churchyard in Providence not seeing "the shade of Poe." One might likewise enjoy the irony of Lovecraft inventing a haunting wholesale for a perfectly respectable (if dilapidated in his era) later Georgian (c. 1764) house of the sort he normally praises.[110]

Lovecraft took the monster under the shunned house from his compendium of American folklore, Charles M. Skinner's *Myths and Legends of Our Own Land* (1896). Specifically, he borrowed it from Skinner's account of a "cellar in Green Street" in upstate Schenectady, New York, where a recurrent mold or fungus took "the shape of a recumbent man." Skinner provides various theories including an overlooked Dutch burial ground, a murder victim, and a vampire imprisoned by an enchantment. Lovecraft combines all of them, replacing the degenerate Dutch with the immigrant Huguenot French, and juicing the vampire (as did Skinner) with the historical 1892 infectious vampire panic in Exeter, Rhode Island.

The hero who battles the quantum vampire again serves as a palpable self-insert for HPL. The hero's wise uncle Elihu Whipple combines Lovecraft's beloved grandfather Whipple Phillips with his learned uncle Dr. Franklin Chase Clark. In similar fashion, HPL blends Providence history into the horror, a key to understanding the phenomenon. In the end, it's hard to say whether modern Providence, "a metropolis with a shifting modern population," is wise or not to forget the surmises and folklore of its older self.

---

110. Although Philip Shreffler reports a story of the original owner Mrs. Stephen (not William) Harris crying out in French when her children died, I would want to find an independent pre-Lovecraft source for the legend before I believe it. By now, Providence ghost tourists repeat Lovecraft's imaginings as authentic folklore, hopelessly muddying the waters.

"Wilcox was a precocious youth of known genius but great eccentricity, and had from childhood excited attention through the strange stories and odd dreams he was in the habit of relating. He called himself 'psychically hypersensitive,' but the staid folk of the ancient commercial city dismissed him as merely 'queer.' Never mingling much with his kind, he had dropped gradually from social visibility, and was now known only to a small group of aesthetes from other towns. Even the Providence Art Club, anxious to preserve its conservatism, had found him quite hopeless."

— H.P. LOVECRAFT, "THE CALL OF CTHULHU"

Only the first act of "The Call of Cthulhu" happens in Providence, but "The Horror in Clay" admirably sets the scene and tone for the whole magnificent fugue. Rich with street names and social observation, it glows with Lovecraft's delight at returning home in April 1926. (He wrote the story out four or five months later, from a 1925 outline.) Providence becomes the meeting place, the liminal zone perhaps, between the narrator Francis Thurston's prosaic Boston and the outré dreams of Cthulhu. George Gammell Angell, a professor at Providence's Brown University, assembles the fragments and clippings of the truth that come to him there from all over the world: Greenland, Louisiana, the Philippines, Paris, and still stranger territories. And that truth reaches up from the "waterfront swarming with foreign mongrels" and kills the eminent WASP on the side of College Hill.[111]

Perhaps befitting the twinning of Providence in this story, Lovecraft introduces twin alter egos. Professor Angell is Lovecraft's aspirational self: scholarly, elderly, independent, occult but respectable, eagerly consulted by men of affairs. His last name is the street on which Lovecraft was born, his middle name is HPL's aunt's family name Gamwell written phonetically ("Gammell"). Henry Wilcox is Lovecraft's "outsider" self: precocious, eccentric, reclusive, dream-plagued, and rejected by the establishment. He quotes Love-

---

111. Lovecraft was perfectly capable of painting that same waterfront in his glowing sunset palette, as in his 1929 poem "The East India Brick Row," which positively exalts the foreign cargoes it brought amid recalling the warehouses' "glow / with hinted wonders from a fire-lashed west."

craft's literal dream-monologue to Angell.[112] Like Lovecraft himself in 1926, Wilcox is "known only to a small group of aesthetes from other towns"—Wilcox is *not* Providence, and HPL clearly fears the truth of this mirror image.

In this story, Providence becomes not just a liminal zone between light and dark, but a balancing point, keeping the world stable yet magical. It hosts both the "adventurous expectancy" of strange dreams and Lascar conspiracies, and the "staid folk of the ancient commercial city" who reject Henry Wilcox' arrant nonsense. On Thomas Street, Henry Wilcox' "hideous" imitation-Breton Fleur-de-Lys Building shelters its debauched modern artists "in the very shadow of the finest Georgian steeple in America." Rhode Island, that "placid island of ignorance in the midst of black seas of infinity," becomes the polar opposite of the black island of R'lyeh. But like all opposites in Lovecraft, they attract and interpenetrate, and thus even Providence gets wet ("slimy") at the edges, at its waterfront. At the end of the day, even Boston falls to Providence, as Thurston prepares to die at the hands of the madness from the sea.

> *"Old Providence! It was this place and the mysterious forces of its long, continuous history which had brought him into being, and which had drawn him back toward marvels and secrets whose boundaries no prophet might fix. Here lay the arcana, wondrous or dreadful as the case might be, for which all his years of travel and application had been preparing him."*

— H.P. LOVECRAFT, *THE CASE OF CHARLES DEXTER WARD*

With *The Case of Charles Dexter Ward* in early 1927, Lovecraft fully limns and fully enters the shadow Providence. In this novel, Providence partakes of all four of Waugh's types of Lovecraftian landscape: the personal, the ideal, the shadow, and the double. Streets, personal names, incidents, and buildings all match the hometown geography and history Lovecraft once

---

112. In a letter of May 21, 1920 to Rheinhart Kleiner, Lovecraft describes a dream in which he tried to sell a clay bas-relief to a museum curator. When the curator rejects the obviously recently carved piece, dream-Lovecraft says, "This was fashioned in my dreams, and the dreams of man are older than brooding Egypt or the contemplative Sphinx or garden-girdled Babylon."

more walked and studied at all hours. The ideal Providence "sunset city" appears in flashes, most ecstatically when Charles Dexter Ward returns home from Europe. Joseph Curwen, and his hideous labyrinths and grave-robberies, lurk in the shadow Providence, home of unthinkable evil connected to the city by ties of history and blood. The double city, as we have seen throughout this Tour, confronts and combines with its opposite ... and this becomes the whole matter of the novel.

Charles Dexter Ward not only doubles his ancestor Joseph Curwen, but also his creator. His last name is the last syllable of "Howard." His appearance embodies Lovecraft's self-image: "tall, slim, and blond, with studious eyes and a slight stoop ... giving a dominant impression of harmless awkwardness rather than attractiveness." He lives at 140 Prospect Street,[113] right around the corner from Lovecraft's home in 1927 at 10 Barnes Street. He has Lovecraft's childhood memories of gazing down from Prospect Terrace at the sunset city below him, and his "famous walks" and nocturnal habits are again Lovecraft's. He has a black cat named Nig, a shortened form of Lovecraft's own childhood pet's name. Like HPL, he spends the years after high school in a period of introversion: three years (1920-1923) for Ward, five years (1908-1913) for Lovecraft.[114] And Ward returns in glory to Providence in May 1926, passing the same landmarks that Lovecraft did in his own return from New York the month before.

Charles Dexter Ward is a novel of returns, from abroad and from the dead. It is Lovecraft's great Gothic, about the shadow of the past returning to haunt the living, echoed by storms and demarcated by bloodlines. Angela Carter memorably calls the novel "a specific declension of outwardness, of the safe public world, and a descent downwards, into the dangerous maze." The story begins in a Georgian mansion in a shining city on College Hill,

---

113. In the novel, Lovecraft gives Ward's address as 100 Prospect Street, but the description of his house makes it clear that he intends the Halsey Mansion at 140 Prospect.

114. Those five years (1908-1913), funnily enough, exactly match the period when Nathaniel Peaslee suffers possession by the Great Race of Yith. We have virtually no documentation or other records of what Lovecraft was up to during that five-year span.

and in the Augustan eighteenth century with reason ascendant. The novel, and Ward, then descend down "the little ancient lanes" into the lower city, and into the witch-haunted 17th-century past, where death and horror have arrived from the satanic woods outside Salem and in coffins through the "riot of iridescent decay" on the "wicked old waterfront" of "polyglot vice and squalor." It climaxes in a pluperfect Lovecraftian hell, an "underground world of nightmare labyrinths" beneath Pawtuxet, and finally ends in a madhouse. It is a Grand Tour, and a Grand Guignol, with Providence as destination and as stage.

> *"Blake's study, a large southwest chamber, overlooked the front garden on one side, while its west windows—before one of which he had his desk— faced off from the brow of the hill and commanded a splendid view of the lower town's outspread roofs and of the mystical sunsets that flamed behind them. ... Against these, some two miles away, rose the spectral hump of Federal Hill, bristling with huddled roofs and steeples whose remote outlines wavered mysteriously, taking fantastic forms as the smoke of the city swirled up and enmeshed them. Blake had a curious sense that he was looking upon some unknown, ethereal world which might or might not vanish in dream if ever he tried to seek it out and enter it in person."*

> — H.P. LOVECRAFT, "THE HAUNTER OF THE DARK"

For what would be his final solo story, Lovecraft returned once more to Providence. He returned not as himself, but like one of his strange magi, as a blend of self and disciple. "Robert Blake" is of course a manqué of the story's dedicatee Robert Bloch, one of Lovecraft's last great protégés. But he lives in Lovecraft's Georgian apartment at 66 College Street and becomes bewitched by Lovecraft's sunset architecture. Even tiny architectural details pay off here. The blaze of the "red Industrial Trust beacon" prefigures the three-lobed eye of the Haunter, trapped in the steeple of a church based on St. John's Catholic Church on Atwells Avenue.[115]

---

115. Unlike the Starry Wisdom church, St. John's still operated in 1935, only closing in 1991. It was demolished in 1992. Its steeple was, however, destroyed by lightning in late June of 1935.

"The Haunter of the Dark" paints Providence as the great maze, each gateway leading to another one both deeper in and further Outside. As Robert Blake looks out his westward window at Federal Hill, or its elfin sunset transfiguration, it becomes a dreamland, "some unknown, ethereal world." The "smoke-wreathed world of dream," the "dream-world never to be trod by living human feet," yields "bewildering mazes of brooding brown alleys" where Blake "twice lost his way." At the center of the maze inside the dream, Blake reaches the "black tower" of the Starry Wisdom church, the "old temple that towered on its high plateau" in "a separate, lesser world." Inside the church, Blake discovers crumbling tomes, ascends to the steeple and enters the tower chamber, the Unholy of Unholies. At this crux, he then looks into an anti-Ark, a box of alien metal, and beholds not the tablets of the Law but a stone of Chaos: the Shining Trapezohedron, within which writhes the Haunter of the Dark.

Providence thus recapitulates Lovecraft's entire world, from Dreamland to Arkham to Dunwich (Blake "dared not" ask directions) to Leng and its "elder Pharos" tower. Blake climbs to enlightenment like the Outsider and gazes on Hadoth. The Trapezohedron itself traveled from Yuggoth through Deep Time and Antarctica to Egypt, and it contains Hyperspace ("vortices of space ... a cold purple haze") and unleashes Apocalypse. In the ultimate center of Providence's labyrinth, Lovecraft places the Outside for Blake to find, to decrypt, and to enter at last.

> "It is still spectral, but its strangeness fascinates me, and I shall find mixed with my relief a queer regret when it is torn down to make way for a tawdry shop or vulgar apartment building. The barren old trees in the yard have begun to bear small, sweet apples, and last year the birds nested in their gnarled boughs."
>
> — H.P. LOVECRAFT, "THE SHUNNED HOUSE"

But the story, and the city, doesn't end there. The Italian inhabitants of Federal Hill bravely encircle the tower with light—hardly abject rurals, or even the "foreign mongrels" of Lovecraft's cities. In an elegiac exorcism of the city, "a sharp flash of belated lightning" destroys the tower and the Haunter: Providence saved by, well, Divine Providence. The human and natural world of roofs and sunsets triumphs over the Outside, Italians and the storm victorious.

In fact, in every one of the Providence stories, the evil is defeated. The narrator shoots Tillinghast's machine to ruins, the younger Whipple burns the spectral werewolf out of the shunned house with sulfuric acid, the *Emma* bursts Cthulhu asunder just as his island sinks, Dr. Willett destroys Joseph Curwen with a mirror image of his own incantation, and Dr. Dexter drops the Trapezohedron "into the deepest channel of Narragansett Bay." To be sure, Lovecraft's stand-ins die in these tales, with the half-exceptions of young Whipple and Henry Wilcox. But as Lovecraft says in his poem "Providence," they die to hallow their city: "thy stern fathers 'neath the mould / Make blest thy sacred ground." Lovecraft's cold cosmic realism cannot withstand a threat to his personal paradise, and his nihilism has no purchase on Prospect Terrace. At the end, the birds return, and we have the small sweet apples—and also just perhaps, in the words of the Rhode Island state motto: "Hope."

APPENDIX I:
OCCULT ITINERARIES
IN LOVECRAFT

"Searchers after horror haunt strange, far places. For them are the catacombs of Ptolemaïs, and the carven mausolea of the nightmare countries. They climb to the moonlit towers of ruined Rhine castles, and falter down black cobwebbed steps beneath the scattered stones of forgotten cities in Asia. The haunted wood and the desolate mountain are their shrines, and they linger around the sinister monoliths on uninhabited islands."

— H.P. LOVECRAFT, "THE PICTURE IN THE HOUSE"

Every so often in Lovecraft's fiction, someone goes to the far corners of the Earth in search of eldritch lore or other horrors. This probably derives from the exaggerated biographies of medieval and other magi, who sought out learning in exotic lands and mountaintop castles. The mathematician (and reputed wizard) Michael Scot studied in Oxford, Paris, and Bologna before voyaging to the former Saracen strongholds of Palermo and Toledo. The mountebank Cagliostro claimed to have learned the true and ancient secrets of Freemasonry in his travels to Egypt, Babylon, Mecca, and Malta. Lovecraft can hardly have his magi do less than Cagliostro, surely.

As the specific lists below demonstrate, Arabia is the place to go for Mythos lore—only Charles Dexter Ward neglects that stop. (In "Call of Cthulhu," Old Castro identifies it as the center of the Cthulhu cult, to boot.) Tibet is the second-best destination, especially if we assume Peaslee slips across the border during his "Himalayas" trip. Egypt is surprisingly neglected, given its featured role in Nyarlathotepist theology.

The Case of Charles Dexter Ward

"It developed that Joseph Curwen had travelled much in very early life, living for a time in England and making at least two voyages to the Orient ..."

Charles Dexter Ward mostly researches his ancestry in Providence graveyards and archives, but widens his search for Yog-Sothothery to:

- Boston libraries

- "Other cities to consult obscure records"

- The (actual) Essex Institute in Salem, Massachusetts, a trove of local New England history

- The South (probably) "to talk with a strange old mulatto who dwelt in a swamp"

- The Adirondacks, in search of "a small village ... whence reports of odd ceremonial practices had come"

- London, especially the British Museum

- Paris, at the Bibliothèque Nationale and "in the library of an unnamed private collector"

- Prague, in the Neustadt to speak with Simon Orne (who himself visited Egypt between 1692 and 1926)

- Castle Ferenczy in Transylvania, to speak with Edward Hutchinson

"History of the *Necronomicon*"

Abdul Alhazred didn't venture terribly far from his birthplace at Sana'a in Yemen. Not in space, anyway. He describes Leng in the *Necronomicon*, but may not have seen it firsthand. His recorded searches brought him to:

- The ruins of Babylon fifty miles south of Baghdad; in Alhazred's time a small village named Babel remained on the mound of mud-brick and soil.

- South of Cairo for "the subterranean secrets of Memphis." The ruins of Memphis still extended "a half-day's journey" across even in the 13th century.

Alhazred visited two specific places (and perhaps others) during his "ten years alone in the great southern desert of Arabia—the Roba el Khaliyeh or 'Empty Space' of the ancients—and 'Dahna' or 'Crimson' desert." The Rub' al-Khali and ad-Dahna actually refer to two different deserts, one in the southeast and the other in the center of the peninsula. A list of Alhazred's Arabian destinations at least starts with:

- Irem, the City of Pillars
- Most likely, the Nameless City: "beneath the ruins of a certain nameless desert town [he found] the shocking annals and secrets of a race older than mankind."

Alhazred spends the last years of his life in Damascus, and in 738 A.D. spectacularly meets his death there. "Or disappearance …"

"THE LAST TEST"

"Three times, however, he had taken long, lone jaunts to strange and distant places in his studies of exotic fevers and half-fabulous plagues; for he knew that it is out of the unknown lands of cryptic and immemorial Asia that most of the earth's diseases spring."

Dr. Alfred Clarendon was "an international figure at thirty," implying travels to the conventional scientific and cultural centers of the 1880s: London, Berlin, Paris, perhaps Geneva, and so forth. But his three "long, lone jaunts" encompass:

- Northern Africa, specifically among the Tuaregs of the Hoggar region (in then French-controlled Algeria) "whose descent from the primal race of lost Atlantis is an old archaeological rumour."
- A study of "the pest [bubonic plague] in China," on which trip he may have talked to the "old man in China calling on Yog-Sothoth."

- A study of "pyemia [staphylococcus infection] in India."

On one of the latter two trips, he visited Tibet, specifically "somewhere in U-tsang." U-tsang being in the southwest of the country on the border with India, this was probably during the pyemia expedition.

On any of the three trips, he could have "talked in Yemen with an old man who had come back alive from the Crimson Desert—he had seen Irem, the City of Pillars, and had worshipped at the underground shrines of Nug and Yeb." The trip to India again seems the most likely, since a voyage from Europe would pass through the Suez Canal and perhaps stop off at Aden or Mocha in Yemen.

"THE HORROR IN THE MUSEUM"

"Before that there had been wild enough stories—accounts of mysterious trips ..."

Evil wax museum curator George Rogers knows many occult secrets, including the secret of making enough money from a wax museum to travel all over the globe. In a brief précis of his career, our narrator Stephen Jones mentions six destinations; in a grandiloquent rant, Rogers expands on one of them and adds a seventh. Consolidated, Rogers' itinerary looks like this:

- Tibet, where perhaps he gathers "proboscidian Chaugnar Faugn"
- African interior
- Arabian desert
- Amazon valley
- Little-known islands of the South Pacific
- Ruined city in Indo-China where the Tcho-Tchos lived
- All the way to Alaska, and up the Noatak [River] from Fort Morton

He may also have traveled to the Arctic one earlier time to collect his "Gnoph-keh, the hairy myth-thing of the Greenland ice."

"THE SHADOW OUT OF TIME"

"As soon as permitted, I haunted the college library at all hours; and shortly began to arrange for those odd travels, and special courses at American and European universities, which evoked so much comment during the next few years."

Nathaniel Wingate Peaslee travels under impulsion by the Yithian consciousness embedded in his body. The Universities probably encompass the usual suspects: Harvard, Oxford, Cambridge, Paris, Berlin—possibly Ingolstadt or Krakow, and mayhap the University of Buenos Aires to see if their copy of the *Necronomicon* was more accessible (or differently recensed) than Harvard's. However, his "long visits to remote and desolate places" are more interesting to seekers after seekers after horror. They include:

- The Himalayas (for a month in 1909)
- "A camel trip into the unknown deserts of Arabia" in 1911
- A chartered ship voyage "in the Arctic north of Spitzbergen" in the summer of 1912
- "The vast limestone cavern systems of western Virginia" later in 1912 for "weeks alone beyond the limits of previous or subsequent exploration"

After his recovery, he travels to Pilbarra in Western Australia via the Red Sea in March-July of 1935.

Peaslee says of the Virginia trip that "no retracing of my steps could even be considered," which I guess is me told.

THE LOVECRAFTIAN WORLD

"It had always existed and always would exist, hidden in distant wastes and dark places all over the world..."

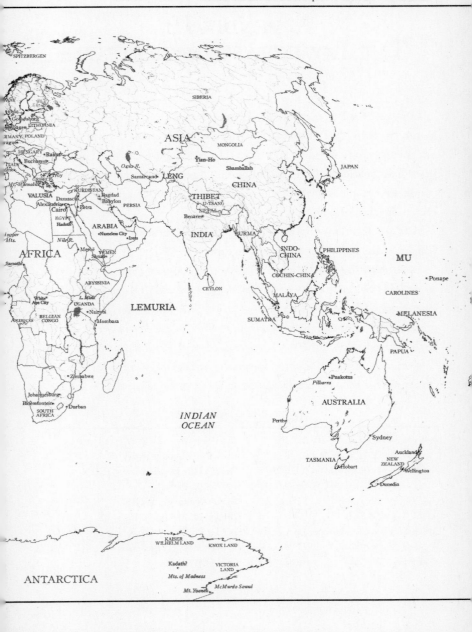

APPENDIX II:
THE LOVECRAFT GAZETTEER

This gazetteer lists every location larger than a single street mentioned in the works of H.P. Lovecraft discussed in this book. Except in the Dreamlands section, towns and cities are not regularly identified as such. Identifiable nationalities (e.g., Burmese, Danes) receive entries as their nation, except in cases where such entries would overload the index (e.g., Dutch, English). Languages are not indexed.

Fictitious locations appear in *italics*, although legendary locations (e.g., Cibola, Shamballah) remain in roman type.

I assembled the first iteration of this gazetteer some time around 1988 on an IBM Selectric typewriter of all things—would that someone could have supplied Lovecraft with such a device! For this version, I gladly and gratefully relied on S.T. Joshi's *Index to the Fiction and Poetry of H.P. Lovecraft*, Appendix 4 in *The New Annotated Lovecraft: Beyond Arkham* by Leslie Klinger, and the "Cthulhu Universalis" index on Joseph Morales' site cthulhufiles.com as backstops, double-checks, and extenders.

NEW ENGLAND

Arkham, Mass.; see pp. 13-18 (ATMM, COLO, DIWH, DOOR, DQUK, DUNW, FEST, FFY, HERB, INNS, NEC, PH, SHHM, SK, TGSK, TIME, UNN, WHIS)

Athol, Mass. (WHIS)

Attleborough, modern Attleboro, Mass. (CDW)

Augusta, Me. (DOOR)

Ayer, Mass. (WHIS)

Aylesbury, Mass. (DUNW, FFY)

Back Bay, Boston, Mass. (PM)

Beacon Hill, Boston, Mass. (AEON, DQUK, PM)

Bellows Falls, Vt. (WHIS)

Biddeford, Me. (DOOR)

Bolton, Mass.; not to be confused with the smaller town of Bolton further w. (COLO, HERB, RATS)

Boston, Mass.; see pp. 122-128 (AEON, ATMM, CALL, CDW, COLO, DOOR, DQUK, DUNW, GM, HERB, HMB, INNS, PH, PM, SHUN, SK, TGSK, TIME, TOMB, UNN, WHIS)

Boynton, Mass. (FFY)

Brattleboro, Vt. (WHIS)

Bristol, R.I. (SHHM)

Brookline, Mass. (CDW)

Brown University, Providence, R.I. (CALL, CDW, HAUN, SHUN)

Caledonia, county, Vt. (WHIS)

Cambridge, Mass. (AEON, ATMM, DUNW, MOU, WING)

Cape Ann, Mass. (INNS)

Cape Cod, Mass. (INNS)

Central Hill, Kingsport, Mass. (FEST, SHHM, SK)

Central Hill Churchyard, Kingsport, Mass. (FEST, SHHM)

Charles, river, Mass. (DQUK)

Charlestown, Boston, Mass. (CDW)

Charter Street Burying Ground, Salem, Mass. (DQUK); as Olde Burying Point (CDW)

Cheapside, Providence, R.I. (CDW, SHUN)

Chepachet, R.I. (REDH)

Chesuncook, Me. (DOOR)

Christchurch Cemetery, Arkham, Mass. (HERB)

Clark's Corners, Mass. (COLO)

College Hill, Providence, R.I. (CDW, HAUN, SHUN)

Conanicut, island, Narragansett Bay, R.I. (CDW)

Concord, Mass. (WHIS)

Concord, N.H. (DQUK)

Connecticut (CDW, TRAP, WHIS)

Connecticut, river, Mass.-Vt. (WHIS)

Copp's Hill, Boston, Mass. (PM)

Copp's Hill Burying Ground, Boston, Mass. (HERB (unnamed), PM)

Cranston, R.I. (CDW)

Danvers, town and asylum, Mass. (CDW, INNS, PM)

Dark Mountain, Vt.; poss. based on Bald Mtn. or Black Mtn. (WHIS)

Dean's Corners, Mass. (DUNW)

Dedham, Mass. (CDW)

Devil Reef, off Innsmouth, Mass. (INNS)

Dunwich, Mass.; see pp. 60-66 (DUNW)

East Greenwich, R.I. (SHUN)

East Providence, Providence, R.I. (FB, SHUN)

Edgewood, R.I. (CDW)

Ellston, Mass.? (NOC)

Elm Mountain, s. of Arkham, Mass. (SK)

Essex, county, Mass. (DIWH, INNS)

Exeter, R.I. (SHUN)

Federal Hill, Providence, R.I. (HAUN)

Fitchburg, Mass. (WHIS)

Gallows Hill, Salem, Mass. (PM)

Gardner, Mass. (WHIS)

Gloucester, Mass. (DQUK, HMB)

Golden Hill, Haverhill, Mass. (TIME)

Granary Burying Ground, Boston, Mass. (DQUK)

Greenfield, Mass. (WHIS)

Greenwich, Conn. (TRAP)

Hardwick, Vt. (WHIS)

Harvard University, Cambridge, Mass. (ATMM, CDW, DOOR, DUNW, GM, MEDU, NEC, TIME, WING)

Haverhill, Mass. (DIWH, TIME)

Hope Valley, R.I. (CDW)

Innsmouth, Mass.; see pp. 221-232 (DIWH, DOOR, FFY, INNS)

Ipswich, Mass. (DOOR, INNS)

Providence, river, R.I. (SHUN)

Rehoboth, Mass. (CDW, SHUN)

Rhode Island (CALL, CDW, DQUK, REDH, SHUN, TGSK)

Riverpoint, usu. River Point, R.I. (CDW)

Round Hill, Vt.; not to be confused with the Round Hill near Rutland to the n.w. (WHIS)

Round Mountain, near Dunwich, Mass.; not to be confused with the Round Mtn. in the Taconic Mts. to the s. (DUNW)

Rowley, Mass. (DOOR, INNS)

Rutland, Mass. (HBG, WHIS)

Saco, Me. (DOOR)

St. John's Churchyard, Providence, R.I. (CDW, SHUN)

Salem, Mass. (CDW, DAT, DIWH, DQUK, DUNW, INNS, NEC, PH, PM, SK, TGSK)

Salem-Village, modern Danvers, Mass. (CDW)

Sefton, town and asylum, Mass. (HERB)

Sentinel Hill, near Dunwich, Mass. (DUNW)

South Londonderry, Vt. (WHIS)

Springfield, Mass. (DUNW)

Stamford, Conn. (TRAP)

Stampers' Hill, Providence, R.I. (CDW)

Stillwater, Mass. (HBG)

Swamp Hollow, Mass. (HBG)

Swan Point Cemetery, Providence, R.I. (CDW)

Townshend, Vt. (WHIS)

Truro, Mass. (DQUK)

Vermont, see pp. 163-170 (INNS, WHIS)

Vermont, University of, Burlington, Vt. (WHIS)

Waltham, Mass. (WHIS)

Wantastiquet, mountain, N.H. (WHIS)

Warren, R.I. (CDW)

West, river, Vt. (WHIS)

West End, Boston, Mass. (TGSK)

Winchendon, Mass. (WHIS)

Windham, county, Vt. (WHIS)

Winooski, river, Vt. (WHIS)

Woonsocket, R.I. (REDH)

Wrentham, Mass. (WHIS)

Y'ha-nthlei, Deep One city off Innsmouth, Mass. (INNS)

Zoar, Mass. (FFY)

UNITED STATES AND CANADA

Adirondacks, mountains, N.Y. (CDW, MAN)

Alameda, Calif. (TEST)

Alaska (ATMM, HOIM)

Aleutian Islands, Alaska (AEON)

Albany, N.Y. (BWS, DAT, EXE, LURK, MAN)

Arizona (ATMM, MOU)

Arkansas (YIG)

Arkansas, river, Kans. (MOU)

Atlantic City, N.J. (CDW)

Attica, N.Y. (DAT)

Banof, valley, Lomar (POL)

Barton, county, Kans. (MOU)

Batavia, N.Y. (DAT)

Bayside, Queens, N.Y. (REDH)

Bellview, plantation, Va. (RATS)

Bend Village, Mo. (MEDU)

Berkeley, Calif. (TEST)

B'graa, town in K'n-yan (MOU)

Big Cypress Swamp, Florida (STAT)

Binger, Okla. (MOU)

Bitterroot, mountains, Ida. (TOTH)

Blue Mountain, forest preserve, Ore. (TOTH)

Brooklyn, N.Y. (REDH, WING)

Buffalo, N.Y. (DAT)

Cactus, mountains, now Cactus Range, Nev. (TJR)

Caddo, county, Okla. (MOU, YIG)

California (CALL, EXE, TEST, WHIS)

Canada (CHAL, HERB, WING)

Canadian, river, Okla. (YIG)

Canton, Ohio (INNS)

Catskills, mountains, N.Y. (BWS, LURK, MAN)

Cape Girardeau, Mo. (MEDU)

Carfax, plantation, Va. (RATS)

Chicago, Ill. (AJ, ERYX, PM, SK, TGSK)

Chorazin, N.Y. (DAT)

Cibola, legendary cities of gold (MOU)

Cicuyé, modern Pecos Pueblo, N.Mex. (MOU)

Cleveland, Ohio (INNS)

Colorado (ATMM)

Columbia University, New York, N.Y. (DAT, TEST, WING); as Columbia College (GM)

Cone Mountain, Catskills, N.Y. (LURK)

Creek, tribal terr., Okla. (YIG)

Daalbergen, N.Y. (TBB)

Daikos, border fortress? of Lomar (POL)

Do-Hna, valley, K'n-yan (MOU)

Dry Gulch, Nev.; not to be confused with the ghost town in White Pine county (TJR)

Ellis Island, N.Y.-N.J. (REDH)

Elizabethtown, modern Elizabeth, N.J. (SHUN)

El Paso, Tex. (EXE)

El Reno, Okla. (YIG)

Esopus, N.Y. (MAN)

Five Nations, confederacy, N.Y. (WHIS); as Iroquois (DAT)

Flatbush, fmr. town, Brooklyn, N.Y. (REDH)

Florida (DOOR, HMB, MOU)

Fort Morton, Alaska (HOIM)

Franklin, county, Ark. (YIG)

Fredericksburg, Va. (SHUN)

French Quarter, New Orleans, La. (TGSK)

Gainesville, Fla. (STAT)

Garden of the Gods, rock formation, Colo. (ATMM)

Germantown, Penna. (CDW)

Goat Hill, San Francisco, Calif. (TEST)

Governor's Island, N.Y. (REDH)

Gowanus, Brooklyn, N.Y. (REDH)

Grand Canyon, Ariz. (MOU)

Greenwich, fmr. town, Manhattan, N.Y. (HE)

Greenwood Cemetery, Brooklyn, N.Y. (REDH)

Grh-yan, hills, K'n-yan (MOU)

Guthrie, Okla. (YIG)

Hampden, Ore. (TOTH)

Harlem, Manhattan, N.Y. (HERB)

Hawaii (AEON)

Hell's Acres, hills, Ore. (TOTH)

Hudson, river, N.Y. (HE, MAN)

Hurley, N.Y. (MAN)

Illinois (HERB)

James, river, Va. (RATS)

Jewel Lake, Nev. (TJR)

Johns Hopkins University, Baltimore, Md. (DUNW)

Kadiphonek, mountain, Lomar (POL)

Kansas (MOU)

Kickapoo, tribal terr., Okla. (YIG)

Kingston, N.Y. (DAT, MAN)

K'n-yan, subterranean realm, Okla. (AEON, MOU, WHIS)

Lake Placid, N.Y. (MAN)

Lefferts Corners, N.Y.; poss. based on Ladew Corners, modern Shandaken (LURK)

Lomar, *anc. country, Alaska and n. Canada* (ATMM, HOIM, MOU, POL, TGSK, TIME)

Louisiana (CALL, MEDU)

L'thaa, *suburb of Tsath, K'n-yan* (MOU)

Manhattan, N.Y. (TEST)

Maple Hill, *Catskills, N.Y.; not to be confused with the Maple Hills near Castleton or Webb, N.Y.* (LURK)

Maumee, Ohio (INNS)

Millbrae, Calif. (TEST)

Milwaukee, Wisc. (HAUN)

Missouri (MEDU, YIG)

Montreal, Que., Canada (MAN)

Mountain Top, *N.Y.* (MAN)

New-Amsterdam, colon. name for New York City (q.v.) (LURK)

Newcastle, Okla. (YIG)

New France, colon. name for Canada (q.v.) (CDW)

New Jersey (CALL, SHUN, WING)

New Mexico (MOU)

New-Netherland, colon. name for New York (q.v.) (DAT)

New Orleans, La. (AEON, CALL, MEDU, TGSK)

New Paltz, N.Y. (MAN)

New York (DAT, EXE, LURK, MAN, WING); unnamed (BWS, TBB); Upstate, see pp. 50-59

New York City, N.Y.; see pp. 43-49 (CALL, CDW, COOL, DAT, DOOR, HE, MAN, MEDU, MOU, PYR, REDH, TEMP, TEST, TIME, WING); as New-Amsterdam (LURK); *as Niyara in the desolate future?* (TATS)

Nith, *plain, K'n-yan* (MOU)

Noatak, river, Alaska (HOIM)

Nome, Alaska (HOIM)

Noton, *mountain, Lomar* (POL)

Norton Mine, *Nev.* (TJR)

Oakland, Calif. (TEST)

Oberlin College, Oberlin, Ohio (INNS)

Ohio (INNS)

Oklahoma, see pp. 155-162 (MOU, YIG)

Okmulgee, Okla. (YIG)

Olathoë, *capital of Lomar* (ATMM, DQUK, IRA, MOU, POL)

Ottawa, Ont., Canada (HERB)

Ozarks, mountains, Ark. (YIG)

Pacific coast, region, U.S. (TEST, UNN)

Paterson, N.J. (CALL)

Pawnee, tribal terr., Okla. (YIG)

Pecos, pueblo, N.M. (MOU)

Pecos, river, N.M. (MOU)

Pennsylvania (CDW, TRAP)

Philadelphia, Penna. (CDW, TEST)

Plattsburg, N.Y. (DOOR)

Princeton University, Princeton, N.J. (CALL, DUNW, MEDU)

Quebec, Que., Canada (ATMM)

Quivira, fmr. Indian country, Kans. (MOU)

Ramapo, mountains, N.Y.-N.J. (TBB)

Red Hook, Brooklyn, N.Y. (REDH)

Rennselaerwyck, N.Y. (MAN)

Rice, county, Kans. (MOU)

Richmond, Va. (ERYX, RATS)

Rio Grande, river, Tex. (EXE)

Riverside, *plantation, Mo.* (MEDU)

Rochester, N.Y. (EXE)

Sacramento, Calif. (EXE, TEST)

St. Louis, Mo. (CALL, HERB, MEDU)

Salmon, river, Ida. (TOTH)

San Diego, Calif. (WHIS)

San Francisco, Calif. (CALL, DAG, EXE, TEST, WING)

San Jose, Calif. (TEST)

San Quentin, town and prison, Calif. (TEST)

Sarkis, plateau on which Olathoë sits, Lomar (POL)

Sausalito, Calif. (TEST)

Scott, county, Ark. (YIG)

South, the, region, U.S.; see pp. 204-212 (BWS, CDW, INNS, MEDU, SK, UNN)

South Carolina (TGSK)

Sugar-Loaf, usu. Sugar Loaf, mountain, N.Y. (MAN)

Tamalpais, modern Kentfield, Calif. (TEST)

Tempest, mountain, Catskills, N.Y.; poss. based on Tremper Mtn. (LURK)

Thapnen, watchtower, Lomar (POL)

Thunder Hill, near Mountain Top, N.Y. (MAN)

Tiguex, pueblos, modern Bernalillo area, N.M. (MOU)

Toledo, Ohio (INNS)

Toronto, Ont., Canada (WING)

Trenton, N.J. (WING)

Tsath, capital city of Kn-yan (MOU)

Tulane University, New Orleans, La. (CALL)

Ulster, county, N.Y. (DAT)

United States (GM, TIME, TRAP); as America (ATMM, CALL, EVC, EXE, HOIM, MEDU, MOON, PYR, RATS, TGSK, TJR, WING)

Virginia (ERYX, HE, MOU, RATS, TIME)

Washington, D.C. (CDW)

Wichita, mountains, Okla. (YIG)

Wichita, river, Okla. (YIG)

Wichita, tribal terr., Okla. (YIG)

Wisconsin (HAUN)

Wisconsin, University of, Madison, Wisc. (WING)

Xinaián, see K'n-yan (MOU)

Zuni, pueblo, N.Mex . (MOU)

EARTH

Abu Roash, Egypt (PYR)

Abyssinia, medieval name for Ethiopia (CDW)

Acolhuacan, medieval kdm., cent. Mexico (EXE)

Acropolis, hill, Athens, Greece (CALL, CDW)

Adare, cape, Antarctica (ATMM)

Admiralty Range, Antarctica (ATMM)

Aegyptus, classical name for Egypt (q.v.) (CATS, VOF)

Aetna, volcano, Sicily (PATG)

Africa (AEON, AJ, ATMM, CALL, CATS, DAT, HOIM, INNS, MEDU, NC, PH, TEST, WING)

Aguas Calientes, usu. Aguascalientes,

Mexico (EXE)

Akurion, rock between Sarnath and Ib (DOOM)

Alexandria, Egypt (PYR, REDH)

Algiers, Algeria (TEST)

Alpheus, river, Greece (PATG)

Alsace, province, France (TEMP)

Altstadt, modern Staré Město, Prague, Czech. (CDW)

Amazon, river, Brazil (HOIM)

Anahuac, Aztec name for Valley of Mexico (EXE)

Anchester, England (RATS)

Andes, mountains, Peru (ATMM)

Angora, modern Ankara, Turkey (DQUK)

Antarctic Ocean (ATMM)

Antarctica, see pp. 75-80 (ATMM, HAUN, MOU, TIME); as Antarktos (FFY)

Anziques, 16th c. kdm., usu. Anziku, lower Congo basin (PH)

Arabia, see pp. 67-74 (ATMM, CALL, DESC, HOIM, NC, NEC, PYR, REDH, SK, TGSK, TIME)

Arabia Deserta, classical name for Arab. interior (ATMM)

Arabian Desert, usu. Eastern Desert, Egypt (PYR)

Arabia Petraea, classical name for n.w. Arabia and Jordan (TGSK)

Arcadia, region, Greece (PATG, TREE)

Arctic, ocean and region (ATMM, HOIM, TATS, TIME)

Arethusa, spring, Sicily (PATG)

Asia (AEON, ATMM, BWS, CRAW, HOU, INNS, PH, REDH, TEST, VOF)

Asturias, province, n. Spain (MOU)

Athens, Greece (TREE)

Atlaanât, ruined pre-Adamite city; orig. Atlânaat, near "Angor-lana" in Persia or Mesopotamia, in E. Hoffmann Price, "The Dreamer of Atlânaat" (1926) (TGSK)

Atlantic Ocean (INNS, TEMP, TIME)

Atlantis, sunken continent (AEON, ATMM, CALL, DESC, HAUN, MEDU, MOU, SHHM, TEMP, TEST, TIME, WHIS)

Attica, region, Greece (HYPN)

Auckland, New Zealand (CALL)

Australia (CALL, PYR, TGSK, TIME)

Auteuil, arrondissement in w. Paris, France (MEDU)

Averoigne, province, s. France; orig. in Clark Ashton Smith, "The End of the Story" (1930) (AEON)

Avon, river, England (PATG)

Babylon, anc. city, Iraq (ATMM, CALL, FEST, FFY, HE, INNS, MEDU, NC, NEC, REDH)

Babylonia, anc. kdm., Iraq (HE)

Bactria, anc. kdm., Afghanistan (TIME)

Bagdad, usu. Baghdad, Iraq (PYR)

Ballylough, County Down, N. Ireland; *or poss. fictional town in Co. Meath* (MOON)

Barcelona, Spain (CDW, COOL)

Bayonne, France (TGSK)

Beardmore, glacier, Antarctica (ATMM)

Belgium (AJ)

Belloy-en-Santerre, Somme valley, France (SK)

Benares, India (TGSK)

Berlin, Germany (TEMP); *as Baling in the desolate future?* (TATS)

Bethlehem, Palestine (FEST)

Bethmoora, deserted city not in Europe; orig. in Lord Dunsany, "Bethmoora" (1910) (WHIS)

Biscay, Bay of (MOU)

Bloemfontein, Orange Free State, South Africa (WING)

Bokhara, also Bukhara, Uzbekistan (TGSK, TRAP)

Borligo, city of the desolate future (TATS)

Brava, Cape Verde Islands (CALL, CDW)

Britain, see pp. 171-178 (CDW, DESC, SHUN); see also Cornwall, England, Scotland, Wales

Bubastis, anc. city, Egypt (DQUK)

Bucharest, Romania (CDW)

Budd Land, Antarctica (ATMM)

Buenos Ayres, usu. Buenos Aires, city and university, Argentina (DUNW, NEC)

Burma (AEON)

Caerleon, Wales (CDW)

Cairo, Egypt (CDW, PYR)

Calagurris, classical name for Calahorra, Spain (VOF)

Callao, Peru (CALL)

Campania, anc. region, s. Italy (VOF)

Canaan, anc. Israel (INNS)

Cape Verde Islands (CALL)

Carcassonne, France (HE)

Carolines, islands, w. Pacific (INNS)

Carthage, anc. city, Tunisia (MEDU)

Castile, region, Spain (TJR)

Caude, village near Angers, France; not on modern maps, poss. error by Lovecraft's source Sabine Baring-Gould (SHUN)

Central Asia, region, Asia (ATMM, HOU); as Tartary (BOOK, TGSK), Turan (REDH)

Ceylon, modern Sri Lanka (AEON; a "Cingalese" cultist)

Chalca, medieval confed., cent. Mexico (EXE)

Chaldaea, anc. kdm., Iraq (AEON, NC)

Chicomoztoc, legendary cavern origin of the Mexica (EXE)

Chihuahua, state, Mexico (EXE)

Chile (AEON)

China (AEON, CALL, CRAW, DAT, INNS, PATG, TEST)

Cimmeria, anc. (Hyborian Age) kdm.; orig. in Robert E. Howard, "Cimmeria" (1928); not to be confused with historical (Ukraine, 8th–7th c. B.C.) Cimmeria (TIME)

Cochin-China, modern s. Vietnam (DAT)

Commoriom, anc. capital of Hyperborea; orig. in Clark Ashton Smith, "The Tale of Satampra Zeiros" (1929) (ATMM, WHIS)

Congo (AJ, HERB, PH, WING)

Congo, river, Africa (AJ)

Constantinople, classical and medieval name of Istanbul, Turkey (NEC)

Copenhagen, Denmark (TRAP)

Corinth, Greece (TREE)

Cornwall, duchy, w. Britain (DQUK, RATS)

Crete, island, Greece (ATMM); as Minoan kdm. (HAUN)

Crimson Desert, also ad-Dahna, cent. Arabia (NEC, TEST)

Croydon, suburb s. of London; *or poss. fictitious town in Pacific n.w.* (TOTH)

Cumae, anc. city, Italy (PATG)

Cyane, spring, Sicily (MOON)

Czecho-Slovakia (CDW)

Dacia, anc. kdm., Romania (TEMP)

Dahna, see Crimson Desert

Damascus, Syria (NEC)

Darien, province, e. Panama (MOU)

Darling Harbour, Sydney, Australia (CALL)

Dashur, Egypt (PYR)

Dath, country of the desolate future (TATS)

De Grey, river, W.A., Australia (TIME)

Denmark (DESC, RATS, TRAP)

Devon, county, w. Britain (MOU)

Dho-Nha, see inner city at magnetic poles.

Dover, England (CEL)

Dublin, city and university, Ireland (REDH)

Dunedin, New Zealand (CALL)

Durban, Natal, South Africa (WING)

Düsseldorf, Germany (AEON)

Easter Island, s.e. Pacific (AEON, DAT, HAUN, INNS, MEDU, TGSK)

Edinburgh, Scotland (BWS)

Egeberg, mansion, Oslo, Norway (CALL)

Egypt, see pp. 98-108 (AEON, ATMM, BWS, CDW, COOL, DQUK, FFY, GM, HAUN, MEDU, NC, NYAR, PATG, PYR, TIME, TOTH); as Aegyptus (CATS, VOF); as Khem (HAUN, PYR)

Eiffel Tower, monument, Paris, France (PYR)

El Dorado, legendary city of gold, S. Amer. (HE)

England, see also Britain (AJ, CDW, CHAL, DQUK, DOOR, HOUN, PYR, RATS, TIME)

Erebus, volcano, Ross I., Antarctica (ATMM)

Etruria, anc. kdm., Italy (VOF)

Europe (AEON, ATMM, CALL, CDW, DAT, DOOR, INNS, MOU, PYR, REDH, TEMP, TIME, TRAP)

Everest, mountain, Himalayas, Nepal (ATMM, NC)

Exham, priory, England (RATS)

Ezbekiyeh, garden, Cairo, Egypt (PYR)

Faussesflammes, chateau, Averoigne, France (AEON)

Ferenczy, castle, Transylvania (CDW)

Fiji (AEON, INNS)

Flanders, region, Belgium (HERB)

Florence, Italy (TIME)

Fortaleza, Brazil (CDW)

France (AEON, CDW, INNS, MEDU, MOU, PM, SHUN, SK, TGSK, WING)

Frankfort, usu. Frankfurt, Germany (PH)

Franklin Island, Antarctica (ATMM)

Fujiyama, volcano, Japan (ATMM)

Gaul, anc. region, France and vicinity (PATG); as Gallia (VOF)

Germany (DAG, MEZ, NEC, PYR, TEMP)

Gethsemane, garden, Jerusalem (CDW)

Ghizereh, island in the Nile, Egypt (PYR)

Giant's Causeway, rock formation, N. Ireland (ATMM)

Gizeh, Egypt (PYR)

Golgotha, hill, Jerusalem (CDW)

Goshen, anc. region, Egypt (HBG)

Gothenburg, Sweden (CALL)

Graham Land, Antarctica (ATMM)

Gray's Inn, London, England (DESC)

Great Sandy Desert, Australia (TIME)

Greece (ATMM, MOON, PYR, REDH, TEMP, WHIS); as Hellas (HYPN, PATG)

Greenland (ATMM, CALL, HOIM)

Guatemala (YIG)

Guinea, region, w. Africa (AJ, CDW, INNS)

Hadoth, valley, Egypt (CDW, OUTS)

Hadrian's Wall, n. Britain (CDW, DESC)

Hanwell, asylum and suburb w. of London (RATS)

Harrow, school and suburb n.w. of London (DESC)

Haute Vienne, department, usu. Haute-Vienne, France (CDW)

Havana, Cuba (CDW)

Haymarket, London, England (HOIM)

Hayti, usu. Haiti (CALL)

Hebrus, river, modern Maritsa R., Greece (PATG)

Heidelberg University, Heidelberg, Germany (DAT, GM)

Helicon, mountain, Greece (PATG)

Heliopolis, anc. city near modern Cairo, Egypt (PYR)

Hellas, classical name for Greece (HYPN, PATG)

Hesperia, Greek legendary paradise of the West (FFY, PATG)

Hexham, England (CDW)

Himalayas, mountains, Asia (ATMM, TGSK, TIME, WHIS)

Hispania Citerior, classical name for e. Spain (VOF)

Hobart, Tasmania, Australia (ATMM)

Hoggar, also Ahaggar, mountains, Algeria (MEDU, TEST)

Holland, province, Netherlands (CDW, DAT, HOU)

Hungary (CDW, DOOR, MEZ)

Huntingdon, England (AJ)

Hyde Park, Sydney, Australia (CALL)

Hyperborea, *anc. civilization in Arctic;* orig. Greek legend turned Theosophist myth, *HPL version orig. in Clark Ashton Smith, "The Tale of Satampra Zeiros" (1929)* (AEON, ATMM, TGSK, TIME)

Ib, prehuman city in Mnar (ATMM, DOOM, NC)

Iberus, river, modern Ebro R., Spain (VOF)

Iceland (CALL)

Ilarnek, city in Mnar (DOOM)

Illyria, classical name for Yugoslavia (VOF)

Implan, hills distant from Sarnath (DOOM)

India (CALL, DAT, SK, STAT, TEST, TGSK, TJR); as East India (AEON, CDW, COOL, INNS, TERR)

Indian Ocean (ATMM, TIME)

Indo-China (DAT, HOIM, INNS)

Inner city at magnetic poles; Dho-Hna? (DUNW)

Innsmouth, Cornwall (CEL)

Ireland, see pp. 171-178 (ATMM, CALL, MOON, WHIS)

Irem, also Iram, legendary anc. city in Arabia (CALL, NC, NEC, TEST, TGSK)

Ismailiya, Egypt (PYR)

Italy (HAUN, NEC, VOF)

Japan (PATG)

Jerusalem, Israel (CDW)

Joanna, spring, W.A., Australia (TIME)

Johannesburg, South Africa (WING)

Kadath, mountains, Antarctica (ATMM, DUNW, MEDU, MOU)

Kafr-el-Haram, village near the Sphinx, Egypt (PYR)

Kaiser Wilhelm Land, Antarctica (ATMM)

Kaliri, tribal terr., Congo basin (AJ)

Kent, county, England (HYPN)

Khem, anc. name of Egypt (q.v.) (HAUN, PYR)

Kiel, Germany (TEMP)

Kilderry, County Meath, Ireland; not to be confused with Kilderry in Co. Kerry (MOON)

Kish, anc. city, Iraq (ATMM)

Klausenburg, modern Cluj-Napoca, Romania (CDW)

K'naa, kdm. or province, Mu (AEON)

Knox Land, usu. Knox Coast, Antarctica (ATMM)

Kurdistan (REDH)

Latin Quarter, Paris, France (MEDU)

Lemuria, sunken continent (ATMM, CALL, DAT, HAUN, MEDU, MOU)

Leng, plateau, Cent. Asia or Antarctica; see pp. 179-189 (AEON, ATMM, HOIM, HOU, TGSK, WHIS)

Leyden, also Leiden, Netherlands (DAT)

Libyan Desert, Egypt (PYR)

Limoges, France (CDW)

Lindum, classical name for Lincoln, England (DESC)

Lithuania (TGSK)

Liverpool, England (CDW, TEMP)

London, England (CALL, CDW, CEL, CRAW, DESC, DQUK, EVC, HE, HOIM, HOU, HYPN, PH, RATS, REDH, WING); *as Loton in the desolate future?* (TATS)

Luarca, Asturias, Spain (MOU)

Luitpold Land, usu. Luitpold Coast, Antarctica (ATMM)

Lydia, anc. kdm., w. Turkey (TREE)

Lyons, France (FEST)

Machu Picchu, anc. city, Peru (ATMM)

Madness, *mts. of, Antarctica* (ATMM)

Maenalus, mountain, Greece (MOON, PATG, TREE)

Magnetic Poles (DUNW)

Malaya (INNS)

Malta, island, Mediterranean (DQUK)

Malwa, region, w. India (PYR)

Man, Isle of, Britain (DQUK)

Marseilles, also Marseille, France (PYR)

Martinique, Fr. West Indies (MEDU, SHUN); as obs. name Martineco (CDW)

McMurdo Sound, Antarctica (ATMM)

Meath, county, Ireland (MOON)

Mediterranean, sea (GM, TIME)

Melanesia, islands, s.w. Pacific (AEON)

Memphis, anc. city near Cairo, Egypt (CDW, FEST, NC, NEC, PYR)

Meroë, anc. city and (usu. Kush) kdm., Sudan (CATS, GM, NC)

Mesopotamia, classical name for Iraq (CHAL, DUNW)

Metz, France (NC)

Mexico (AEON, EXE, MOU, TEST, TJR, YIG); also Aztec (EXE, MOU, TJR, YIG)

Mexico City, Mexico (EXE)

M'gonga, correctly Mgonga, fmr. German border post, Tanzania; not to be confused with the arch. site Mgonga near Iringa (WING)

Midian, anc. kdm., n.w. Arabia (PH)

Mlolo, lake, Uganda (WING)

Mnar, anc. country (ATMM, DOOM, NC)

Mombasa, Kenya (WING)

Mongolia (DAT, TEST, TGSK)

Mont St.-Michel, France (PM)

Mouski, market, Cairo, Egypt (PYR)

Mu, sunken continent in Pacific; orig. in James Churchward, Lost Continent of Mu (1926) (AEON, MEDU)

Nairobi, Kenya (WING)

Nameless City, Arabia (ATMM, DESC, NC, NEC)

Nan-Matol, usu. Nan Madol, arch. site, Ponape (AEON)

Nansen, mountain, Victoria Land, Antarctica (ATMM)

Nantes, France (SHUN)

Natal, province, South Africa (WING)

Nath, anc. city, poss. near Egypt (TOTH)

Neapolis, classical name for Naples, Italy (TREE)

Neb, rock tombs, Egypt (OUTS)

Nemorensis, Lacus, modern Lake Nemi, Italy (VOF)

Nepal (DAT, TGSK, WHIS)

Netherlands (REDH)

Neustadt, modern Nové Mĕsto, Prague, Czech. (CDW)

New Spain, colon. name for Mexico (q.v.) (MOU, TJR)

New Zealand (AEON, CALL)

Nile, river, Africa (NC, OUTS, PATG, PYR, TEMP)

Nis, valley; orig. in Edgar Allan Poe, "The Valley of Unrest" (1831) (LURK, MEM)

Niyara, city of the desolate future (TATS)

N'kai, black subterranean realm beneath Yoth (MOU, WHIS)

N'Kini, jungle belt, Uganda; not to be confused with Nkini (now Nkéni) r. valley in Congo Rep. (WING)

North America (ATMM)

North Sea (DESC)

Northam Keep, Yorkshire, England (DESC)

Norway (CALL, REDH)

Nyangwe, Congo Dem. Rep. (WING)

Old Town, also Gamlebyen, Oslo, Norway (CALL)

Olympus, mountain, Greece (HYPN, PATG, WS)

Onga, tribal terr., Congo basin (AJ)

Ophir, unk. anc. country in Bible (CATS)

Orient, the, obs. term for e. Asia (AEON, CDW, HOU)

Oslo, Norway (CALL)

Otaheite, usu. Tahiti (q.v.), Fr. Polynesia, s. Pacific (INNS)

Oxford University, Oxford, England (AJ, ATMM, DESC, HE, TJR)

Oxus, river, modern Amu Darya, w. Turkestan (NC)

Pacific Ocean, see pp. 37-42 (AEON, ATMM, CALL, DAG, HOIM, INNS, MOU, TIME)

Palmyra, anc. city, Syria (ATMM)

Panama Canal (ATMM)

Paphos, anc. city, Cyprus (PATG)

Papua, region, New Guinea (TIME)

Paris, France (CALL, CDW, CRAW, DUNW, HE, MEDU, NEC, REDH, SHUN)

Parnassus, mountain, Greece (PATG)

Parry, mountains, Antarctica (ATMM)

Pentelicus, mountain, Greece (HYPN)

Persia (AEON, DQUK, REDH)

Perth, W.A., Australia (TIME); *as Perath in desolate future?* (TATS)

Peru (AEON, TIME)

Petra, anc. city, Jordan (ATMM)

Philippines (AEON, CALL)

Philistia, anc. kdm., Palestine (DAG, INNS)

Phoenix Park, Dublin, Ireland (REDH)

Phrygia, anc. kdm., w.-cent. Turkey (RATS, VOF)

Pilbarra, W.A., Australia (TIME)

Pnakotus, ruined city of the Great Race, Australia; see pp. 109-114 (TIME);

unnamed in HPL, name orig. in Lin Carter, "Zoth-Ommog" (1976)

Poland (COLO, DIWH, HERB, INNS, REDH, TGSK)

Polynesia, islands in cent., s. Pacific (AEON, INNS, TIME)

Pompeii, Italy (AEON)

Pompelo, classical name for Pamplona, Spain (VOF)

Ponape, Caroline Is. (AEON, INNS)

Port Royal, Jamaica (CDW)

Port Said, Egypt (PYR)

Portugal (AJ, CALL, CDW, INNS, MOU, SHHM)

Poseidonis, sunken capital of Atlantis; orig. Theosophical name for Plato's Atlantis (SHHM)

Prague, Czech. (CDW)

Pretoria, Transvaal, South Africa (WING)

Prussia, province, Germany (TEMP)

Ptolemaïs, anc. city, Egypt (PH)

Pyramids, monument, Gizeh, Egypt (OUTS, PYR)

Queen Alexandra Range, Antarctica (ATMM)

Queen Mary Land, Antarctica (ATMM)

Querétaro, Santiago de, Querétaro, Mexico (EXE)

Rakus, Romania; possibly Racos, or Rákosd (CDW)

Red Sea, btwn. Africa and Arabia (TIME)

Regent's Park, London, England (HOIM)

Relex, see also R'lyeh (MOU)

Rhine, river, Germany (PH)

Rhineland, province, Germany (TEMP)

R'lyeh, sunken city, s.e. Pacific (ATMM, CALL, EXE, INNS, MAN, MEDU, TGSK, WHIS); *as Relex* (MOU)

Roba el Khaliyeh, usu. Rub' al-Khali, desert, Arabia (NEC)

Rokol, country far from Sarnath (DOOM)

Rome, Italy (ATMM, CDW, NC); empire of (CDW, DESC, PYR, RATS, TIME, VOF)

Ross Island, Antarctica (ATMM)

Ross Sea, Antarctica (ATMM)

Rotterdam, Netherlands (HOU)

Roumania, usu. Romania (CDW)

Sahara, desert, n. Africa (MEDU, TEST)

St. Eloi, also Sint-Elooi, Belgium (HERB)

St. Eustatius, Neth. Antilles (CDW)

St. Thomas, U.S. Virgin Is. (TRAP)

Sakkara, also Sakkarah; anc. necropolis, Egypt (AEON, PYR)

Samarcand, usu. Samarkand, Uzbekistan (HE)

Samoa, islands, cent. Pacific (ATMM)

San Mateo, mountains, Mexico; not to be confused with the actual San Mateo Mts., N.Mex. (EXE)

Sanaá, usu. Sana'a, Yemen (NEC)

Santa Cruz, usu. St. Croix, U.S. Virgin Is. (TRAP)

Sarnath, doomed city in Mnar (DOOM, NC)

Scandinavia, region, Europe (REDH, TRAP)

Scotland, see also Britain (CDW)

Scythia, anc. nation, Ukraine (GM, MOON, VOF)

Shamballah, usu. Shambhala, Buddhist legendary city in inner Asia (DAT, TOTH)

Shrewsfield, England (RATS)

Siberia, region, e. Russia (ATMM)

Sicily, island, Italy (MOON, PATG, PM)

Sierra de Malinche, usu. La Malinche, volcano, Mexico (EXE)

Somerset, county, England (MOU)

Sorbonne, university, Paris, France (MEDU)

South Africa (TIME, WING)

South America (ATMM, CALL, SK)

South Pole, Antarctica (ATMM, MOU)

South Seas, usu. South Pacific (INNS)

Southwark, London, England (HOIM)

Spain (CDW, DUNW, MOU, NEC, VOF)

Sphinx, monument, Gizeh, Egypt (CALL, CATS, PYR)

Spitzbergen, island, Arctic Ocean (TIME)

Stonehenge, monument, Salisbury, England (CDW, DESC, RATS)

Suez Canal, Egypt (PYR, TIME)

Suffolk, county, England (TIME)

Sumatra, island, East Indies (INNS)

Sumeria, anc. country, Iraq (CHAL)

Surinam (CDW)

Surrey, county, England (CEL)

Sussex, county, England (CHAL, TOMB)

Sydney, city and university, N.S.W., Australia (CALL)

Syracuse, Sicily, Italy (TREE)

Syria (REDH, VOF)

Tahiti, island, Fr. Polynesia, s. Pacific (AEON); as Otaheite (INNS)

Tallaght, suburb s. of Dublin (MOON)

Tartary, medieval name for cent. Asia (BOOK, TGSK)

Tasmania, island and state, Australia (ATMM)

Tenochtitlan, Aztec name for Mexico City (EXE)

Tegea, Greece (TREE)

Tepanecapan, medieval kdm., cent. Mexico (EXE)

Terror, Mount, volcano, Ross I., Antarctica (ATMM)

Than, river, Nis (MEM)

Thebes, anc. city, Egypt (FFY, PYR)

Thebes, anc. city, Greece (PATG)

Thibet, usu. Tibet (DAT, DQUK, HOIM, REDH, TEST)

Thrace, anc. region, Bulgaria (PATG)

Tlaxcala, state, Mexico (EXE); also as
   Tlascalteca

Torreón, Coahuila, Mexico (EXE)

Totten Land, usu. Totten Glacier, Antarctica
   (ATMM)

Transvaal, province, South Africa (WING)

Transylvania, region, Romania (CDW)

Troad, anc. region, n.w. Turkey (RATS)

Troy, anc. city, Turkey (PATG)

Tsan-Chan, cruel future empire (TIME); *also
   Tsan Chan* (BWS)

Turan, obs. name for cent. Asia (REDH)

Tyre, anc. city, Lebanon (CALL)

Uganda (WING)

Ukala, modern Kakamega, Kenya (WING)

U-tsang, usu. Ü-Tsang, province, Tibet
   (TEST)

*Uzuldaroum, second capital of Hyperborea;
   orig. in Clark Ashton Smith, "The Tale of
   Satampra Zeiros" (1929)* (ATMM)

Valencia, Spain (COOL)

Valley of Kings, necropolis, Egypt
   (COOL)

Valparaiso, Chile (AEON, CALL)

*Valusia, prehuman serpent empire, Europe;
   orig. in Robert E. Howard, "The Shadow
   Kingdom" (1929)* (ATMM, DAT, HAUN,
   TIME)

Vera Cruz, usu. Veracruz, city and state,
   Mexico (EXE)

Victoria Land, Antarctica (ATMM)

Vienna, Austria (CDW)

Virgin Islands, Caribbean (TRAP)

Wales, see also Britain (DAT, RATS, WHIS)

Weddell Sea, Antarctica (ATMM)

Wellington, New Zealand (AEON)

West Indies (CALL, CDW, MEDU,
   TRAP); as West India (SHUN)

Western Australia, state, Australia (TIME)

Wijtgaart, fmr. town, Leeuwarden,
   Netherlands (MAN)

Wilhelmshaven, Germany (TEMP)

Xochimilco, fmr. city, Mexico City, Mexico
   (EXE)

*Yaanek, volcano, identified with Mt. Erebus,
   Antarctica; orig. at North Pole in Edgar
   Allan Poe, "Ulalume" (1847)* (ATMM)

Yaddith-Gho, mountain, K'naa, Mu (AEON)

Yarat, country of the desolate future (TATS)

Yemen (NEC, TEST)

Yhe, vanished country or continent, Pacific (TIME)

*Yian, city in China or Sinkiang; orig. in Robert
   W. Chambers, "Maker of Moons" (1896)*
   (WHIS)

*Yian-Ho, city in China or Sinkiang; poss.
   variant of Yian (q.v.)* (DAT, TGSK)

Yin, gardens (FFY)

Yorkshire, county, England (CDW, DESC)

Yoth, red-litten realm beneath K'n-yan (MAN,
   MOU, WHIS)

*Yuanario, capital of the desolate future; present-
   day Rio de Janeiro?* (TATS)

Yucatan, usu. Yucatán, state and region,
   Mexico (TEMP)

Zimbabwe, medieval city, Zimbabwe
   (MEDU)

Zin, vaults beneath a city in Yoth (CDW,
   MOU); not to be confused w. the biblical
   "wilderness of Zin" in s. Israel

Zobna, anc. country n. of Lomar (POL)

Zululand, fmr. kdm., South Africa (MEDU)

DREAMLANDS

Ai, *river in Mnar* (DOOM, IRA)

Aira, *unattained city* (IRA)

Akurion, *rock between Sarnath and Ib* (DOOM)

Aphorat, *city?* (DQUK)

Aran, *mountain in Ooth-Nargai* (CEL, DQUK)

Arinurian Streams (CRAW)

Baharna, *city in Oriab* (DQUK)

Basalt Pillars of the West (DQUK, WS)

Bnazic Desert (DOOM, IRA)

Camorin, *groves in Cathuria* (WS)

Cathuria, *land of hope* (DQUK, WS)

Celephaïs, *city in valley of Ooth-Nargai* (CEL, DQUK)

Cerenarian Sea (CEL, DQUK)

Cydathria, *country near Mnar* (DOOM, IRA)

Cytharion, *paradise city of Seven Suns* (CRAW)

Dothur, *country near Mnar* (DOOM)

Drinen, *in the E.* (IRA)

Dylath-Leen, *city at the mouth of the R. Skai* (DQUK)

Enchanted Wood (DQUK)

Hatheg, *town n. of Ulthar* (CATS, DQUK, OG)

Hatheg-Kla, *mountain n. of Hatheg* (DQUK, OG, SHHM)

Hlanith, *city on the Cerenarian Sea* (DQUK)

Ib, *prehuman city in Mnar* (DOOM)

Ilarnek, *city on the R. Ai, Mnar* (DOOM, DQUK, IRA)

Ilek-Vad, *city on the Twilight Sea* (DQUK, SK, TGSK)

Implan, *hills distant from Sarnath* (DOOM)

Inganok, *city near Leng; occas. misprinted 'Inquanok'* (DQUK)

Jaren, *city in Narthos valley* (IRA)

Kadath, *mountain in the Cold Waste* (DQUK, OG, MEDU, SHHM)

Kadatheron, *city on the R. Ai, Mnar* (DOOM, DQUK, IRA)

Karthian Hills (IRA)

Kiran, *city on the R. Oukranos* (DQUK)

Kled, *jungles on the R. Oukranos* (DQUK, SK, TGSK)

Kra, *stream* (IRA)

Lelag-leng, *seaport near Sarkomand* (DQUK)

Leng, *plateau; see pp. 179-189* (CEL, DQUK, FFY, WHIS)

Lerion, *mountain, source of the R. Skai* (DQUK, OG)

Liran, *desert* (IRA)

Lomar, *frozen northern land* (DQUK, IRA, OG)

Middle Ocean, *near Mnar* (DOOM)

Mnar, *country* (DOOM)

Mtal, *coastal province* (DOOM)

Narath, *city* (SK)

Naraxa, *a river of Celephaïs* (CEL, DQUK)

Narg, *a river of Cathuria* (WS)

Nariel, *islands in the Sarnath-era Middle Sea* (DOOM)

Narthos, *valley of Jaren* (IRA)

Ngranek, *mountain in Oriab* (DQUK, OG)

Nir, *city in valley of the R. Skai* (CATS, DQUK, OG)

Nithra, *river of Aira* (IRA)

Ogrothan, *port city on the Cerenarian Sea* (DQUK)

Oonai, *city* (IRA)

Ooth-Nargai, *valley* (CEL, DQUK)

Oriab, *island in the Southern Sea* (DQUK)

Oukranos, river (DQUK, SK, TGSK)

Parg, forested country across the R. Skai from Dylath-Leen (DQUK)

Pnath, underworld vale; occas. misprinted 'Pnoth' (DOOM, DQUK, HAUN)

Rinar, city (DQUK)

Rokol, country far from Sarnath (DOOM)

Runazar, country in Pegāna; orig. in Lord Dunsany, "The King That Was Not" (1905) (CDW)

Sarkomand, deserted city below Leng (DQUK)

Sarnath, doomed city in Mnar (DOOM, IRA)

Selarn, city west of Inganok (DQUK)

Serannian, city in the clouds (CEL, DQUK)

Sidrak, mountain near Teloth (IRA)

Sinara, caravan city on the Zuro R. (IRA)

Six Kingdoms, political grouping incl. Dylath-Leen (DQUK)

Skai, river (CATS, DQUK, OG, SHHM, SK, TGSK)

Sona-Nyl, land of fancy (DQUK, WS)

Southern Sea (DQUK)

Stethelos, country below the great cataract (GM, IRA)

Tanarian Hills, around Ooth-Nargai (CEL, DQUK)

Teloe, paradise city (CRAW)

Teloth, city on the R. Zuro (IRA)

Thalarion, daemon city (DQUK, WS)

Thok, mtn. peaks above Pnath (DQUK, FFY)

Thorabonia, or Thorabon, northern city or country (DQUK)

Thraa, city on the R. Ai, Mnar (DOOM, DQUK, IRA)

Thran, city on the R. Oukranos (DQUK, SK, TGSK)

Thurai, mountain (OG)

Ulthar, city beyond the R. Skai (CATS, DQUK, OG, SHHM, SK, TGSK)

Urg, village btwn. Inganok and Leng (DQUK)

Xari, river in Narthos valley (IRA)

Xura, land of pleasures unattained (DQUK, WS)

Yath, lake on Oriab (DQUK)

Yian, city of silver bells; orig. in Robert W. Chambers, "Maker of Moons" (1896) (WHIS)

Yin, gardens (FFY)

Zakarion, city (EXO)

Zar, land of forgotten dreams (DQUK, WS)

Zin, vaults beneath Leng (DQUK)

Zuro, river of Teloth (IRA)

OUTER SPACE

Aldebaran, star in Taurus (DQUK, FEST, POL)

Algol, star in Perseus (BWS)

Altair, star in Aquila (MOU, VOF)

Antares, star in Scorpio (DQUK)

Arcturus, star in Boötes (POL, TGSK); red worlds orbiting (BWS)

Argo Navis, constellation in southern sky (DIWH)

Callisto, as "the fourth moon of Jupiter" (BWS)

Capella, star in Auriga (BWS)

Cassiopeia, constellation in northern sky

(POL, SHHM, VOF)

Cepheus, constellation in northern sky (VOF)

Charles' Wain, also Ursa Major, constellation in northern sky (DQUK, POL); see also Great Bear

Coma Berenices, constellation in northern sky (MEDU, POL)

Corona Borealis, constellation in northern sky (HYPN)

Cygnus, constellation in northern sky (COLO, VOF)

Deneb, star in Cygnus (COLO, VOF)

Dionaean Plateau, Venus (ERYX)

Dog Star, also Sirius, star in Canis Major (FEST)

Dragon, also Draco, constellation in northern sky (SHHM)

Eryx, highland, Venus (ERYX)

Fomalhaut, star in Piscis Austrinis (DQUK, FFY, VOF)

Ghooric Zone (FFY)

Great Bear, also Ursa Major, constellation in northern sky (PATG, SHHM, WHIS); as Charles' Wain (DQUK, POL)

Hali, Lake of; orig. in Robert W. Chambers, "The Repairer of Reputations" (1895) (WHIS)

Hydra, constellation in southern sky (DIWH)

Jupiter, planet (TGSK, TIME); fourth moon of (BWS)

Kath, extrasolar planet (TGSK)

Kynarth, planet beyond Yuggoth (TGSK)

Kythanil, planet orbiting Arcturus; misprinted 'Kythamil' (TGSK)

Little Bear, also Ursa Minor, constellation in northern sky (DQUK)

Magellanic Clouds, galaxies (WHIS)

Mars, planet (TGSK)

Mercury, planet (TIME)

Milky Way, galaxy (BWS, CRAW, COLO, DQUK, MOU); as Via Lactea (VOF)

Moon, of Earth (as location only); see pp. 25-36 (ATMM, DQUK)

Mthura, extrasolar planet (TGSK)

Neptune, planet (TGSK, WHIS)

Nithon, moon of Yuggoth? (FFY)

Nython, triple star (TGSK)

Nova Persei, nova in Perseus (BWS)

Orion, constellation in the northern sky (FEST)

Orion's Sword, asterism in Orion (BWS)

Perseus, constellation in the northern sky (VOF)

Pleiades, star cluster, Taurus (SK)

Pluto, planet; see also Yuggoth (ATMM, TIME, WHIS)

Polaris, pole star (POL); named only "the Pole Star" in the story text

Saturn, planet (CDW, DQUK, PM)

Seven Suns, world of, planet of Nyarlathotep (WHIS)

Shaggai, planet more distant than Yuggoth (HAUN)

Shonhi, extragalactic planet; occas. misprinted 'Stronti' (TGSK)

Thog, Outside planet (FFY)

Vega, star in Lyra (CDW, DQUK, MOU, VOF)

Venus, planet (CDW, DAT, ERYX, TIME)

Yaddith, extragalactic planet (DAT, FFY, HAUN, TGSK)

Yekub, extragalactic planet; named by Robert E. Howard (CHAL)

Yith, extragalactic planet (TIME)

Yuggoth, planet; usu. Pluto (AEON, FFY, HAUN, HOIM, MEDU, TGSK, WHIS)

STORY KEY

AEON: "Out of the Aeons"

AJ: "Facts Concerning the Late Arthur Jermyn and His Family"

ATMM: *At the Mountains of Madness*

BOOK: "The Book"

BWS: "Beyond the Wall of Sleep"

CALL: "The Call of Cthulhu"

CATS: "The Cats of Ulthar"

CDW: *The Case of Charles Dexter Ward*

CEL: "Celephaïs"

CHAL: "The Challenge From Beyond"

COLO: "The Colour Out of Space"

COOL: "Cool Air"

CRAW: "The Crawling Chaos"

DAG: "Dagon"

DAT: "The Diary of Alonzo Typer"

DESC: "The Descendant"

DIWH: "The Dreams in the Witch House"

DOOM: "The Doom That Came to Sarnath"

DOOR: "The Thing on the Doorstep"

DQUK: *The Dream-Quest of Unknown Kadath*

DUNW: "The Dunwich Horror"

ERYX: "In the Walls of Eryx"

EVC: "The Evil Clergyman"

EXE: "The Electric Executioner"

EXO: "Ex Oblivione"

FB: "From Beyond"

FEST: "The Festival"

FFY: *Fungi From Yuggoth*

GM: "The Green Meadow"

HAUN: "The Haunter of the Dark"

HBG: "The Horror in the Burying-Ground"

HE: "He"

HERB: "Herbert West—Reanimator"

HMB: "The Horror at Martin's Beach"

HOIM: "The Horror in the Museum"

HOU: "The Hound"

HYPN: "Hypnos"

INNS: "The Shadow Over Innsmouth"

IRA: "The Quest of Iranon"

ITV: "In the Vault"

LURK: "The Lurking Fear"

MAN: "The Man of Stone"

MEDU: "Medusa's Coil"

MEM: "Memory"

MEZ: "The Music of Erich Zann"

MOON: "The Moon-Bog"

MOU: "The Mound"

NC: "The Nameless City"

NEC: "History of the *Necronomicon*"

NOC: "The Night Ocean"

NYAR: "Nyarlathotep"

OG: "The Other Gods"

OUTS: "The Outsider"

PATG: "Poetry and the Gods"

PH: "The Picture in the House"

PM: "Pickman's Model"

POL: "Polaris"

PYR: "Under the Pyramids"

RATS: "The Rats in the Walls"

REDH: "The Horror at Red Hook"

SHHM: "The Strange High House in the Mist"

SHUN: "The Shunned House"

SK: "The Silver Key"

STAT: "The Statement of Randolph Carter"

TATS: "Till A' the Seas"

TBB: "Two Black Bottles"

TEMP: "The Temple"

TERR: "The Terrible Old Man"

TEST: "The Last Test"

TGSK: "Through the Gates of the Silver Key"

THM: "The Thing in the Moonlight"

TIME: "The Shadow Out of Time"

TJR: "The Transition of Juan Romero"

TOMB: "The Tomb"

TOTH: "The Tree on the Hill"

TRAP: "The Trap"

TREE: "The Tree"

UNN: "The Unnamable"

VOF: "The Very Old Folk"

WHIS: "The Whisperer in Darkness"

WING: "Winged Death"

WS: "The White Ship"

YIG: "The Curse of Yig"

BIBLIOGRAPHY

This book uses the texts of Lovecraft's fiction and poetry from The H.P. Lovecraft Archive (at hplovecraft.com) maintained by Donovan Loucks.

Barrell, Joseph. "Rhythms and the Measurements of Geologic Time." *Bulletin of the Geological Society of America* 28 (December 4, 1917): 745-904.

Bergier, Jacques. *Extraterrestrial Visitations From Prehistoric Times to the Present.* Chicago: Henry Regnery Company, 1973.

Berruti, Massimo. "The Unnamable in Lovecraft and the Limits of Rationality." Research seminar presentation, Univ. of Helsinki, 2005.

Bright, William. *Native American Placenames of the United States.* Norman, Okla.: Univ. of Oklahoma Press, 2004.

Brush, S.G. "Early History of Selenogony." In *Origin of the Moon; Proceedings of the Conference, Kona, HI, October 13-16, 1984,* 3-15. Houston: Lunar and Planetary Institute, 1986.

Burleson, Donald R. "Hawthorne's Influence on Lovecraft." In *Lovecraft and Influence,* edited by Robert H. Waugh, 35-44. Lanham, Md.: Scarecrow Press, 2014.

— "Lovecraft and the World as Cryptogram." *Lovecraft Studies* 16 (Spring 1988): 14-18.

— "The Mythic Hero Archetype in 'The Dunwich Horror.'" *Lovecraft Studies* 4 (Spring 1981): 3-9.

Callaghan, Gavin. *H.P. Lovecraft's Dark Arcadia: The Satire, Symbology and Contradiction.* Jefferson, N.C.: McFarland, 2013.

Cannon, Peter. "Lovecraft in Hawthornian Perspective." In *H.P. Lovecraft: Four Decades of Criticism,* edited by S.T. Joshi, 161-165. Athens, Ohio: Ohio Univ. Press, 1980.

— "Sunset Terrace Imagery in Lovecraft." *Lovecraft Studies* 5 (Fall 1982): 3-9.

Cannon, Peter, and Joshi, S.T., annots. *More Annotated Lovecraft,* by H.P. Lovecraft. New York: Dell Publishing, 1999.

Card, Jeb J. *Spooky Archaeology: Myth and the Science of the Past.* Albuquerque: Univ. of New Mexico Press, 2018.

Cardin, Matt. "The Master's Eyes Shining with Secrets: H.P. Lovecraft's Influence on Thomas Ligotti." *Lovecraft Annual* 1 (2007): 94-125.

Carter, Angela. "Lovecraft and Landscape." In *The Necronomicon,* edited by George Hay, 171-181. Jersey: Neville Spearman, 1978.

Clute, John, et al. *The Encyclopedia of Science Fiction.* Online 3rd edition, 2011.

Colavito, Jason. *The Cult of Alien Gods: H.P. Lovecraft and Extraterrestrial Pop Culture.* Amherst, N.Y.: Prometheus Books, 2005.

— "What Was the Scholomance? Horror, Ancient Myth, and the Origins of the Devil's School." Jasoncolavito.com blog post, 2011.

Coli, Waltraud Berger, and Lobban, Richard A. *The Cape Verdeans in Rhode Island: A Brief History.* Providence: Rhode Island Publications Society, 1990.

David-Néel, Alexandra. *Magic and Mystery in Tibet* [1929]. New York: Dover Publications, 1971.

Derie, Bobby. "The Shadow Out of Spain." In *Weird Talers: Essays on Robert E. Howard and Others,* 19-51. New York: Hippocampus Press, 2019.

Eckhardt, Jason. "The Cosmic Yankee" [1991]. In *An Epicure in the Terrible: A Centennial Anthology of Essays in Honor of H.P. Lovecraft,* 2nd ed., edited by David E. Schultz and S.T. Joshi, 78-100. New York: Hippocampus Press, 2011.

— *Off the Ancient Track: A Lovecraftian Guide to New-England & Adjacent New-York.* 2nd ed. West Warwick, R.I.: Necronomicon Press, 1990.

Evans-Wentz, W.Y. *The Fairy-Faith in Celtic Countries* [1909]. New York: Citadel Press, 1990.

Faig, Kenneth W. *Lovecraftian Voyages.* New York: Hippocampus Press, 2017.

Gingerich, Owen. "Report on the Progress in Stellar Evolution to 1950." In *Stellar Populations; Proceedings of the 164th Symposium of the International Astronomical Union, held in the Hague, the Netherlands, August 15 -19, 1994,* 3-20. Dordrecht, Neth.: Kluwer Academic Publishers, 1995.

Godwin, Joscelyn. *Arktos: The Polar Myth in Science, Symbolism, and Nazi Survival.* Grand Rapids, Mich.: Phanes Press, 1991.

Goudsward, David. *H.P. Lovecraft in the Merrimack Valley.* New York: Hippocampus Press, 2013.

Granzier-Nakajima, Riako. "Rhode Island and the Great Depression: An Analysis of Reactionary Legislation." Bachelor's thesis, Univ. of Arizona, 2016.

Grundhauser, Eric. "Bradford College." *Atlas Obscura* blog, n.d.

Haden, David. "The Catskill Mountains." In *Lovecraft in Historical Context: A Fifth Collection,* 8-81. Self-published, 2014.

— "Locating 'The Mound.'" In *Lovecraft in Historical Context: A Third Collection.* Self-published, 2012.

— "Of Rats and Legions: H.P. Lovecraft in Northumbria." In *Lovecraft in Historical Context: The Fourth Collection*, 109-124. Self-published, 2013.

— *Walking With Cthulhu: H.P. Lovecraft as Psychogeographer, New York City 1924-26.* Self-published, 2011.

Hamblin, William. "Thoth's Dagger." In *Curse of the Chthonians*, 2nd ed., edited by Sandy Petersen, 91-117. Oakland, Calif.: Chaosium, 2011.

Harman, Graham. *Weird Realism: Lovecraft and Philosophy.* Winchester, Hants.: Zero Books, 2012.

Harms, Daniel. *The Cthulhu Mythos Encyclopedia.* 3rd ed. Lake Orion, Mich.: Elder Signs Press, 2008.

Hite, Kenneth. *Tour de Lovecraft: The Tales.* 2nd ed. Alexandria, Va.: Atomic Overmind Press, 2020.

Houellebecq, Michel. *H.P. Lovecraft: Against the World, Against Life* [1991]. Translated by Dorna Khazeni. San Francisco: Believer Books, 2005.

Ingebretsen, Edward J., S.J. *Maps of Heaven, Maps of Hell: Religious Terror as Memory from the Puritans to Stephen King.* Armonk, N.Y.: M.E. Sharpe, Inc., 1996.

Isaacson, Kja. "Deep Time in the Nineteenth-Century British Novel: Temporality, Science, and Literary Form." Ph.D. thesis, Univ. of Ottawa, 2017.

Joshi, S.T. *I Am Providence: The Life and Times of H.P. Lovecraft.* 2 vols. New York: Hippocampus Press, 2013.

— *An Index to the Fiction and Poetry of H.P. Lovecraft.* West Warwick, R.I.: Necronomicon Press, 1992.

— *An Index to the Selected Letters of H.P. Lovecraft.* West Warwick, R.I.: Necronomicon Press, 1980.

— *Lovecraft's Library: A Catalogue.* 4th ed. New York: Hippocampus Press, 2017.

— "Lovecraft's Other Planets" [1982]. In *Lovecraft and a World in Transition: Collected Essays on H.P. Lovecraft*, 232-242. New York: Hippocampus Press, 2014.

Joshi, S.T., annot. and ed. *The Case of Charles Dexter Ward* [1927], by H.P. Lovecraft. Tampa, Fla.: Univ. of Tampa Press, 2010.

Joshi, S.T., and Schultz, David E. *An H.P. Lovecraft Encyclopedia.* New York: Hippocampus Press, 2001.

Klinger, Leslie, annot. and ed. *The New Annotated H.P. Lovecraft,* by H.P. Lovecraft. New York: Liveright, 2014.

— *The New Annotated H.P. Lovecraft: Beyond Arkham,* by H.P. Lovecraft. New York: Liveright, 2019.

Kneale, James. "'Ghoulish Dialogues': H.P. Lovecraft's Weird Geographies." In *The Age of Lovecraft,* edited by Carl H. Sederholm and Jeffrey Andrew Weinstock, 43-61. Minneapolis, Minn.: Univ. of Minnesota Press, 2016.

Kramer, Bret. "New England's Native Americans in Lovecraft's Fiction." *Sentinel Hill Press* blog (October 28, 2015).

Lai, Rick. "The Lost Tales of Robert Bloch." *Lovecraft eZine* (July 25, 2017).

Leiber, Fritz. "A Literary Copernicus" [1949]. In *Lovecraft Remembered,* edited by Peter Cannon, 455-466. Sauk City, Wisc.: Arkham House, 1998.

— "Through Hyperspace With Brown Jenkin: Lovecraft's Contribution to Speculative Fiction" [1966]. In *Lovecraft Remembered,* edited by Peter Cannon, 472-483. Sauk City, Wisc.: Arkham House, 1998.

Lévy, Maurice. *Lovecraft: A Study in the Fantastic* [1985]. Rev. ed. Translated by S.T. Joshi. Detroit: Wayne State University Press, 1988.

Livesey, T.R. "Dispatches from the Providence Observatory: Astronomical Motifs and Sources in the Writings of H.P. Lovecraft." *Lovecraft Annual* 2 (2008): 3-87.

— "Green Storm Rising: Lovecraft's Roots in Invasion Literature." In *Lovecraft and Influence,* edited by Robert H. Waugh, 83-94. Lanham, Md.: Scarecrow Press, 2014.

Loucks, Donovan K. "Antique Dreams: Marblehead and Lovecraft's Kingsport." *Lovecraft Studies* 42-43 (Autumn 2001): 45-52.

Lovecraft, H.P. *Collected Essays.* Vols. 3-5. Edited by S.T. Joshi. New York: Hippocampus Press, 2005-2006.

— *In the Spirit of Revision: Lovecraft's Letters to Zealia Brown Reed Bishop.* Edited by Sean Branney and Andrew Leman. Glendale, Calif.: H.P. Lovecraft Historical Society, 2015.

— *Letters to C.L. Moore and Others.* Edited by David E. Schultz and S.T. Joshi. New York: Hippocampus Press, 2017.

— *Letters to James F. Morton.* Edited by David E. Schultz and S.T. Joshi. New York: Hippocampus Press, 2011.

— *Letters to Maurice W. Moe and Others.* Edited by David E. Schultz and S.T. Joshi. New York: Hippocampus Press, 2017.

— *Letters to Robert Bloch and Others.* Edited by David E. Schultz and S.T. Joshi. New York: Hippocampus Press, 2015.

— *O Fortunate Floridian: H.P. Lovecraft's Letters to R.H. Barlow.* Edited by S.T. Joshi and David E. Schultz. Tampa, Fla.: Univ. of Tampa Press, 2007.

— *Selected Letters.* 5 vols. Edited by August Derleth, Donald Wandrei, and James Turner. Sauk City, Wisc.: Arkham House, 1965-1976.

— *Supernatural Horror in Literature* [1934]. Edited and annotated by S.T. Joshi. New York: Hippocampus Press, 2000.

Lovecraft, H.P., and Derleth, August. *Essential Solitude: The Letters of H.P. Lovecraft and August Derleth.* 2 vols. Edited by David E. Schultz and S. T. Joshi. New York: Hippocampus Press, 2008.

Lovecraft, H.P., and Howard, Robert E. *A Means to Freedom: The Letters of H.P. Lovecraft and Robert E. Howard.* 2 vols. Edited by S.T. Joshi, David E. Schultz, and Rusty Burke. New York: Hippocampus Press, 2009.

Lovecraft, H.P., and Smith, Clark Ashton. *Dawnward Spire, Lonely Hill: The Letters of H.P. Lovecraft and Clark Ashton Smith.* Edited by David E. Schultz and S. T. Joshi. New York: Hippocampus Press, 2017.

Lubnow, Fred S. "The Lovecraftian Solar System." *Lovecraft Annual* 13 (2019): 3-26.

Machen, Arthur. *Things Near and Far.* London: Martin Secker, 1923.

Mariconda, Steven J. "Lovecraft's Concept of 'Background'" [1986]. In *H.P. Lovecraft: Art, Artifact, and Reality,* 46-56. New York: Hippocampus Press, 2013.

Marten, Robert. "Arkham Country: In Rescue of the Lost Searchers" [1998]. In *A Century Less a Dream: Selected Criticism on H.P. Lovecraft,* edited by Scott Connors, 77-111. Holicong, Penna.: Wildside Press, 2002.

McInnis, John Lawson, III. "H.P. Lovecraft: The Maze and the Minotaur." Ph.D. thesis, Louisiana State Univ., 1975.

McRoy, Jay. "There Goes the Neighborhood: Chaotic Apocalypse and Monstrous Genesis in H. P. Lovecraft's 'The Street,' 'The Horror at Red Hook,' and 'He.'" *Journal of the Fantastic in the Arts* 13, no. 4 (2003): 335-351.

Miéville, China. "Introduction." In *At the Mountains of Madness: The Definitive Edition,* by H.P. Lovecraft, xi-xxv. New York: Modern Library, 2005.

Miller, David. *Dark Eden: The Swamp in Nineteenth-Century American Culture.* Cambridge: Cambridge Univ. Press, 1989.

Murray, Will. "Illuminating 'The Elder Pharos.'" *Crypt of Cthulhu* 20 (Eastertide 1984): 17-19.

— "In Search of Arkham Country" I & II [1986, 1989]. In *The Fantastic Worlds of H.P. Lovecraft,* edited by James Van Hise, 97-113. Yucca Valley, Calif.: Self-published, 1999.

— "Roots of the Miskatonic" [1987]. In *The Fantastic Worlds of H.P. Lovecraft,* edited by James Van Hise, 94-96. Yucca Valley, Calif.: Self-published, 1999.

Nevins, Jess. *The Encyclopedia of Pulp Heroes.* Tomball, Tex.: Self-published, 2017.

Norris, Duncan. "Lovecraft and Egypt: A Closer Examination." *Lovecraft Annual* 10 (2016): 3-45.

O'Brien, Edward W. "Lovecraft's Two Views of Arkham" [1990]. In *Dissecting Cthulhu: Essays on the Cthulhu Mythos,* edited by S.T. Joshi, 196-201. Lakeland, Fla.: Miskatonic River Press, 2011.

Pardoe, Rosemary, and Nicholls, Jane. "The Black Pilgrimage." *Ghosts & Scholars* 26 (1998): 48-54.

Pearsall, Anthony. *The Lovecraft Lexicon: A Reader's Guide to Persons, Places and Things in the Tales of H.P. Lovecraft.* Tempe, Ariz.: New Falcon Publications, 2005.

Perridas, Chris. "Constellation Felis: Is it Slyly Mentioned in 'The Dreams in the Witch House'?" *H.P. Lovecraft And His Legacy* blog (October 11, 2006).

Peters, Art. *Legends of the Mounds: A Collection of Legends, Stories and History of the Mounds in North Caddo County.* Hinton, Okla.: Self-published, 2014.

Poe, Edgar Allan. *The Collected Works of Edgar Allan Poe: Tales and Sketches.* Edited and annotated by Thomas Ollive Mabbott. Cambridge, Mass.: Harvard Univ. Press, 1978.

Powell, Arthur E. *The Solar System.* London: Theosophical Publishing House, 1930.

Price, Robert M. "A Critical Commentary on the *Necronomicon.*" *Crypt of Cthulhu* 58 (Lammas 1988): 1-63.

— "HPL and HPB: Lovecraft's Use of Theosophy." *Crypt of Cthulhu* 5 (Roodmas 1982): 3-9.

— "Introduction: Lovecraft's Cosmic History." In *The Antarktos Cycle,* edited by Robert M. Price, ix-xiii. Oakland, Calif.: Chaosium, 1999.

— "Introduction: Ontogeny Recapitulates Phylogeny." In *The Innsmouth Cycle,* edited by Robert M. Price, vii-xiv. Oakland, Calif.: Chaosium, 1998.

— "'St. Toad's' Revisited." *Crypt of Cthulhu* 20 (Eastertide 1984): 21.

— "Two Biblical Curiosities in Lovecraft." *Lovecraft Studies* 16 (Spring 1988): 12-13, 18.

— "What Was the 'Corpse-Eating Cult of Leng'?" *Crypt of Cthulhu* 2 (Yuletide 1981): 3-8.

Price, Robert M. [as Laban Shrewsbury] "Apocalyptic Expectation in 'The Call of Cthulhu.'" *Crypt of Cthulhu* 9 (Hallowmass 1982): 9-10.

Price, Robert M. [as Alonzo Hasbrouch Typer] "St. Toad's Hagiography." *Crypt of Cthulhu* 9 (Hallowmass 1982): 25-26.

Quinn, Dennis. "Endless Bacchanal: Rome, Livy, and Lovecraft's Cthulhu Cult." *Lovecraft Annual* 5 (2011): 188-215.

Rajala, J.-M. "Locked Dimensions Out of Reach: The Lost Stories of H.P. Lovecraft." *Lovecraft Annual* 5 (2011): 3-90.

Redding, Moses Wolcott. *Ecce Orienti, or, Rites and Ceremonies of the Essenes.* 2nd ed. New York: Redding & Co., 1872.

Ridgely, J.V. "The Continuing Puzzle of *Arthur Gordon Pym:* Some Notes and Queries." *Poe Newsletter* 3, no. 1 (June 1970): 5-6.

St. Armand, Barton Levi. *The Roots of Horror in the Fiction of H.P. Lovecraft.* Elizabethtown, N.Y.: Dragon Press, 1977.

Salmonson, Jessica Amanda. "Introduction: Sarah Orne Jewett's 'Imaginative Realism.'" In *Lady Ferry and Other Uncanny People*, by Sarah Orne Jewett, xv-xxiv. Ashcroft, B.C.: Ash-Tree Press, 1998.

Salonia, John. "Cosmic Maenads and the Music of Madness: Lovecraft's Borrowings From the Greeks." *Lovecraft Annual* 5 (2011): 91-101.

Schuchert, Charles, and Dunbar, Carl O. *A Textbook of Geology, Part II.* New York: John Wiley & Sons, 1933.

Schultz, David E., annot. and ed. *Fungi From Yuggoth: An Annotated Edition,* by H.P. Lovecraft. New York: Hippocampus Press, 2017.

Scott-Elliot, W. *The Story of Atlantis & the Lost Lemuria.* London: Theosophical Publishing House, 1925.

Shershow, Scott Cutler, and Michaelsen, Scott. *The Love of Ruins: Letters on Lovecraft.* Albany: State Univ. of New York Press, 2017.

Sederholm, Carl H., and Weinstock, Jeffrey Andrew. "Introduction: Lovecraft Rising." In *The Age of Lovecraft,* edited by Carl H. Sederholm and Jeffrey Andrew Weinstock, 1-42. Minneapolis, Minn.: Univ. of Minnesota Press, 2016.

Shreffler, Philip. *The H.P. Lovecraft Companion.* Westport, Conn.: Greenwood Press, 1977.

Skinner, Charles M. *Myths and Legends of Our Own Land.* Philadelphia: J.P. Lippincott Co., 1896.

Taylor, Justin. "A Mountain Walked or Stumbled: Madness, Apocalypse, and H.P. Lovecraft's 'The Call of Cthulhu.'" *The Modern Word* blog, 2004.

Tierney, Richard L. "Cthulhu in Mesoamerica." In *HPL,* edited by Meade and Penny Frierson, 48-49. Birmingham, Ala.: Self-published, 1972.

Wallace, Bill. "The Untravelled Roads 'Round Arkham." In *Essays Lovecraftian,* edited by Darrell Schweitzer, 76-78. Baltimore: T-K Graphics, 1976.

Waugh, Robert H. "Landscapes, Selves, and Others in Lovecraft." In *An Epicure of the Terrible,* 2nd ed., edited by David E. Schultz and S.T. Joshi, 230-255. New York: Hippocampus Press, 2011.

— "Lovecraft, Citizen of Rome." In *Monster of Voices: Speaking for H.P. Lovecraft,* 267-293. New York: Hippocampus Press, 2011.

Wetzel, George T. "The Cthulhu Mythos: A Study" [1955, rev. 1971]. In *H.P. Lovecraft: Four Decades of Criticism,* edited by S.T. Joshi, 79-95. Athens, Ohio: Ohio Univ. Press, 1980.

Wilk, Stephen R. *Medusa: Solving the Mystery of the Gorgon.* Oxford: Oxford Univ. Press, 2000.

INDEX OF LOVECRAFT WORKS

CLIENTS AND COLLABORATORS

AdC: Alphonse de Castro
AHC: Anna Helen Crofts
AM: A. Merritt
CLM: C.L. Moore
CME: C.M. Eddy, Jr.
DWR: Duane W. Rimel

EHP: E. Hoffmann Price
FBL: Frank Belknap Long
HH: Harry Houdini
HDH: Hazel Drake Heald
KJS: Kenneth J. Sterling
REH: Robert E. Howard

RHB: Robert H. Barlow
SHG: Sonia Haft Greene
WBT: Wilfred Branch Talman
WL: William Lumley
WVJ: Winifred V. Jackson
ZB: Zealia Bishop

GENERAL INDEX

Voodoo, 209n., 214

Voormis, 199

Wales, 8, 86, 165, 176, 178

"Walking, or the Wild" (Thoreau), 215, 217

Wandrei, Donald, 14, 44-45, 93, 124, 165, 213, 245

Ward, Charles Dexter, 56, 123, 125, 171, 208, 245-46, 251, 255, 256; see also *The Case of Charles Dexter Ward*

Warren, Harley, 10, 68, 205, 215, 217, 233

Waugh, Robert H., 4, 47, 92n., 116-17, 125, 226n., 250; "Landscapes, Selves, and Others in Lovecraft," 226n.

Weird Tales, 37, 149

Weiss, Henry George, 40

Wells, H.G.: *The Time Machine,* 149, 190, 201; *The War of the Worlds,* 149, 151

West Shokan, N.Y., 50

Wetzel, George; "The Cthulhu Mythos," 22, 96

Whateley, Wilbur, 61, 64, 83, 97, 123, 241

Wilbraham, Mass., 62-63

Wilcox, Henry, 20, 40, 49, 133, 135, 237, 249, 250, 254

Wilk, Stephen, 31n.

wind, motif, 157-58; *The Wind* (Scarborough), 157

witches, 7, 10, 14-15, 30, 61n., 64, 71, 224, 226, 230, 252

Woods, the, **6-12,** 14, 20, 23-24, 29, 87-88, 92, 94, 116, 161, 161n., 166-69, 176, 218, 252, 255; Wild Man of the, 7-9; *see also* Enchanted Wood, Shub-Niggurath

Wooley, Natalie, 41

Yaanek, Mt., 77

Yaddith, 84, 152-53, 201, 242

Yekub, 149; Cube of, 76, 197, 202; Yekubians, 152

"Yellow Peril," 41, 238

Yemen, 70, 256, 258

Y'ha-nthlei, 72, 231; name of, 222n.

Yhe, 39

Yian, 54, 55, 185-86, 188

Yian-Ho, 55, 183, 185

Yig, 26, 105n., 157, 159

Yith, Great Race of, 18, 69, 75, 76n., 83, 85, 88, 93-94, 110-11, 113-14, 145-46, 149, 152, 197, 199-200, 202, 205, 240, 251n., 259; planet, 110, 149

y'm-bhi, 210

Yog-Sothoth, 16, 55, 64-66, 83, 96, 132-33, 135, 142, 241, 257; Yog-Sototl, 159

Yoth, 85, 86, 162

Yuga cycle, 199

Yuggoth, 145-47, 169, 187, 196, 253; fungi from, *see* Mi-Go; see also *Fungi From Yuggoth* (poems)

Zin, vaults of, 20

Zkauba, 135, 152-53

zombies, 18, 210n.

zoogs, 9, 23, 29

ABOUT THE AUTHOR

Kenneth Hite is the multiple Origins, Golden Geek, and ENnie Award-winning author, co-author, or designer of over 100 roleplaying game books and supplements, including *GURPS Horror, Call of Cthulhu d20, Trail of Cthulhu, Bookhounds of London, Night's Black Agents*, the *Delta Green RPG, The Fall of DELTA GREEN, The Day After Ragnarok*, and *Vampire: the Masquerade 5th Edition*. He has annotated Robert W.  Chambers' *The King in Yellow* for Arc Dream Publishing, and written on the narrative of horror roleplaying in *Nightmares of Mine*, on the Dracula variations in *The Thrill of Dracula*, and on the narrative structure of *Call of Cthulhu* in the *Second Person* anthology from MIT Press. His other works include the Mythos miscellany *Dubious Shards*, several Cthulhu Mythos short stories, *The Nazi Occult* and *The Cthulhu Wars* for Osprey Publishing, and a series of Lovecraftian children's books: *Where the Deep Ones Are, The Antarctic Express, Cliffourd the Big Red God*, and *Goodnight Azathoth*. An Artistic Associate at Chicago's WildClaw Theatre, he served as dramaturg for their stage production of *The Shadow Over Innsmouth*. Half of the multiple-award-winning podcast *Ken and Robin Talk About Stuff*, he lives in Chicago with his wife Sheila, the mandatory Lovecraftian cat and a spare, sixteen thousand or so books, and a sense of adventurous expectancy.